Praise for
Richard Bandler's
Guide to Trance-formation

"This wonderful book is for anyone interested in making their life significantly better. It is a gold mine of insights and techniques from one of the greatest geniuses of personal change. As you use the techniques in *Richard Bandler's Guide to Trance-formation*, you will exponentially increase your ability to make dramatic, life-enhancing differences. It is by far one of the most entertaining and professionally stimulating books I have read. It will change your life!"

—**Paul McKenna, Ph.D.,**
coauthor of *I Can Make You Thin*
and host of TLC's *I Can Make You Thin*

"For years, anyone wanting to learn directly from Richard Bandler had two choices: pay hundreds or even thousands of dollars to attend a live training or settle for material in books that, while excellent, were ten to thirty years behind the cutting edge. With this new book, *Richard Bandler's Guide to Trance-formation*, the cutting edge has finally arrived—and it's sharper than ever!"

—**Michael Neill,**
author of *You Can Have What You Want*

"*Richard Bandler's Guide to Trance-formation* will be of interest to you only if you want more happiness, unlimited success, complete freedom, and deep inner peace. If not, I'd leave it alone."

—**Robert Holden, Ph.D.,**
author of *Happiness NOW* and *Success Intelligence*

"Richard Bandler gets better and better. This book summarizes his previous work in NLP and adds a wealth of new material. The examples and exercises are clear, informative, and helpful. However much one may know about NLP already, this book is well worth reading and using as a resource. There is no substitute for learning from the master himself."

—Dr. Robert Lefever,
Director of The PROMIS Recovery Centre,
London, England, and NLP Trainer

RICHARD BANDLER'S

GUIDE to

TRANCE-
formation

MAKE YOUR LIFE GREAT

HARPER
element

To my son Jay,

my daughter Elizabeth,

and to Dr. Glenda Bandler—

the three shining lights in my life.

HarperElement
an imprint of HarperCollins*Publishers*
77–85 Fulham Palace Road,
Hammersmith, London W6 8JB

www.harpercollins.co.uk

and *HarperElement* are trademarks
of HarperCollins*Publishers* Ltd

First published in the USA in 2008 by Health Communications, Inc.
This edition 2010

13 5 7 9 10 8 6 4 2

A catalogue record of this book is
available from the British Library

ISBN 978-0-00-730198-0

Printed and bound in Great Britain by
Clays Ltd, St Ives plc

Mixed Sources
Product group from well-managed
forests and other controlled sources
www.fsc.org Cert no. SW-COC-1806
© 1996 Forest Stewardship Council

FSC

FSC is a non-profit international organisation established to promote the
responsible management of the world's forests. Products carrying the FSC
label are independently certified to assure consumers that they come
from forests that are managed to meet the social, economic and
ecological needs of present and future generations.

Find out more about HarperCollins and the environment at
www.harpercollins.co.uk/green

Contents

PART 1:

PATTERNS OF PROCESS AND ELICITATION
How People Create Their Reality, and How We Can Know

Foreword

WOW! WHAT AN HONOR to write the foreword for one of my favorite books of all time.

Back in 1985, I was working as a radio broadcaster and went to interview a local hypnotist for my programme. It had been a particularly bad week—I'd split up with my girlfriend, the people in the apartment next to where I was living seemed to be having a "who can make the most noise" contest, and to top things off, that morning I'd had a flaming row with my boss.

When I sat down in his office, the hypnotist said, "Rather than try and explain how this works, I think you'd benefit from a demonstration." Skeptically, I replied, "Let the healing begin."

To my delighted surprise, in only a few minutes I felt relaxed and quite euphoric. Even more impressive to me was that while I knew there were still issues I had to deal with in my life, they no longer carried any emotional charge. I just knew that I could handle them.

How could it be that easy? Didn't therapy take months, or even years? Wasn't I supposed to tell him all about my childhood?

When I asked him what he had done to me, he explained that he had used something called Neuro-Linguistic Programming, or NLP. With NLP, he was able to notice patterns in my language and behavior that let him know exactly what I was doing in my brain to create my experience. He explained to me that hypnosis was just one of the many tools in this amazing new technology. I was hooked from that moment forward!

He lent me a book by Dr Richard Bandler—the first edition of the book you are holding in your hands right now. Not only did I read it, but my life began to change for the better almost immediately.

Several years later I met Richard at a seminar in London and we became friends. The more I learned from him, the more I wanted to know.

Even though I was at the top of the TV ratings and filling theatres every night with my hypnotism show, I began spending my weekends sitting with small groups of people in hotels and teaching them the basics of NLP. This book was our bible—the most powerful and practical guide to NLP and hypnosis ever written.

I flew to San Francisco and started to harass Richard. "I would really like to put on a training session in London with you," I said. Years later we had become the biggest NLP training organization in the world. I feel very privileged to train by his side.

This book has made a massive difference to my life and to the lives of so many people around the world. Not only does it eloquently detail many easy techniques you can use straight away, it beautifully captures the spirit of Richard's humorous and creative style of presentation, a style we refer to as "stand-up therapy."

What is so exciting about this new edition is that Richard has continued to evolve NLP and hypnosis far beyond what they were when it was first published nearly 20 years ago. Inside, you will find not only an introduction to "classical NLP" and "Ericksonian Hypnosis," but also the very latest innovations and developments from one of the true creative geniuses of our time.

We cannot control everything that happens to us, but using these techniques gives us control over the way we feel about the events of our lives, and consequently what we decide to do in response. I hope you use this amazing book to unleash your power and redesign your destiny. May each page fill you with the delighted fascination that I felt when I first read it.

Hang on—your life might just be about to change for the better!

PAUL MCKENNA, PH.D.

A Note from the Editor

I AM DEEPLY PRIVILEGED to have been invited to edit this book by Richard Bandler on the subject of hypnosis and Neuro-Linguistic Programming. Once or twice in a lifetime, one may encounter a true rainmaker, someone who makes the impossible possible to the benefit of those around him. From the very first page I read of his first book, *The Structure of Magic I,* so many years ago, I recognized him as one of these rare beings. Since then, I have studied with Richard for many years and have benefited hugely from his training and his personal attention, which he has always given with the utmost kindness, generosity, and patience.

I cannot pretend that editing his writings has been an easy task—not because of a lack of material to include (few people on this planet can be as consistently creative and productive as Richard), but because it has been difficult to know what to leave out.

This is not a definitive book of Richard Bandler's work. No single book could hope to be that. Rather, it is one of a series of new works written in his own voice to introduce newcomers to Neuro-Linguistic Programming and his endlessly creative development of this and related fields.

In this book, Richard returns to his roots—hypnosis, altered states, trance-work . . . he declines to call it one thing. From the time he met Milton Erickson nearly forty years ago, he has been deeply interested in how the alignment of conscious and unconscious processes can cure apparently intractable illnesses, remove deep-seated emotional problems, and create shining futures for those prepared to do the work. But he has also been driven to seek the boundaries to what is possible . . . limits, he says, that he has not yet found.

The principles, processes, techniques, and exercises he writes about here may seem simple, but do not be deceived. They are profoundly effective, and Richard's ability to teach with apparent simplicity, together with humor and a kind of laid-back energy, conceals highly complex and ambitious underpinnings. With Richard, it's never "what you see is what you get." What you get is not only what you get; it's always far more than you ever noticed him giving or you expected to receive.

The book is divided into three main sections. The first addresses the structure, process, and elicitation of the patterns of human consciousness (how people create their unique worlds and how we can know how someone else is thinking), the second explores altered states and their role in accelerated learning, and the third outlines some of the applications of these principles, processes, and techniques in optimizing human behavior.

The Resource Files at the back of the book are intended mainly for those people not yet conversant with Richard's work. Rather than slow the narrative with too much background information, the relevant files are flagged in the main body of the work, leaving readers, NLP and hypnosis newcomers, or experienced practitioners to consult them according to their needs.

Unique transcripts of Richard at work with real clients close the book.

I am especially grateful for the help and support Richard has given in so patiently filling in some of the many gaps in my own knowledge; in supporting me in the writing of my own book, *Magic in Practice*; and in the founding of the Society of Medical

NLP, created to promote his approach to healing and health to the medical profession. Already, hundreds of doctors and allied health professionals (and their patients) have benefited from training in Medical NLP.

I hope you enjoy reading *Richard Bandler's Guide to Trance-formation* as much as I have editing it.

GARNER THOMSON

Introduction

IT'S BEEN FOUR DECADES since I started writing my first book, *The Structure of Magic, Volume 1. The Structure of Magic* was a book about how psychotherapists unconsciously use language.

Since that time, I've studied and modeled unconscious behavior, not just of psychotherapists and hypnotists and great communicators, but of experts in sports and many other fields, as well as of people who made profound changes in their lives with or without psychotherapists—people who were great learners, great inventors, great innovators.

My career modeling these people, and developing behavioral technologies aimed at helping people solve problems and achieve goals, has been long and in many cases very successful, even where other "experts" have been unable to help.

This book represents a little of some of the old things that I did, patterns that were in my books, including *Trance-formations, Frogs into Princes*, and *The Structure of Magic*. Many of these things, I feel, are still useful. They worked then, and they work now, so I offer them to you in the hope that you can learn from my years of experience.

I want to make clear the very real difference between my work and psychotherapy. People who know me know I always reject the "therapists' label" for the following reason: most therapists looked for what was wrong and tried to get the client to understand what it was, so that the client could get better. These therapists believed insight was the magic key to change. However, years and years of psychoanalysis didn't seem to do much more than give people reasons to stay stuck in their old ways, or even to reinforce the condition by repeatedly revisiting the problems of the past.

Other psychologists wanted to "condition" their patients away from their bad behavior toward what they thought of as good behavior. Then, of course, psychiatrists saw the medicalization of psychology as a major step forward; now therapists and doctors could give drugs to people so they didn't necessarily get better, but they didn't seem to care as much.

Still other people believed in an entirely mechanical approach to the brain and its functions. They saw it as a broken or malfunctioning machine in need of a physical tune-up. I once met a neurosurgeon who told me he didn't believe there was a single psychological problem that couldn't be solved by the application of "a bit of cold steel." He was an expert in performing frontal lobotomies—operations where they removed part of the prefrontal cortex. It's true that people stopped being depressed or anxious, but then they just ambled around like sheep. I asked him why he and his colleagues stopped at the frontal lobe. Why not remove the whole brain? Then he'd solve every problem anyone had ever had.

Things have moved on since then. They don't do that many frontal lobotomies anymore. Increasingly powerful drugs can get the same result. People who get out of hand can just be chemically shut down.

I, on the other hand, was never that interested in the client's problem as such. I also didn't want to just fix clients and send them away. I wanted to teach clients how to solve the presenting problem and other problems that might arise long after they left my office. Then, when I saw how that could work, I wanted to lay the same kind of foundations for other people in the helping professions—not just for therapists, but for anyone in the business of giving lessons to other human beings. I wanted them to understand that people need not necessarily be lost or broken or stuck for the rest of their lives, and they didn't have to be treated as disabled. They simply had choices to make other than the one that caused them problems.

I believe in the human learning process. Human beings learn automatically. We learn a language effortlessly because we're born with the wiring already in place for us to accumulate the means of communicating with other people of our kind. We are powerful language-learning machines, but we are also behavior-learning machines.

Some of the behaviors we learn turn into bad habits, and some turn into profoundly good habits. But the fact that we learn anything at all means we can learn something else—something more useful, quicker, and better.

We know now that it doesn't have to take time and hard work. In fact, human beings learn best when they learn fast, and when they learn to make things unconscious so that the behavior can run automatically.

Of course, whenever we're learning something new, it feels awkward at first. But we very quickly acclimatize to behaviors we persist in practicing. When we first learn to ride a bicycle, we have the balance, the steering, the pedaling to think about, all at the same time—and, at first, it seems impossible.

Then there is a magic moment when it all comes together, without effort. From that point, for the rest of our lives, we can always pedal and steer, even if we haven't ridden a bicycle in years.

Being an optimist, my hope is that everything in this book gets taken even further. People often say an optimist is someone who sees a glass as half full, but a true optimist looks outside the glass entirely. We look at where the liquid comes from, and how it gets where it is. We look at the kind of containers it can be put in and how we can move it from here to there. We look at all the possibilities, and then we begin to understand that we don't just fill that glass, but we can fill vessels of all kinds, with different liquids, and move them around all over the world. In other words, we look for what we can apply elsewhere in other ways so we can start to do all sorts of things that have never been done before.

This is what successful and creative people do naturally. People who are successful in business—in fact, people who are successful in any field—don't just look at the short run, the immediate problem or challenge. They don't just look at what is. They look beyond, at how things got that way and how they can be better. Successful people apply their principles to solve many more problems and do many more new things for as many people as possible.

So now it's time to learn to ride a new kind of bicycle, a bicycle that's about personal freedom. I'm always fond of saying that the chains of the free are only in people's minds. Your fears, your doubts, your confusions, your habits, and your compulsions are all by-products of how you're thinking, and how you're thinking dictates how you're feeling and behaving and living your life.

If you have fears, it's not that heights or spiders or meeting new people, for example, scare you; it's that you *learned* how to be afraid of heights, spiders, and new people. Babies are born with only two fears: the fear of falling and the fear of loud noises. All other human fears are learned. Therefore, if you learned to be afraid, you can learn to be unafraid. If you learned to do something one way, you can learn how to do it totally differently and better. Learning is the way to personal freedom. Hypnosis and NLP are tools to make this easy and fun.

PART 1

PATTERNS OF PROCESS
AND ELICITATION

HOW PEOPLE CREATE THEIR REALITY,
AND HOW WE CAN KNOW

One

PATTERNS, LEARNING, AND CHANGE
How to Take Charge of Your Brain

I HAVE WRITTEN MANY BOOKS and talked to many hundreds of thousands of people about hypnosis and NLP, and people are still confused about the similarities and differences between the two. In this book I hope to simplify the issue. My attitude is that at some level or other, everything is hypnosis. People are not simply in or out of trance but are moving from one trance to another. They have their work trances, their relationship trances, their driving trances, their parenting trances, and a whole collection of problem trances.

One characteristic of trance is that it is patterned. It's repetitive or habitual. It's also the way we learn.

After we're born, we have so much knowledge and expertise to acquire—everything from walking, talking, and feeding ourselves to making decisions about what we want to do with the rest of our lives. Our brains are quick to learn how to automate behavior. Of course, this doesn't mean the brain always learns the "right" behavior to automate; quite often, our brains learn to do things in ways that make us miserable and even sick.

We learn by repetition. Something we do enough times gets its own neuronal pathways in the brain. Each neuron learns to connect and fire with the next one down, and the behavior gets set.

Sleeping and dreaming are important parts of the learning process.

Freud thought of dreams as merely "wish fulfillment"—and

maybe for him they were. I regard dreaming as unconscious rehearsal. If I do something I've never done before, I tend to go home, go to sleep, and do it all night long. This is one of the functions of rapid eye movement (REM) sleep. REM sleep is the way the unconscious mind processes what it's experienced during the day. It's literally practicing repetitively to pattern the new learning at the neurological level. Quality information and quality material are important to the learning process. If the brain isn't given anything specific to work with, it processes nonsense.

If we plan to take control of our learning, we need to understand that it's not only repetition that is important but speed as well. The brain is designed to recognize patterns, and the pattern needs to be presented rapidly enough for the human to be able to perceive the pattern for what it is.

Most people have drawn a series of stick figures in the margins of their schoolbooks, then flipped through them to make the figure appear to move. Each page has on it a static image, but the brain will find a pattern—in this case, movement—if the images run rapidly enough.

We wouldn't be able to enjoy movies without this process. We'd never be able to understand the story if we only saw one frame a day.

So, when we dream, we're running through things to learn, and we're not doing it in real time. "Internal" time differs from clock time in that we can expand or contract it. We learn at extraordinary speed—we can do maybe eight hours worth of work in five minutes before waking up. Sleep researchers support this idea. Subjects who report massively long and complex dreams are found through neural scanning to have been dreaming for only minutes, or even seconds, at a time.

Sleep, therefore, is one of the ways we program and reprogram ourselves. If you doubt your own ability to do this, try this out tonight:

As you're settling down to go to sleep, look at the clock, and tell yourself several times very firmly that you're going to wake up at a specific time. Set the alarm if you like, but you will wake up a second or two before it goes off.

This is something I've encountered in several different cultures. Some people gently bang the pillow with their heads the same number of times as the hour they want to get up.

Others tap their heads or their forearms to set their wake-up time. Whichever way it's done, the principle is the same; you somehow "know" you have an internal clock that you can set, using a specific ritual, and no matter how deeply you sleep, it will wake you as effectively as any alarm.

If we can program ourselves to do one little thing—such as waking without an alarm—we can program our minds to do many things. We can decide to go to the supermarket. Maybe we need bread, milk, peanut butter, and a couple of cartons of juice. We can drive five miles to the supermarket, walk through a thousand products, maybe talking to someone on our cell phone, and still remember the juice, peanut butter, milk, and bread.

Academics sometimes challenge me for something they call "evidence." They want to know the theory behind what I do; they want me to explain it, preferably with the appropriate research references. I've even had people ask for the correct citations for things that I've made up. The way I see it, it's not my job to prove, or even understand, everything about the workings of the mind. I'm not too interested in why something should work. I only want to know *how*, so I can help people affect and influence whatever they want to change.

The truth is, when we know how something is done, it becomes easy to change. We're highly programmable beings—as unpopular as that idea still is in some quarters. When I started using the term "programming," people became really angry. They said things like, "You're saying we're like machines. We're human beings, not robots."

Actually, what I was saying was just the opposite. We're the only machine that can program itself. We are "meta-programmable." We can set deliberately designed, automated programs that work by themselves to take care of boring, mundane tasks, thus freeing up our minds to do other, more interesting and creative, things.

At the same time, if we're doing something automatically that we shouldn't be doing—whether overeating, smoking, being afraid of elevators or the outside world, becoming depressed, or coveting our neighbor's spouse—then we can program ourselves to change. That's not being a robot; that's becoming a free spirit.

To me the definition of freedom is being able to use your conscious mind to direct your unconscious activity. The unconscious mind is hugely powerful, but it needs direction. Without direction, you might end up grasping for straws . . . and then finding there just aren't any there at all.

Two

DOING MORE OF
WHAT WORKS
The Secret of Effortless Change

VIRGINIA SATIR, THE FAMILY THERAPIST, once said something that has stayed with me for many years. She said: "You know, Richard, most people think the will to survive is the strongest instinct in human beings, but it isn't. The strongest instinct is to keep things familiar."

She was right. I've known people willing to kill themselves because they can't face the thought of life without the partner who's died or left them for someone else. Even thinking about how things could be different overwhelms them with fear.

There's a reason for this. One of the ways we make models of the world is by generalizing. We survive and prosper by making things familiar, but we also create problems for ourselves.

Each day you see new doors, but at a practical level you know each is still just a door. You don't have to figure out what each one is and how to open it. You shake hands with thousands of people, and even though it's a brand-new hand each time, it's not a new event, because somehow you've made it "the same." It's been filed in the compartment in your brain called "shaking hands."

But if you go to a country such as Japan where traditions differ, and you stick out your hand and someone bows to you instead, that action completely shatters the pattern. You have to come back to your senses to figure out how to respond in that new situation.

But that's the way it's supposed to work. When we're really thinking properly, we make everything familiar until the pattern doesn't function anymore. Then we review it and revise the way we're thinking.

Sometimes, though, we make something familiar, and even when it doesn't function anymore, we stick with it, and that's when it starts to make our lives dysfunctional. Instead of redefining the situation and coming up with a new behavior, we keep doing the same thing . . . only harder!

Pop psychologists talk about "the comfort zone" when they should more accurately be calling it "the familiarity zone." People persist in situations that are extremely uncomfortable simply because they're used to them. They're unaware that they have choices, or perhaps the choices they present to themselves—like being alone for the rest of their lives because they'd left an abusive partner—are so terrifying that they refuse to change.

For years, psychologists have tortured rats by making them do things like run mazes for bits of cheese. The interesting thing about these experiments is that, when the scientists change the position of the cheese, the rats only try the same way three or four times before starting to explore other possible routes. When humans replace the rats, however, they just keep on and on and on, in the hopes that if they just do the same thing often enough they'll get the desired result.

Apart from proving that rats are smarter than people, these experiments show us that people will often stick to their habits until they're forced to change . . . or die to avoid that change.

All the work I do to accomplish change is based on one important principle. I go in and find out what works and what doesn't work. I slice away what isn't working and replace those areas with new states of consciousness that work better. It's as simple as that.

The way I see it, there are three steps to making enduring change:

1. People must become so sick of having the problem that they decide they really want to change.
2. They have to somehow see their problem from a new perspective or in a new light.
3. New and appealing options must be found or created, and pursued.

As Virginia also said, if people have a choice, they'll make the best one. The problem is, they often don't have choices.

In these cases, hypnosis proves a valuable tool. By definition, we have to alter our state of consciousness to do something new. Hypnosis not only facilitates this but it allows us to minimize or remove the impact of past experiences and to create and install in their place newer, more useful, and more appropriate states. With hypnosis, we can help people discover choices and explore them. And, since time distortion is a characteristic of the phenomenon we call "trance," just as it is of dreaming, we can lead people through choices very rapidly. The learning tool of altered states permits us to familiarize the subject with a new experience in a fraction of the time it would take for them in an ordinary waking state.

For this to happen, we need somehow to reduce the impact on the subject of their past negative experiences, to make way for new and more useful ways of experiencing oneself and one's world. The way I work (and the techniques outlined in this book) permits a person who had been held prisoner by his past to make room for change.

Some of the patterns in this book lead people to "relive" their past in a new way, while other activities allow people to look at their past, and it just doesn't feel like it quite belongs to them anymore.

But, to do any of this really creatively means that we need to understand how people create their representations of their world, as well as how we can help them build new and more resourceful alternatives. Why they behave the way they do is far less important than *what* they're doing to set up their problem states and *how* they maintain them. When we know that, even the most impossible problem can have a solution.

When I started out, I asked some psychiatrists what were their most difficult clinical problems. Without hesitation, most of them said, "Phobias."

This answer is easy to understand. Phobics always have their phobic responses, and they always have them immediately. They never forget.

People often describe themselves as "phobic," when in reality they're suffering from some kind of anxiety disorder. Anxious people have to work up to their anxiety attack; phobics don't. They see or even just think *elevator* and instantly go, *"Aaargh!"* They never make an exception.

Phobias can either be learned, say, from a parent or caregiver, or instantly acquired by some emotionally overwhelming incident. Phobias are a graphic demonstration of the brain's ability to learn something really quickly—often in a single pass.

Addressing phobias intrigued me for several reasons. Not only was I ready to respond to the challenge of doing the "impossible," but I knew how useful it could be if people could learn to use the brain's ability to learn quickly and easily to acquire more useful responses. Think of how different someone's life would be if they learned to feel instantly and completely delighted every time they saw their partner—and vice versa.

Even though people are often disabled by their phobias, they are always incredibly creative and committed to having them. They need to experience a unique trigger, make complex decisions, and have responses in less time than it takes to describe it. If they fear heights, they have to know precisely what "high" is to have the response.

One of the weirdest height phobias I ever encountered was in Michigan. I asked three hundred people if anyone had a really outrageous phobia, and a very distinguished gentleman, aged about fifty, raised his hand and said, "I'm afraid of heights."

This didn't seem particularly outrageous, but when I invited him up on to the stage, which was just a couple feet high, he turned pale and said, "No."

I reached out my hand and said: "Step up on just one step," but he stepped backward and his knees gave way. To me, that's a real, flaming phobia. I went down in the front of the audience, turned him around, ran him through the Phobia Cure (see Chapter 16), then asked him what he did for a living.

He said, "I'm an airline pilot." Something about my reaction or expression prompted him to say, "I know what you're thinking, but once you're in the plane it's not the same."

He explained that walking up a flight of stairs was impossible for him. He could only fly planes, such as 747s, that were accessible by a ramp. He told how, when he was in the air force, he had to close his eyes, then be lifted backward into the cockpit. Once he was inside an F-16, he was fine. He couldn't climb a ladder to the plane, but he could fly it at twice the speed of sound and drop napalm across Vietnam without a second thought.

His problem had to do with the distinctions he made in his mind of how high "high" was. It had nothing to do with going up; it was all to do with looking down. Once he was high enough up, he was okay. He even told me: "If I get in an elevator and I go up to the eighth or ninth floor I can look out the window, or off the balcony, and I'm fine. But if I get off on the first floor, I've got a problem."

If he was in one of those glass elevators, he wouldn't be able to look out. He couldn't cope with walking around and looking out of the first floor, but felt quite safe if his room was on the sixteenth floor. The only thing was, he had to go up to his room with his back to the glass, staring at the wall or the door.

How he developed his phobia to such an elegant degree is probably all very complicated, but it doesn't really matter. What's significant is that he made the distinction that being at a certain height meant he could fall—but if it was much higher, he was safe. As soon as he got high enough, the phobia simply stopped functioning.

Somewhere in his brain were a starting point and a cutoff point—both very specific, and both functioning entirely outside his conscious awareness. His starting point for a height phobia was the lowest I've ever seen.

When he left the air force and became a commercial pilot, he had no problem flying people around in 747s, but he couldn't take a single step up. Of course, I did everything I could to get him fixed as quickly as possible. I don't want crazy people in the cockpit of my plane. I want people who are completely unflappable, with great sensory acuity, so they know exactly where real danger begins and ends.

Interestingly, phobias often make a kind of sense. People usually become phobic about something that could actually harm them under certain circumstances. When people come to me and say, "I want to be completely fearless around spiders," or "I don't want to be bothered by heights, no matter how high up I go," I always make them step back and take a realistic look at what they are requesting. In some countries, such as Australia or Africa, having no fear of spiders would be extremely stupid. Some spiders are very poisonous. Likewise, a man with a phobia of heights who told me he wanted to be able to dance fearlessly along the rail of a balcony four floors up needs a reality check.

The outcome in curing phobias should always respect the fact that part of the person's brain has actually been working very efficiently to help them avoid danger. The real problem is overreaction. The brain needs a new perspective to be able to change.

At the time I began investigating phobias, everyone was arguing over the right approach to psychotherapy. There were dozens, if not hundreds, of different schools of psychology, all fighting over who was right. The interesting part was that none of them was successful. Nobody was actually managing to cure anyone of their problems. To me, it seemed particularly foolish for a group of people who couldn't do something to be arguing about the best way to not do it.

These therapists were limited by their own unconscious patterning, which predisposed them to failure. They were all looking at the *content* of the client's experience—the "why"—to discover what was wrong and find ways to put it right. They were paying too much attention to trying to interpret what their clients were saying, and not noticing what they were doing.

I approached it differently. I advertised in the newspaper for people who'd had phobias they'd recovered from and offered to pay them money just to sit down and talk about their experiences.

I didn't really expect to get more than a few, but it turned out there were many, many former phobics who were happy to talk about themselves.

They all told me more or less the same story. They said things like: "One day, I'd just had enough. I said: 'That's it! No more!'" Then they all said: "I looked at myself and for once I saw how stupid it was to be acting the way I was and I started to laugh . . . ," and then they changed.

I noticed that when they made the change, they switched to *watching* themselves doing the behavior. Those people who lost the phobia were no longer thinking of the experience as if seeing it through their own eyes but were literally recalling it from a different point of view—that of an observer. No matter how scary the phobia had been, it no longer affected them the same way when they took up this detached or "objective" point of view. Inadvertently, they'd discovered how to dissociate from the problem experience.

People who still had their phobias, on the other hand, were looking at spiders or planes or elevators as if they were actually there. Because they were representing the thought from a point inside the experience, part of their brains responded as if the experience was actually happening and plunged them even deeper into a state of panic.

Even though each of them had differing stories to tell about their particular phobias, the only difference I could see was in the way they were representing the experience of their phobias to themselves. So I had some people with phobias apply what I had learned. I had them "step out" of their bodies and watch their responses as if from across the room. And it worked. They got rid of their phobias really quickly. Their brains simply shifted the way they perceived their situation, and their problems went away.

The psychiatrists responded by sending me more and more people with phobias. Some of them were extremely creative and entertaining in the way they had set up their problems. For example, one man had developed a phobia about leaving Huntington, Ohio. He'd be driving along quite happily, then come to the city limits, skid to a halt, and freak out. He hadn't been able to leave town in four and a half years.

Since I was always trying to find easier and faster ways of doing things, I had him imagine he was Superman. I got him to float out of his body and fly alongside, watching himself driving his pickup truck. He flew for a couple of miles, then saw himself begin to get nervous, jam on the brakes, and start to panic . . . *but he flew on!*

What made the difference was a trick. Inside his mind, not only was he calmly flying along, but he also left town for the first time in years. Now, since part of his brain could perceive *that* experience as real, I could start to put together the stimulus he had with the response he desired. We sent him out to go for a drive, and he was away for hours. When he came back he was astonished. He said he'd driven to the city limits, come to a bridge leading out of Huntington, all the time waiting for his phobia to kick in—but he just drove on.

Needless to say, some psychiatrists were deeply skeptical. They kept telling me that change had to be painful and slow, and I said, "Well, that hasn't been my experience. I've changed rapidly, many times, without any trouble."

Actually, we all have. Maybe you read something in a book that changed your life in a second. Someone might have said something that instantly changed not only the way you did certain things but the entire quality of the experience you were having.

Suddenly, without actually realizing it, something happened that switched off the problem and turned on the solution.

It fascinated me that among all the warring factions, a few therapists scattered around the country seemed capable of acting as genuine change agents, and I was driven by curiosity to know how they did it. That was my rule then and remains my rule now: if you want to find out how to do something you can't yet do, find someone who can and ask them. Now we call that process "modeling," and some people have turned it into an unnecessarily long and complicated process.

When I first began investigating modeling, I was astonished to find that highly successful people were flattered to be asked how they got that way and were usually happy to talk. The only problem was that they didn't always know how they came to be the way they were.

Exercise:
Changing Feelings by Dissociation

1. Recall an experience that still causes you sadness or distress. As you remember it, make sure you are reexperiencing it as if it were happening right now. See everything through your own eyes, feel all the feelings—including the associated emotions—through your own body. Pay particular attention to any sounds; these might include anything that was said by you or any other significant participants in the original scenario. It may also include your own self-talk. Make a mental note of the degree to which this memory still causes you pain.

2. Now pretend or imagine you can step back out of the experience so you can see yourself there, as if on a screen. Push the entire scene away from you, further and further, noticing, as it moves into the distance, how the colors begin to leach away and the detail diminishes. Push it as far away as you need to push it to notice a distinct difference in the way you feel about the events.

Note: Unless you particularly wish to have the discomfort back, you can leave the experience where it is—or even spin it away into space and have it explode into the sun.

Three

REPRESENTING "REALITY"

The Birth of Personal Freedom

NEURO-LINGUISTIC PROGRAMMING WAS born many years ago, partly out of the events one night in a hypnosis seminar. The people there were achieving deep hypnotic states and demonstrating dramatic hypnotic phenomena.

Some of them were doing things like limited vision and positive hallucinations; others were controlling their blood pressure. One young girl even speeded up the way her eyes worked, but not the rest of her, so she could see the world in slow motion. Without any training at all, she was able to run rings around a martial artist friend of mine. From her point of view, everything was slowed all the way down. To the observer, she was moving twice as fast as the other guy.

Of course, different people were able to achieve different levels of competence, and that set me thinking.

Already, those psychologists studying hypnosis had decided there was such a thing as "hypnotizability" that could be measured—meaning that one person could be more or less hypnotizable than another.

I didn't really believe that. I wasn't impressed with the idea of a hypnotizability scale. I kept asking, "Has anybody got one? Has anyone even seen one?"

What the research really told me, though, was that if you use the same input with some people, they will respond differently than others. In the case of hypnosis, some people go deeper, others not. To me, the analogy was simply that if you keep punching a group of research subjects at the same height, you'll hit some in the head and hit the really tall ones in the knee. The whole thing begged the question: What was one person doing with his brain that the other wasn't? It seemed to me that these psychologists were really measuring not hypnotizability, but their own incompetence.

Some philosophers and scientists have suggested that the world we perceive ourselves in is only a representation of reality, whatever that is. Hans Vaihinger, Alfred Korzybski, and Gregory Bateson all made the same observation. They all discussed variations on the theme of "our experience of reality is not the same as reality itself." Some very old cultures came to the same conclusion. They realized thousands of years ago that what was outside the mind was not the same as what was inside the mind. Part of their way of dealing with it was to meditate for years to become enlightened and dissolve the "illusion."

But the problem remained for the rest of us. Even if we accepted that our experience was constructed in our minds, what then? What could we do with that knowledge? What difference would it make?

In volume one of *The Structure of Magic*, I wrote: "We as human beings do not act directly on the world. Each of us creates a representation of the world in which we live—that is we create a map or model which we use to generate our behavior. Our representation of the world determines to a large degree what our experience of the world will be, how we will perceive the world, what choices we will see available to us as we live in the world."

My point was that those people in that workshop who could create positive or negative hallucinations, or become selectively amnesiac, or anesthetize their arms, were representing their world differently from those who could not do those things. They changed their way of looking at things; they changed their beliefs. The intriguing thing is that, in some cases, *not only did their subjective experience change with the suggestion, but their physiology did, too.*

Hypnosis, therefore, was central to the development of NLP because it allowed us to explore altered states. We could push boundaries with it, because it was a tool that allowed us to begin to learn what was possible. Once we saw some of the things that were possible, we could begin to look at how they happened and what we needed to do to replicate the outcomes. In this sense, NLP may be thought of as the underlying "structure" of hypnosis.

It wasn't possible to turn to psychology for help, because not only were most of the "experts" fighting with each other to decide whose theory was correct, they were also focused only on why people became ill or stuck, or how they came to fail.

I once spent a whole winter house-sitting for a psychiatrist friend, and out of sheer boredom I read every book he had. It was a fascinating experience. The hundreds of texts by all these important doctors and professors could tell you everything you needed to know about how people got sick or stuck—but not one of them had even the glimmer of an idea of how to help them get better. It didn't even seem to occur to them that it might be a useful direction to follow.

That was a question I found myself asking again and again. How do people get better? Some of them *do* get better, sometimes with the help of doctors or psychologists. Others just get better all by themselves.

But my interest went beyond that. I wanted to know how people achieved their goals and what made some of them exceptional in their field. I wanted to know how some people achieved excellence.

A few therapists at the time were getting far better results than those of their colleagues. They lived and practiced in different parts of the country; their methods were different; and they didn't know anything about each other or the way they worked. But those who knew them and saw their work described their results as magical—and they were, compared with the results of most of their peers.

Their followers praised their talent or genius or intuition, as if that explained their abilities, but nobody at the time really understood how they came to be this way, least of all the therapists themselves.

As a scientist and a mathematician, I knew there had to be a structure, and I wanted to know what that structure was. I knew that, if it could be identified, it should be possible to replicate it and even teach it to other people. Everybody could become magicians in their own right.

I spent some time with John Grinder studying these therapeutic wizards very closely. Initially, we focused on family therapist Virginia Satir, Gestalt therapist Fritz Perls, and Milton Erickson, the grandfather of modern hypnotherapy. We watched them at work, and instead of getting caught up in the content of what they were doing, we looked at the syntax of what they were saying and doing. As soon as we looked at it that way, the patterns popped out everywhere—in the questions they asked, the words they used, the gestures they made, in the tonality and rate with which they spoke. We started to notice that, even though they were all very different personalities, they shared many characteristics.

The interesting thing was that they all acted intuitively. They all had their own maps or models of therapy; there were similarities and there were differences. Often they had no idea at all why some-

thing they had done had been successful, but all shared a belief that
the client's model of the world could be changed. Regardless of what
they did or thought they were doing, each believed in helping to
expand and enrich the clients' subjective experience.

Neuro-Linguistic Programming (NLP) takes the position that
no two people share precisely the same experiences. The map or
model they create to make sense of and navigate around the world
is partially based on these experiences and the distinctive ways in
which each processes them. Therefore, each person's model varies
to some degree from the model created by every other person. We
live in different realities, some richer, and some very much poorer,
than others.

This fact alone doesn't always cause problems. We have something called consensual, or shared, reality, which means we all,
more or less, agree to operate according to the same hallucinations—
and this is a useful thing. We need to have certain rules by which
we all function. We need to agree on what is up and what is down.
We need to know the difference between left and right—something I discovered for myself the first time I visited the United
Kingdom and found out that they drive on the other side of the
road from Americans. Stepping off the sidewalk and looking only
one way is not a good idea if you're still operating according to a
map that applies to somewhere else.

Now, if a map or a model adequately represents the reality it is
describing, the person who has created it is likely to be functioning adequately in her or his world. But experience shows us that
most people who come to us in pain feel blocked and limited and
without any sense of options or choices. In other words, it's not
the world they live in that's limited; it's the poverty of their maps
that keeps them suffering and in pain.

It follows, then, that it's often much more productive—and a lot easier—to change the map someone has been using rather than the territory in which the person is functioning. The therapists we modeled were showing us this approach in their behavior.

Despite the fact that some people, usually psychotherapists, believe change is only possible with a lot of time and effort—and then only if the client isn't resistant—hypnosis, the effective therapists, and those people who "just changed" showed us that change could be a lot quicker and easier. The tools to do this were not available at the time, so I had to create them. Through NLP, I have been able to develop learnable principles, processes, and techniques that make change systematic and easy.

As I pointed out in Volume I of *The Structure of Magic*, perception and experience are active, rather than passive, processes. We all create our subjective experience out of the "stuff" of the external world. One of the reasons that we don't all end up with the same model is that our experiencing is governed by certain restrictions or constraints: the constraints of our individual nervous systems (neurological constraints), the societies in which we function (social constraints), and our unique personal histories (personal constraints).

The NLP model we advanced at the time to explain this process was simplified, but it's held up remarkably well over the years. Basically, the model suggested that we each use our five senses slightly differently from each other to process incoming information. The models we make depend on which senses we favor, what information we take in and how much we leave out, and how we interpret whatever does get through. To summarize briefly:

Neurological constraints. We receive information about the world through five sensory input channels—visual, auditory, kinesthetic (feelings), smell (olfactory), and taste (gustatory). Rather than each sense being given equal weight with every other sense, each of us favors one or two over the others. Of course, we know there's considerable overlap in the parts of the brain responsible for processing our senses, but one or the other usually dominates in experience. This is known as your sensory preference or preferred sensory system.

Social restraints. As members of a particular society, we are subject to a number of mutually agreed-upon filters, the most significant of which is the language we are born to speak.

The more specific our language is, and the more distinctions we can make, the richer our experience will be. This concept is central to the practice of Neuro-Linguistic Programming and hypnosis. Words are power, and the language patterns you will learn from this book will help harness this power for yourself and for others.

Individual constraints. As its name suggests, the third category of constraints develops out of our personal experience. We are each born into a particular set of circumstances, and as we grow up we encounter an increasing number of experiences, which in turn give rise to unique likes and dislikes, habits, rules, beliefs, and values. The maps we create from these can become rich and useful, or limited and destructive, and unless we understand how we create our subjective world, we will continue to live in confusion and pain.

People don't make themselves miserable out of choice, even though it sometimes looks that way. NLP doesn't see people as bad, crazy, or sick. Our viewpoint is that they are operating out of an impoverished map, limited in the number of choices they have. To put it another way, they mistake the model for reality. This is what we mean when we say: *The map is not the territory.*

The richness and poverty of our maps are created by three fil-
tering mechanisms: deletion, distortion, and generalization. These
are all processes we need to carry out to manage the information
that is coming at us so we are not overwhelmed. Problems occur
when the wrong information is deleted, distorted, or generalized,
creating patterns that either don't support our well-being or
actively diminish it.

Deletion. Deletion occurs when we pay attention to certain
parts of our experience at the expense of others, which we do
naturally. Think about being in a crowded room, talking to a
friend. You automatically screen out the buzz of other people's
conversation . . . until you hear your name spoken by someone on
the other side of the room.

Deletion is a necessary and useful mechanism for making sure
your world is manageable in size, but in certain circumstances it
can create pain and suffering. For example, I've never met a
depressed person who can remember a time when he was really
happy. As far as depressives are concerned, they've always been
unhappy. Equally, sufferers of chronic pain often don't notice
those times when their pain is reduced or nonexistent. Certain
people believe the world is a hostile place and simply fail to notice
how many people act in a caring or supportive way.

Distortion. Distortion is a quality that all creative people have
in abundance. We need to be able to shift the meaning of—to
distort—present reality to be able to create something new. (Great
writers and artists are experts in distortion.) However, as pattern-
making beings, we are equally inclined to distort reality in ways
that cause us pain and distress.

Some years ago I was in a restaurant, listening to a couple at
the next table having a fight. The man said something really

nice—obviously wanting to make peace with his partner—and she snapped back: "Oh, you're just saying that to make me feel better!"

Of course he was trying to make her feel better—nothing wrong with that, as far as I could see. But she distorted into a hostile act his attempt to make peace. So I leaned over and said: "Yeah, he's really bad that way. Imagine wanting to make the woman he loves feel good." For a moment, they were both stunned. Then they laughed and started to talk to each other in a much nicer way.

Generalization. The third mechanism is generalization—the process by which a person takes one or two experiences and decides that this is the way all things are meant to be, all the time.

Generalization is useful as a tool in learning. If we cut ourselves when we are careless with a sharp implement, we generalize to the extent that we believe "all" sharp instruments are capable of injuring us, so we treat them with respect. We have learned over many hundreds of thousands of years to stay alive by applying generalization.

Generalization, as has already been mentioned, is the mechanism by which people all over the planet know how to open doors, simply because they've generalized information out of one or two formative experiences, but generalization is also at the root of many problems. When I was still at school, teachers believed we left-handers should be forced to write with our right hands. Their method of instruction was to patrol our desks and whack us with rulers when they found us writing with the "wrong" hand.

Later, I got to do more things my way. As a person who was still left-handed, I reversed all the doors in my house to make things easier for myself. Everywhere else, the front door opened inward. Mine opened outward; it just felt better that way.

However, friends of mine would come along, try to get in, then say, "Hey, your door's jammed." I'd come along, open it the other way, and then next time they came along, the same thing would happen. Their motor programs just couldn't cope with an exception to their generalization about the way doors "should" be.

Generalization can have serious consequences on people's lives when they fail to undo generalizations that no longer work. Someone who was mistreated as a child may decide that all men (or women) or all authority figures are to be feared and disliked. A person who experiences several failed relationships may decide that love is for losers and withdraw into a lonely existence. Sexual dysfunction among some men persists because they believe a single incident will necessarily apply to all physical encounters.

Basically, generalization occurs when someone applies a single rule to all situations that resemble the one in which the original rule was formulated. The context has been altered from "one" to "all," from "sometimes" to "always."

Understanding this mechanism gives us insight into much behavior that otherwise seems strange or even bizarre. If we recognize that the rule makes sense in the appropriate context, we can start to help people restore the behavior to the situation or situations in which it originated, or help to create new and more appropriate behaviors. Based on this NLP approach, we can say, at some level, that all behavior has positive intent.

Freedom can only start to come when we restore information to an impoverished map. Once we begin to explore how each individual reality is constructed, we open ourselves and others to a whole range of options and opportunities. Rather than trying to take away people's discomfort or unwanted responses—to make people "not have" depression or anxiety or an eating disorder—

we create new choices for them in the belief that, when they have more and better choices than before, they will make them on a more consistent basis.

Exercise: Identifying Your Sensory Preferences

You can do this exercise with a partner or by yourself. If you are alone, it helps greatly to speak out loud, possibly into a voice recorder so you can review your experiences later.

1. Imagine as clearly as you can a walk along a beach. It can be a beach you know or an entirely imaginary one. Your goal is to describe in as much detail as you can the experience, cycling through each of your five senses. First, describe everything you see—the color of the sky and the ocean, the seagulls in the air, the white foam flying into the air as waves crash against the black rocks, the colorful clothes of children playing in the sand, and so on. Then move to another sense—hearing, for example—and describe everything you can hear, from the sound of your feet on the beach to a ship's horn in the distance. Continue until you have completed your description in all five senses.

2. Now, review your description and notice whether it was easier to make pictures, hear sounds, or feel sensations, such as the temperature of the air against the skin. Was it easy to imagine the smell of salt in the air, or the taste of a hot dog bought from an oceanfront stand? One of these senses will dominate. This is your sensory preference.

Note: Having a preference for one sensory modality does not mean you do not use the other senses, or that you use your preferred modality in all situations. We all tend to use all senses in processing information, but some are used to a greater or lesser degree.

Four

LANGUAGE AND CHANGE
The Gentle Art of Casting Spells

I USED THE TERM "INCANTATIONS" in *The Structure of Magic I* to describe the use of language in change-work for a very good reason. Words—as occultists, philosophers, psychologists, and writers know all too well—have magical effects. When I invite clients to "sit for a spell," the ambiguity is deliberate. I want them to begin to be open to the possibility of change—and to the fact that the change may seem magical; often, it is.

One important aspect to helping people change is making sure they feel you understand their problem, then to move them as quickly as possible from their problem state to the solution you have prepared for them. Words are the primary means by which you can help create this kind of change.

Watching Virginia Satir work, I noticed that she tended to reflect her clients' sensory predicates—those words and phrases that signify which of the five senses is dominant at the time of speaking.

Someone might say: "I just feel everything's getting on top of me and I can't move forward or back. I just don't see a way through this." She would reply: "I feel the weight of your problems is stopping you from finding your direction, and the best route you can take isn't clear yet . . ."

She did this intuitively and achieved really close connections with her clients.

On the other hand, I often observed therapists who had no concept of the sensory preferences of their clients and just spoke the same way to everybody they met. In response to "I'm weighed down by all my problems," a less enlightened therapist might respond, "Well, you need to listen to what I'm saying so you can see some light at the end of the tunnel." These therapists were talking a different language from their clients, and their clients felt as if they were somehow not being listened to or understood.

Couples sometimes end up in trouble by not recognizing these differences. One person—the visual partner—might express love in the form of gifts and flowers, but the other—the auditory partner— still feels neglected because the words "I love you" are never actually spoken out loud.

Once you have successfully matched the other person's preferred sensory system, you can begin to lead them in new directions, to increase their ability to process effectively and make enduring change. We do not want the subject to stay stuck in one processing mode; this lack of flexibility landed the person in trouble in the first place.

One of my objections to the Montessori method was just this. Originally, when a kinesthetic child was identified, he was taught only by kinesthetic methods. Likewise, visual children were taught only visually, and auditory children were taught strictly by auditory methods, thereby stunting their growth and possibilities. They were stuck on one channel, whereas real learning involves crossing into other sensory channels to optimize an individual's potential.

Expanding a client's experience by expanding the limits of his or her subjective model is central to the methods adopted by all the truly effective therapists and teachers I have studied. Other characteristics of effective therapists and teachers include:

- They tend to be proactive and directed toward outcomes rather than formalized in their approach.
- Their sensory acuity is well developed and they respond to the patient in the moment, rather than invoking a concept of what should be done.
- They demonstrate behavioral flexibility, trying different approaches, and work toward developing the same quality in their clients.
- They share a belief—not necessarily made explicit—that the structure of the client's problem is more significant for making change than its content.
- They see problem clients as a challenge and an opportunity to learn.
- They regard the client's condition as an attempt to deal with a problem, rather than a sign that the client is broken or stuck.
- They have certain unconscious or intuitive skills and behavior patterns in common.

Among these commonalities was the kind of questions they asked. Somehow these people seemed to have the ability to ask questions that put the client on the way to recovery. When we analyzed the effective therapists and teachers, we found that they focused less on gaining more information about the possible origins of the problem, and they paid more attention to helping the client retrieve deleted, distorted, and generalized information. In this way, the client was able to reconfigure her or his internal map. The syntactic distinctions, published as the Meta Model in Volume I of *The Structure of Magic*, were intended to explore the underlying, full sensory representation (the deep structure) of the thoughts and utterances (the surface structure) made after information had been filtered out by the processes of deletion, distortion, and generalization. A simplified version of the model is laid out in Resource File 4 (page 311), and I suggest you spend some time studying and practicing the different patterns and their challenges. The section that follows is intended to give a feeling for what is possible with mastery of the model.

Over the years, some people have come to see the Meta Model as a form of therapy, possibly because the book included a transcript of a therapy session, identifying a client's violations of the Meta Model together with the therapist's challenges. But the Meta Model has nothing to do with therapy. It is a powerful, recursive, linguistic pattern used to uncover quality information. That's why, when I use the Meta Model, I always ask for the biggest chunk of information first. I start the opposite way to that laid out in *The Structure of Magic I*.

The purpose of the Meta Model is to be meticulous, to ask the kind of questions that will help you find out how somebody's problem works so that you make sure you alter just the problem, and not everything else in the person's life.

Somebody comes in and says, "I'm depressed."

I challenge the generalization (the Universal Quantifier) within the statement by asking, "*Every* moment of *every* single day? Even in the shower?"

They might admit, "Well, not always."

I then ask, "So how do you know when to be depressed?"

Some people respond, "I'm depressed whenever I have spare time."

With the Meta Model as a tool, there's no reason to quit. I ask, "How do you know when it's spare?"

They say, "Because my mind races . . ."

"Ah, the racing mind," I go. Now I start to get quality information. I ask, "When your mind is racing, what exactly is it doing?" and this is where all the details emerge of how the subject is creating the experience: pictures going by, voices yakking away, feelings slopping from here to there, or any combination.

What actually happens with this approach is that you're defining the experience as volitional instead of outside the person's control. You say things like: "So if you make a picture of X, then you say that to yourself Y, then you feel Z . . ." This is all process, and once expressed as a process, it presupposes that the process is open to change.

If we accept the other way of saying things, "I have depression" or "The problem is my frustration," the speaker has taken a verb and turned it into a noun (nominalization), and in so doing has also deleted information such as the fact that he's making the pictures, saying those negative things in his head, and feeling those bad feelings.

Every sentence has a lost performative (an indication as to who is responsible for the action being complained of), and as soon as you restore that performative, you're returning responsibility and power to the client. I use the phrase, "So, what you're saying to me is . . . ," to restore the lost performative.

They might say: "I'm not happy" and claim they've "never really" been happy.

I can choose to challenge them by questioning the "never," or I can say something like: "So, you're saying to me that you can never be happy."

They'll say, "Well, yes."

I'll ask, "And how do you know that?"—because they're making a comment about their state of mind, not about the nature of reality.

They'll usually respond: "Well, I just know it, because . . ."

I'll say: "No, no, I don't want to know why. I want to know *how* you know."

They'll say something like, "Well, because I've never really been happy."

I'll follow up with: "Well, if you've never tried something, how do you know whether you like it or not? Maybe happiness isn't all it's cracked up to be. Maybe really happy people are actually miserable. They could be just pretending. It could all be a big con."

Then they say, "Okay, I know because I've had moments when I've been happy."

I say, "Ahh, so there have been moments. What was that like?"

Using the Meta Model requires a certain amount of finesse and elegance. Just asking the questions by rote is not going to get the results you want. There should always be the presupposition of change in the language you use. For example, often, as I'm bringing someone out of trance, I tell them to "go back and remember this bad feeling for the last time." Nobody ever questions it. I say: "Have you got it?"

They say, "It's really hard now."

I say, "Work at it more."

Now, whether they get the feeling back a little or a lot doesn't matter. They've already accepted the presupposition that the bad feeling can and will be felt "for the last time."

Meta Model questions are designed to gather information. You can think of the model itself as a sword that chops up meaning. It slices things out, sorting what works from what doesn't, always moving toward whatever outcome you want.

So, whatever it is they want, your message is, "Okay, we chop away all the things that won't get you there."

People will tell you they want something like "being comfort-able about public speaking." The presupposition in there, right to start with, is that what they're asking for is a good thing. You could challenge what the Meta Model calls the Universal Quantifier by asking, "Are you saying you want to fall asleep in front of your audiences?"

They'll say, "No, of course not. No, maybe, it's . . . I'd like people to admire me."

You might respond, "For no particular reason? You want them to just to hang around obsessively admiring you?"

They'll say, "Wow, no. I don't want that, I want . . ."

You slice away the nonsense until finally they explain, "Look, okay, so, I want to be relaxed, but alert. I want to engage my audience's attention and see that they're enjoying themselves," and so on.

Then they realize they've been going inside, seeing themselves terrified, sweating, voice cracking, everybody in the audience laughing, and you say: "Good plan. That'll get you into the right state."

Not only do they see that their old behavior was not a good plan, but that they've been doing it habitually and also uncon-sciously. By asking the Meta Model questions, you bring their behavior up into consciousness, make it move a little slower, then start slicing away the nonsense. It tells you everything you need to know, including what to do next.

One of my favorite cases, which I wrote about in *Magic in Action*, involved a woman who had psychotic episodes whenever anyone she was expecting to meet was late. She'd been in therapy for eight years, had three different therapists that I knew about, and whenever anyone asked her why she had these responses, she'd say, "I don't know."

But when the woman said, "I have a problem I'm too close to," I knew the solution was to push away the pictures. She was making pictures of horrible road accidents that became progressively closer, bigger, and more detailed, until she smelled the burning metal and felt the warm blood spattering on her skin. That would scare anyone. She let me know that we needed to push the images out, make them less and less distinct until they disappeared. We did, and it worked, all in a fifteen-minute session.

MAKING THE DIAGNOSIS WRONG

I'm not trying to diagnose people with this approach; I'm trying to make the diagnosis wrong. If people come in and say they're depressed, I want them laughing their asses off as quickly as possible, so, after that, every time they think about being depressed they burst out laughing.

I want to give them a better problem. Often I listen to clients and think: "What a sad little problem. They need something bigger and better." They need to find the answer to questions like: *How much pleasure can I stand? How much can I get done in a lifetime? How can I feel really great every time I go into a meeting or see my husband or wife?*

If people don't ask the right questions, their brains don't learn. I always know when the questions are coming, so I throw out a better question. I say, "Stop and say to yourself, 'It's time to do something. What should I do?'" I just switch the Referential Index (who is saying what). It's not elegant, but it works.

All the above examples illustrate how the Meta Model works. The questions lead us directly to where we want to go, because we're looking at the syntax of the question, not its content. If you fall into content, you'll drown because content is infinite. We all know how little kids going "why?" can go on forever. The fact that a psychiatrist might do that means therapy can last for years.

It doesn't matter to me why something happened. I don't try to read minds or encourage clients to read their own minds. I want answers that point me in the direction of making change. You have to know how to ask just the right questions, and then you have to know how to give just the right suggestions, in just the right way, so that you maximize the result that you want. Being able to move smoothly back and forth between knowing how something happens and what to do about it is what good NLP is about.

This is where the Milton patterns become so important. The Milton Model (see Resource File 5, page 316) is sometimes said to be the mirror image of the Meta Model, but while the Meta Model is applied to gain quality information, the Milton Model— derived from the patterns modeled from Erickson's work—uses language in an "artfully vague" way to induce trance and promote change.

It's often assumed I knew a lot about hypnosis before I heard about Milton Erickson, but when Gregory Bateson first told me about Milton, I knew nothing. So I gathered his collected works, all his journal articles, everything I could find written by him, and read it all. What I found interesting was that he was claiming to get results that nobody else said they could achieve.

I was intrigued by Milton's claims, so I went out and got every book—literally hundreds of books—about hypnosis and read them all. I tried out everything, a lot of it on an extraordinary neighbor I had at the time. She was agoraphobic and had allergies and all sorts of things wrong, and we fixed them all. So, by the time I got to actually see Milton, I had quite a lot of experience, and I'd already analyzed his language patterns, from the journal articles and the transcripts.

It was fairly apparent that most of the people who knew about him were as mystified by him as they were by Virginia Satir and by Fritz Perls.

Virginia, who achieved consistently good results, didn't claim to have the right approach to therapy. She just said that people could be helped more easily if all the family members were involved, rather than just the individual. Also, her ability to observe patterns and predict behavior was extraordinary. On one occasion, when I drove her to see a family whose epileptic daughter had been labeled a juvenile delinquent, she said, "Watch what happens. In the middle of this session, the girl is going to have a seizure. The moment I start talking to one or other of the family members, she's going to fall down in a fit." Sure enough, that's exactly what happened. This was the sort of thing that happened around Virginia. But one of the most important qualities she had was that she was absolutely relentless. She was warm and sweet and kind, but she didn't give up. It didn't matter to her if it took twelve hours. She would keep working until she got the change she was after.

Virginia was an exquisite hypnotist, something she strongly denied at first. I showed her videotapes of her and Erickson, and for the first ten minutes they said exactly the same things. Virginia had nicer tonality than Milton. He sounded a little like Boris Karloff. She sounded like the sweetest person on the earth.

It was superb hypnosis, but she said it was just a centering exercise. She'd talk about people's uniqueness, how each was the only one in the world with those fingerprints, and so on. Then I'd turn on the Milton tape, and he'd talk about the individuality of his patients, how their fingerprints were unique—the same concepts, in the same order.

It took her time to admit it, but, finally she came around, and even asked me to use hypnosis to help her with a personal problem.

Virginia had met Milton and thought he was creepy and didn't want anything to do with him. I have to admit, I understood why she felt that way. He was in a wheelchair, having had polio twice, and was suffering from postpolio syndrome. He wore purple pajamas, induced trance, and communicated covertly more or less all the time, even when he didn't need to. But he did it to amuse himself. Interestingly, though, despite their differences, Virginia and Milton were, in my opinion, the best at getting results.

Fritz's work was very hypnotic, too. Telling clients to hallucinate dead relatives in empty chairs—what is that if it isn't deep trance hypnosis?

In reality, Fritz didn't actually have a very good track record fixing clients. Everybody was impressed with his work, but he didn't get good results. He couldn't get an insomniac suddenly to be able to sleep, for example, and he was very open about the fact that he couldn't work with psychotics or schizophrenics. He only worked with "neurotics."

On one occasion, though, he did help a client get over his impotence by having him think about his nose and then his genitals and his nose again. He couldn't explain how it worked; he just said it was something that fit his theory. Now, of course, we know that in the motor cortex, the wiring for the muscles of the nose and the genitals are right next to each other. If you move your nose, typically your genitals will move; typically, if you flare your nostrils or move the nose up and down, you stimulate your genitals.

When the patterns I identified were first published as the Milton Model, Milton was very pleased, even though he implied they only reflected a part of his repertoire. Milton's approach could be very complicated. He very strongly identified with the concept of "being a hypnotist" and insisted that all his clients become exceptional hypnotic subjects before they went any further.

I was more interested in how far I could push this thing called hypnosis, so I tried everything that he ever claimed you could do. This was not because I wanted to disprove it, but because if I could produce the same effects, then I knew there would be a world of things that hadn't even been tried.

I tried things no one had ever tried before. I wanted to find out what effects could be achieved with light trance and deep trance; I wanted to see how far we could go. I have to admit that a lot of my clients went through a lot of demanding stuff so I could find easier ways of doing things.

The people who really should get credit for my work are the clients who came to me at the end of their ropes. In fact, nobody came to me first. They only came to me because everybody had given up on them. They always said, "You're my last hope," and I'd always respond, "Boy, you're in big trouble then."

But I didn't give up. From Virginia Satir I learned to be relentless. I learned that if something doesn't work, you just do something else. Failure is when you stop, and I never stopped.

In practice, Erickson didn't use all the patterns that became known as the Milton Model, nor do I. Since I paid attention to Erickson, Satir, and Perls, as well as to those "ordinary" people who accomplished things by themselves, it became possible to create a technology that was universal in its application, was fast, and that anyone could learn. Quite simply, the language we use has a direct impact on the listener's neurology. The language we use when talking to and about ourselves also affects our own neurology.

Not everybody will use Milton patterns the same way. The people who become really familiar with them will find they have certain preferences and will naturally develop their own distinctive styles.

TEMPORAL PREDICATES

For my part, I find temporal predicates—words that refer to time and its passage—incredibly powerful. I use temporal predicates as linkage—"*when* you sit here breathing in and out, *then* you will relax, and *as* you think about this for the last time . . ." But there are many more ways temporal language can be used.

Inducing confusion increases suggestibility—for example:

> *[B]efore you stop yourself from preventing the idea that you don't know what's coming later, it'll be here, but before we start to continue with what isn't important about what you don't know, you'll find that you've just begun to go backwards, because the past is just a future moving by now . . .*

This passage demonstrates how language patterns can be layered. Aside from the temporal predicates, that last sentence is stacked with ambiguities—words and phrases that could have more than one meaning, leaving the unconscious room to explore alternatives that have not been explicitly stated.

Another reason I regard temporal predicates as particularly important is to make clear the very important distinction between the past and the future. The best thing about the past is that it's over. When people don't deal with the past as if it's over, then they're not free to go into the future. That's why I particularly love the ambiguity that "the past is just a future moving by now . . ." (I suggest that you reread that sentence very carefully to find out for yourself how many meanings it contains.)

SEMANTIC DENSITY

I often talk about people being angry or sad or depressed "for the last time." I like what are known as "semantically dense" predicates, something linguistics spends a lot of time discussing. For instance, one doesn't lurk up to somebody openly. The verb "lurk" has all kinds of connotations that don't need to be stated, so when you say that somebody is walking around the edge of a crowd, as opposed to lurking around the edge of a crowd, the semantically denser phrase has greater impact.

Temporal predicates—words like "last," "first," "after," "again"— all have semantic density. Phrases including the word "when" ("when you start to do X, you'll find something important") and "next" ("the next time you see him, you'll feel Y") really allow you to aim posthypnotic suggestions to maximum effect.

I think of temporal predicates as targeting devices that allow you to place feelings, amplify them or diminish them, with great power and precision.

Temporal predicates, of course, are directly connected to presuppositions. Presuppositions literally "presuppose" or assume that something is present, even though they are not explicitly stated. A question such as, "When you get up, could you close the door?" contains a number of presuppositions: that the listener will get up, that there is a door, that he is capable of closing the door, and so on.

Many syntactic environments for presuppositions are based on temporal predicates. The "when" in the previous example is a temporal predicate that supports the presupposition. I find these to be extremely powerful, especially when you talk about doing something "for the last time," or about feeling something "never again and again and again."

There are also wonderful, simple, and effective words like "stop." Most people don't think of "stop" as a temporal predicate, but when I see people beginning to go into a behavioral loop that's going to run ad infinitum, where they start to get a bad feeling or a panic attack, I say to them, "Stop"—and, amazingly, they usually do.

Add to that a phrase such as "back up," and you have even more effective tools. When someone is sitting down, there's no way to physically back up, so when you say, "Stop. Back up and feel something else this time," they know at a deep level what to do.

Another word that is temporal in nature is "new." "New" implies that you're going to do something in the future so "this old feeling that's going past isn't going to be as satisfying as when you find new feelings coming . . . now."

"Now" is one of the most powerful temporal predicates in the hypnotist's repertoire. People, especially in altered states, can be very passive, so you have to tell them what to do, when to do it, when to start . . . and now, of course, is a good time. If I tell people to "go deeper," it doesn't mean they will. I tell them exactly when to do anything I want them to do: "Your arm will drop . . . now"; "In exactly two minutes you'll find these thoughts coming into your head, now, and then you'll find . . ."

Ambiguity is a useful pattern when working with somebody who has a suspicious conscious mind and doesn't trust himself. Then I'll talk "through" them to their other parts, trying to come in from the back door to the front door, instead of the front door to the back. Of course, if I have the subject's cooperation, I'll use it. I'll get the conscious mind and the unconscious mind doing the same thing. The more you can line up a person's resources, the better off you are.

PUNCTUATION AND SCOPE AMBIGUITIES

The categories known as punctuation and scope ambiguities need special attention. Not only are they effective in themselves, but they are also modified by temporal predicates. "Time and again and again you'll start to have old feelings disappear"; "Those same old feelings will come up for the last time just before you feel them now disappearing . . ."

These patterns are very hard for the conscious mind to follow, but very easy for the language-processing centers of the brain to compute. I don't know how many times I've given people suggestions, and they looked at me and said, "What?" . . . and then carried them out to the letter, at precisely the right time, because they were given specific temporal markers.

Now, take a minute or two to find a new idea . . .

Milton used the phrase "Your unconscious now" ("you're unconscious now") many, many times. It's a great ambiguity, but as soon as you slam that temporal predicate after the word "unconscious," it also becomes a command. "Your unconscious now . . . wants new ideas," "Your unconscious now wants to know even more unconscious now . . . You'll see that you're not doing what you can see the future coming now . . ."

All of those kinds of temporal phrases give you great room to put content on either side. It's about deciding a direction and aiming where you want things to go. What you're doing in hypnosis is leading someone's consciousness down a certain path, and you have to decide whether that path leads into their past or their future. Some things you want behind them and some you want in front. Some you want gone forever.

LANGUAGE IN ACTION

Forewarned is forewarned . . . and the more warned you are about where you're not going . . . you need to have signs in your mind that say, *Stop, go back, you're going the wrong way.* In the United States, they put those on freeway on-ramps so you don't go on the wrong one and end up going against traffic. I install them in people's minds. I say: You need a sign in your head that says, *Go back, you're going the wrong way!*

Now, stop, go back, and remember that idea you just thought about, only just get to the sign at the entrance. *Bad idea. Go back. You're going the wrong way* . . . now. And then see the signs of where you should go. *Pleasure ahead. Happiness coming. Choices ahead. Past behind.* Leave it behind, now, so when you go ahead of time—because it's not enough to be in the now—you need to be ahead of the now, because the future is coming, the past is behind, so never, yeah, never do never again. Never forget what you shouldn't remember. And always remember what you shouldn't forget . . . now. And then you'll do it correctly. Because, once again (I love that "once again"), you'll find tomorrow is much better.

Yes to day (I love that one, too. That's full of logical ambiguity, "yes to day"). And when it comes to hope, yes to day has no bearing. Now . . .

Notice how densely the language patterns are stacked. When

you have temporal predicates and presuppositions, and when you stack presuppositions—at least three at a time—it becomes extremely difficult for the listener to track consciously, so it produces a very strong effect on the listener's unconscious.

Another pattern I'm particularly fond of is "the more, the more" pattern. I use that one all the time, especially with negations stacked one on top of the other. *"The more you try to stop yourself from preventing what you know that you don't understand, the more you will, because, as you try to continue to not do something you won't be able to not see what's going on."*

The purpose is to overload the unconscious, and once that happens, the doors open up and you can flood in the suggestions.

I often say that I'm not a hypnotist so much as a "hypno-ranter." Where most people are providing gentle, nondirective suggestions, I'm slamming things in from every side, and every way that I can.

Speaking to the unconscious processes inside somebody with semantic density is an art form. It's almost like being able to write good poetry, but it doesn't come from nowhere. It's not an innate talent. It's something you develop, and the way you develop it is through practice.

I recommend that you spend two days on one kind of syntactic environment and the next two days on another. You can refer to Resource Files 4 and 5 (pages 311 and 316) for further explanation and inspiration, but to be able to generate language patterns without needing to think about them, you should write down pages and pages of each pattern. Reconfigure your brain so that it all becomes familiar and easy.

If you don't have a lot of examples of what makes things different, it's very hard to make yourself familiar with it. Hypnotic language patterns, hypnotic states—these are the building blocks. If you didn't know all the letters of the alphabet it would be very hard for you to write anything.

People often consider me to be a very complicated person. It's true that I know a lot of really complicated things, but when I work with human beings, there's nothing complicated about it at all. I have broken things down for years and learned how they work, and then I've practiced putting them into effect. I studied language patterns so that I can automatically and unconsciously generate them in many sophisticated forms. I don't need to think about them anymore. I just do it, while keeping my eye on where I want to be.

These are the things that set people free.

Exercise 1: The Meta Model

1. Refer to Resource File 4. Begin to practice noticing Meta Model patterns, spending two days on each. Pay special attention to the language you hear, noting the violations that occur. Television interviews with politicians are a rich source of Meta Model violations.
2. As you become more familiar with each pattern, jot down some of the challenges you would use in a real-time situation.

Exercise 2: The Meta Model

1. Working with a partner, discuss a real or imaginary prob-lem. The listener notes Meta Model violations and chal-lenges them, always seeking to recover information that has been deleted, distorted, or generalized.
2. Change places and repeat.

Exercise 1: The Milton Model

1. Review the examples given in Resource File 5, then cre-ate at least twenty of your own.

Exercise 2: The Milton Model

1. Decide on an outcome you would like for a client. Choose three to five Milton Model patterns, and create a conversational induction by linking the patterns with conjunctions or temporal connections. Repeat the pattern three times, so that each induction comprises between nine and fifteen examples of hypnotic language.

Five

DIRECTIONS OR OUTCOMES
Planning to Succeed

ALL THE SUCCESSFUL PEOPLE I've studied share two important qualities: they know where they're going, and they're prepared to put in whatever work is necessary to get them from where they are now to where they want to be. This is what I would like readers of this book to develop, both for themselves and for the people they will be able to help: their friends, family, and clients.

Great golfers practice, practice, practice. Baseball players spend their time in the batting cages, having people pitch to them for hour upon hour upon hour. Professional musicians spend more time practicing than they do performing. I worked with a close-up card magician once, and he would sit there doing the same trick again and again and again. Interestingly, whenever any of these people make a mistake or fall short of their goal, they never complain that they were doing it wrong or underperforming, or failing—they simply laugh or shrug and do it again until they get it right.

The magician's strategy was to make a movie of how his hands were supposed to move when the trick worked perfectly. Then he'd move around and step into the image—slide his hands into the hands that could do the trick perfectly—and try to replicate the action.

Most successful athletes do this, or something similar. They know what perfection looks like. They see it being done perfectly, then step inside it, and carry out the action, knowing they've succeeded when they get a good feeling.

It's important to realize that they don't feel bad when they don't get it right; they simply don't feel anything at all. But when they start to get it right, they feel good, and the better they get, the better they feel—so it builds an addiction to trying. Even if they only get it right one out of ten times, that feeling makes it worthwhile. They push right through the nine times for the buzz of the tenth. After a while, they get it twice out of ten, then four times, and so on, and they keep going because they become hooked on the good feeling.

By contrast, many people just feel bad whenever what they decide should happen doesn't work out that way. This is why I often say, "Disappointment takes adequate planning."

Unlike the failure-punishment approach to learning, attaching good feeling to action builds a feed-forward loop that gets people to improve their activity based on feeling better and better. When this strategy is properly in place, people don't mind not getting it right the first time, or even the fourth time, because they know how good it will feel when it does work out.

What works for athletes or magicians works for all of us. We're all playing games of some kind or another—work games, relationship games, parenting games, recreational games—and it's as well we learn to play them to the best of our ability. We need to move in useful, appropriate, and desirable directions. If we try to get through by avoiding discomfort or pain, we're walking backward, and we don't know what we're going to fall into. If we build feed-forward loops so we're moving toward pleasure rather than away from pain, we're walking toward something we want, and we know in which direction we're going.

Many Neuro-Linguistic Programmers talk about getting good outcomes. I talk about setting good directions. It's an important distinction. I want people to have a direction so they keep going. I want them to become involved in the *process* of living. Whenever people come to me and say, "I want to be happy," I always say, "I'm sorry all the Seven Dwarf jobs are gone. You're going to have to be a little more specific than that."

You can't just be happy, but you can learn to do things happily. Living happily entails paying attention to and enjoying the process of doing whatever it is you happen to be doing. It's not just that something goes *bing!* and suddenly you're happy. You learn to be happy by following the old adage about stopping to smell the roses, but you have to enjoy looking at them, and touching them, and walking by them, and everything else about them. You can learn to enjoy everything. You can learn to enjoy sleeping, and waking up, and making breakfast, and going to work. The more things you make pleasant, the happier life will be.

One of my approaches to help people improve their lives is to get them into a light trance, create good feelings for them, and then aim them in a direction where they can see themselves behaving differently. Everyone can learn to behave differently to some degree or other. And everyone can learn to create good feelings. They first have to know what this will be like; then and only then can they go about planning how to do it for themselves.

Planning, of course, takes a little time, but it's time well spent. Since most people are doing it anyway (do you think the person who has anxiety isn't planning to have an attack when he goes into a supermarket, or the OCD sufferer isn't planning to behave compulsively at certain specific times of the day?) you might as well do it properly, making sure you get the result you want.

The first step is always to build choices. This is not quite the same as making the right choice or doing the right thing, then hoping that will make you feel good. That's the basis of many self-development programs. It's also a formula for disappointment. The reason is simple: we often know what we *ought* to do and how we *ought* to feel . . . and not doing that makes us feel terrible.

This usually occurs when we lack the flexibility to make choices. If we have only one response, we're stuck. If we have two, we can oscillate backward and forward. If we have three or more, it starts to feel a lot better.

When I talk about having choices, I don't mean this conceptually. I mean viscerally. It's about learning to feel differently and making sure the better feeling occurs when you're moving in the direction you want to go. When Virginia spoke about having a choice, she didn't talk about knowing about it intellectually. You need to experience neurologically what the options are before you can exercise voluntary choice.

We may all agree that when riding in a plane it's a better choice to be calm than to be terrified, but that doesn't mean you have the choice to be calm—at least, not until you can *either* feel calm *or* terrified. Then you have choice.

Many of us know what we should be doing and don't do it. We know we shouldn't eat the chocolate cake, but we do it. I'm a diabetic and I eat desserts, and I know I'm not supposed to, and I know it so well that I take extra insulin before I go to dinner to compensate for it. But if you don't plan, bad choices will hurt you. For example, lots of men know they shouldn't be looking at other women when they're married, but they just can't stop themselves. They don't really have the choice to not care. They don't know how to shrug it off because they don't know how that feels.

To me, having choice means that you're capable of feeling more than one thing; for most people, it's straight stimulus-response. Thinking inside is not voluntary. Choice is when you can think on purpose, not when you're a victim of your thoughts. Choice means having different sets of possibilities, and then picking between them. Choice means that you get to choose intentionally with a clear idea of the direction or outcome your choice will provide for you, not that you choose and then feel regret because you should have chosen something else.

Most people who complain of being stuck will argue about what it is that keeps them that way—how strong it is, how overwhelming, how unique. The point is, as long as they think of it that way, it will overwhelm them. But it's not really strong and it's certainly not unique. They've just become habituated to representing it that way and have not yet understood that there are other choices to be made.

All I'm really trying to get people to do is to go into states they really go into anyway, but to stay there and to trust the natural processes in themselves more. Rather than exploring in exquisite detail the really horrible pictures that scare them, they should be thinking about which pictures they should be whiting out. Not exploring the origins or discussing the meaning—just whiting out, the way movies fade out at the end.

The pattern is simple: white out the image you don't want, and then immediately replace it with something you prefer. Just take hold of the brightness control and turn it all the way to white and make the image disappear in a blur. If you do it five times, it becomes difficult to recall the picture, even if you try.

It seems that the unconscious understands this simple procedure as a command: not this, that. Not A-to-B, but A-to-C. Once your unconscious accepts the message, it just keeps doing it.

Instead of thinking the thoughts that aren't doing you any good, you get yourself to think the thoughts that will get you where you want to go.

Importantly, it does this without fear. Contrary to what many religious leaders and bad parents and teachers believe, it isn't fear that really propels people forward. Fear stops us short. That's why we have it. This is generally known as the fight/flight response, but, whether you fight or flee, you're still bouncing back and forth inside the primeval nervous system, not the part of the mind that has developed to design and follow plans.

MOVING AWAY FROM THE PAST

Since people worry so much about the past, I've almost completely moved away from taking it into consideration. In helping people overcome difficulties, I mostly just blank them out and replace them with things toward which people are strongly drawn.

It's often said that people can be motivated to either run away from negative experiences or be drawn toward positive things. I work by accentuating people's desires, hopes, and dreams, and making them absolutely irresistible.

If they talk about compulsions, I want them to be compelled to move in the direction they want, in the same way as if, when they spot a roll of hundred-dollar bills lying in the road, they snatch it up. Their brains don't react with, "Oh, you don't know where it's been. It might have germs on it." They just go for it.

They need to have the same immediacy of response when they have ideas in their head about things that are worth doing: valuing their relationships, telling their children they love them, going out and trying to get the jobs they want. They need to recognize and focus on what is important and rewarding, not on what's terrible about life.

I want them to come to their senses and start to figure out how to please the people they care about, how to act in situations where they need to impress somebody important, and how to make sure they don't do stupid things. Instead, they're building up anxiety and worrying about being anxious and becoming even more anxious as a result.

You don't avoid trouble and achieve your dreams by thinking of everything stupid you could do and examining every negative feeling you get—and then trying to ensure those things don't happen. That just keeps you trapped.

The choice is simple. Either you plan and take action to move you in the direction you want to go, or you try to cope with the thoughts, feelings, and experiences that threaten to overwhelm you. The first process is called "thinking"; the second is "reacting." You either react or you think and plan.

I teach lessons on how to think and plan, and I've learned to do it very quickly. When people walk in and start to tell me what's wrong, typically I've seen it and heard it all before. I imagine most people in my profession have. I pretty much know what direction people need to go in, but they're still giving me a list of what they need to stop thinking about and what they want to not feel.

What they're not yet aware of are all the things they need to live happily and successfully.

For years and years I've told people not just to listen to what their clients are saying, but also to notice what they're not talking about, because what's *not* there is what they need.

If somebody can't spell, for example, it's not because there's something wrong with them; it's because they don't have a good spelling strategy. If somebody is shy, that's because they don't think people will like them. That's different from thinking that people won't like them. They're simply not planning on people liking them for who they are, so, when they meet new people, they feel nervous and awkward, and they're not being themselves, so people don't like them. It's a self-fulfilling prophecy.

Since I'm always looking for the shortest route to get people where they want to be, comfortably and with the greatest degree of enjoyment, the techniques I use change at the same time as I change. Over the years, I've abandoned many of the processes that were considered revolutionary in their time—not because they don't work, but because I've found something that allows me to get the same result quicker and more easily.

However, I am able to do this because I built a foundation of experience. I know how these tools and techniques work, and therefore I'm in a position where I can keep developing them. But first I needed to accumulate those foundations on which to build, and I urge you to do the same.

BUILDING YOUR SKILLS

If you become proficient in understanding the patterns discussed here and practicing the skills, you will not only be able to use them with confidence on yourself, your family, your friends, and your clients but you will be able to develop approaches of your own, and help evolve the field even further.

Exercise: Stealing a Skill

1. Decide on a "role model"—someone whose physical performance you would like to replicate. Spend as much time as possible studying your role model in the flesh, on videotapes, or on DVD recordings. Simply relax while watching them, softening your vision and hearing and seeing the flow of the performance.

2. When you feel as familiar as possible with your role model's performance, close your eyes, relax, and re-create your role model performing a sequence of actions at the highest level of excellence. See and hear everything there is to build a model of that competence.

3. When you have watched this performance for some time, move around the mental image of your role model and step inside. Imagine you are able to see through the eyes of excellence, hear through the ears of excellence, and feel the feelings of excellence.

4. Run through the same sequence of actions but from within, noticing this time how your body feels as you do this. Repeat several times until you have a sense of familiarity.

5. Step out of your role model's body, with the intention of retaining as much of the skill as possible as you return to normal waking consciousness.

6. As soon as possible (and as much as possible) practice the borrowed skill, noticing how this exercise improves your performance.

7. Repeat the entire exercise, combining it with whatever real-time practice you do, at least once a day for the first twenty-one days, then at least once a week as maintenance.

Relaxing, going inside, and starting to experience new realities is, by definition, a trance state. It's an important skill to develop, especially with the power of trance. There's a real difference between the visceral vividness of a hypnotic dream and simply thinking about something. Being told how to do something is different from relaxing deeply and going into a state where you live through an experience, using all your senses. One alters the neurology, and the other really doesn't.

STEPS TO ACHIEVEMENT

One of the earliest techniques I developed was the Visual Squash. This was designed to fill in the gaps between the present state and the desired state and to build energy and enthusiasm to maintain movement toward that end.

What makes this technique different from all other goal-setting, planning, and motivational approaches is that it doesn't leave you with an artificial sense of well-being, but with strong, positive feelings that intensify as you follow a series of specific, achievable steps.

Coupled with effective planning, the Visual Squash still proves a valuable tool in setting your direction and identifying the key actions to take.

Exercise: The Visual Squash

1. Create a vivid representation of yourself the way you are now (your present state), with all your difficulties.
2. See yourself the way you would be if you got through all the problems. Be very clear on how you will be behaving, what you will be saying and feeling. Make the image as clear and as rich in detail as possible. Use all your senses.
3. Place one image in each of your hands outstretched in front of you with a space separating them. This space represents the unexplored territory and unspecified steps that lie between the two states.
4. Begin to make a series of images or movies of the logical steps from one state to the other. Adjust each picture or movie, frame by frame, changing whatever needs to be changed, until each is a fully representational, progressive stage of the process of change.
5. When you have between ten and twelve stages in front of you, begin slowly to close your hands, collapsing all the stages into a single process.
6. Bring your clasped hands toward your body and pull the new state into your body, making a new feeling that represents action and success.
7. Spin that feeling faster and faster, intensifying it and allowing it to spread throughout your body, so it permeates every muscle, every organ, every nerve, and every cell. As you do this, look at where you want to go and decide clearly what you need to do first. Then see yourself taking the second step, then the third, and keep spinning and intensifying the feeling until you feel compelled to get up and go for it.

FOOLPROOF PLANNING

Sometimes, when people make step-by-step plans to achieve a specific outcome, they find themselves engulfed in even more problems. The outcome is so overwhelmingly large or complex, they are unable to distinguish between steps that will carry them in the direction they want to go and steps that will lead them astray. The planning method below clarifies direction and outcome but also ensures that only the relevant steps are included in the plan.

Be sure you observe the conditions of well-formedness when planning. In NLP a particular outcome is well-formed—and most likely to be achieved—when it is:

1. Stated in positives (that is, what is wanted, not what is not wanted).
2. Initiated and maintained by the individual (to maintain proaction and self-efficacy).
3. Ecological (either confined to the context where it is desired, or unlikely to negatively impact other areas of the subject's life).
4. Testable in experience (sensory based; expressed in what the subject will see, hear, feel, and, perhaps, taste and smell).

These conditions of well-formedness are offered as a simple checklist to ensure that you and/or the person you are working with are clear and focused in your undertakings.

Exercise: Foolproof Planning

1. Step into a full sensory representation of the way you will be behaving, talking, thinking, and feeling when you are completely on track with your new and preferred direction. To intensify the experience, imagine going through an entire "ideal" day with your new resources already in place, spinning and building on your good feelings.
2. Ask yourself what needs to be done immediately before you could have your perfect day. Make a note of your answer.
3. When you have identified that, ask yourself the same question: what needs to be done immediately before you achieve that step. Write down the answer.
4. Repeat until you have moved backward to your starting point. You should now have all the key steps needed to carry you from your present state to your desired state.
5. Carefully give each step a start and finish date, making sure that they all complete within your overall timescale.

Note: Complex tasks can be broken into separate components, each of which can be reverse-engineered as above, making sure that none of the start-finish dates clash.

Six

SEEING INSIDE THE
BLACK BOX
Accessing Cues, Predicates, and Strategies

THE BEHAVIORISTS, INSPIRED BY B. F. Skinner, tried to solve the problem of thinking by eliminating the brain—literally. They explained all behavior as the result of a stimulus that went into the "black box" (otherwise known as the brain, the most sophisticated organ in the universe) and came out as a response. They decided what happened in between the "S" and the "R" shouldn't be taken into consideration, because it couldn't be observed.

They were wrong.

People leak clues from every pore about how they're processing information. In fact, people can't avoid communicating, even when they choose to say nothing.

Still, the psychologists and psychiatrists got themselves deeper into trouble because they insisted on defending their theories and trying to interpret their patients' experience, rather than listening to and observing what was going on with the person in front of them.

Some said you could get at truth through free association, others by analyzing dreams. Some really believed (and still believe) that the more times victims of trauma go over and over their traumatic experiences, the better they'd feel. If that were true, all sufferers of conditions such as Post-Traumatic Stress Disorder would fix themselves, since obsessively going back, over and over, their past experiences is a characteristic of their problem.

The biggest mystery to me is how the entire field of psychology could miss the fact that when people think, their eyes move in particular directions. Even now, some researchers question this—despite the evidence right there in front of them.

Furthermore, the directions in which they move their eyes are patterned. When right-handed people are making remembered images, their eyes tend to go up and to the left; when they create pictures of things they haven't actually seen before, their eyes go up and to the right. When they talk to themselves, their eyes go down to the left (sometimes they look straight ahead and defocus); and, when they experience deep feelings, their eyes go down to the right. With left-handed people, this pattern is often reversed.

I noticed this pretty early on in my work. It's actually quite difficult to miss when you're on stage and you ask four hundred people to remember something that happened to them, and four hundred pairs of eyes go all the way up and to the left as they're thinking, "Hmm. Now, let's see . . ."

It's just as difficult to miss that when people are depressed they look down, their eyes flicking from one side to another, as they talk to themselves about how downright bad they're feeling.

Despite the controversy this observation aroused in the mainstream, people were intuitively aware of this behavior. Actors followed these patterns in silent movies. You could even see this in Betty Boop cartoons from the 1920s. But the entire field of psychology missed this, simply because the psychologists themselves were not really observing human behavior, nor listening to people talk. They claimed they were, but really they were *interpreting* behavior—and when you do that you're too busy to pay full attention to the person in front of you.

I was able to notice this, and a whole lot of other things about human behavior, because I approached everything not as a psychologist but as an information scientist. I was more interested in noticing what was happening and finding out what that meant than I was in developing a theory and trying to force the client's behavior to fit it.

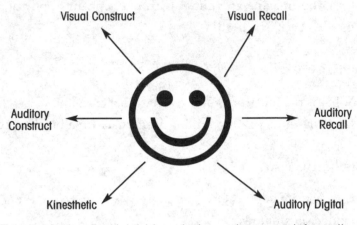

Figure 6.1. How most right-handed people access information; left-handers are often reversed.

Good NLP practitioners routinely calibrate to their subjects' individual responses by asking certain questions, then checking the results. Some people may demonstrate idiosyncratic eye-accessing patterns, but they will always be consistent. Their eye-accessing cues will be organized systematically for them.

Here are some suggestions for the kind of questions you might ask:

Visual Recall (Eidetic memory):

• How did you get here today?
• Were there many people on the bus?

- Have they finished painting the door downstairs? What color is it now?

Visual Constructed:

- How would you look if you lost the weight you want?
- Can you imagine an animal with an elephant's body and a giraffe's neck and head?

Auditory Recall:

- What is the fourth word of the national anthem?
- Can you think of the sound of fingernails on a blackboard?

Auditory Constructed:

- Can you imagine the sound a snowflake would make as it landed on a pillow?
- Can you sing the first three notes of "Three Blind Mice" inside your head—backward?

Auditory Digital (Words or sounds; self-talk):

- What do you say inside your head to get yourself up in the morning?
- What exactly are you saying to yourself right now when you say you can't relax?

Kinesthetic:

- Can you feel what it's like to stroke a cat's fur?
- Which of your hands is warmer than the other?

PATTERN: Calibrating Internal Processing Part 1

1. Create a list of several questions for each of the organizational categories. Make them as conversational as possible.
2. Test your questions with several partners and keep a record. Rotate through the categories systematically to test the consistency of their responses (and the specificity of your questions).

When people first learn about eye-accessing cues, they go out into the world and suddenly find themselves in the middle of a Fellini movie. People talking to each other or trying to make their minds up about what to buy in the supermarket roll their eyes around in the most bizarre ways—totally unaware they are doing it, and totally unaware they are giving away huge amounts of information about how they're thinking.

But it is important to listen as well as watch. It takes some effort to take one's attention away from the content of someone's problem—the story of why they think they got to be the way they are—and place it on how they are expressing themselves. When you do watch and listen, another interesting pattern emerges—that of representational system predicates, or preferred sensory predicates.

We know from Chapter 3 that people have sensory system preferences. People use a wide range of words and phrases that provide clues as to which of the senses they are using to process information.

Here are some examples (see Resource File 2 on page 308 for further examples):

Visual: "I see what you mean." "I get the picture."
Auditory: "That sounds about right." "I hear what you're saying."
Kinesthetic: "That feels right." "I came to grips with that."

Matching eye-accessing cues with sensory predicates will often confirm the speaker's preferred processing method, but it can also be a useful indicator of information that is outside of the speaker's conscious awareness—for example, a particular incident may have dropped out of conscious awareness, but visual or auditory recall cues suggest it may be influencing the person at an unconscious level.

I firmly believe that the human brain stores everything that ever happens to us. Using deep hypnosis, I have had people regress to childhood, sitting on a parent's knee, and being able to recall every word of a book they last saw forty years ago, before they'd even learned to read.

So, when someone tells me, "I can't draw. I just don't have any talent," and their eyes keep flicking to their left, I can be reasonably sure they're unconsciously recalling someone telling them that, maybe many years before.

That's the point when I ask my favorite Meta Model question: "How do you know?"

Inevitably, they'll say, "I don't know. I just can't."

Be aware that the word "just" almost always signals that the speaker is at the edge of their conscious awareness, and that by persisting, you can help them reconnect with their unconscious model.

The process this person might eventually come up with could be something like this: "Well, I get this picture of my grade-school art teacher leaning over me and saying in this really dismissive voice: 'You're never going to be able to draw. You don't have the

talent,' and then I get this sinking feeling in the pit of my stomach that I got every time my father told me how stupid I was, and
I just can't seem to get anything right, so what's the point of even
trying? There have been enough people in my life who've said it,
so it must be true."

Some psychotherapists will see a lifetime's work, a new Porsche,
and a house on the beach in a statement like this. The experienced
NLP practitioner will notice something else.

Not only is the speaker driven by remembered images of critical people and the statements they made, but these statements
cause certain feelings that in turn remind him of all the other critical people and the statements they made . . . and so on, in a
never-ending loop.

The sequence of visual, auditory, and kinesthetic constructs is
what we call a strategy. People have strategies for doing everything, from getting out of bed in the morning to deciding the
right person to marry. The characteristic of any strategy is that
the person using it has to go through the same sequence of steps
to get a predictable result.

Can the person draw? Almost certainly he can. The problem
thus far has been that the strategy he has been using to feel bad
about "having no talent" is entirely different from the strategy
used by people who draw and paint extremely well.

I discovered this point while watching a man painting at the
side of the river. He kept looking up at the scene, looking down at
his canvas, painting a stroke or two, looking up again, and so on.

Eventually I went up to him and asked him directly: "How do
you know how to get what you see down on your canvas?"

He thought a bit, then said, "Well, as I'm looking at the scene
I want to paint, I feel this wire in my mind that goes from my

brush to the scene outside, and, as I mentally trace the details of the scene, the wire moves my hand in the same way and I can feel the marks I see on my canvas are right."

Since then, I've taught this strategy to hundreds of people, all of whom believed they couldn't draw or paint and now are very competent and enthusiastic artists.

A major key to helping people optimize their thinking is to understand how they use their senses and how they sequence their internal processing to have a particular result. If you wish formally to elicit and record strategies, the annotation system in Resource File 6 is often used (see page 327). However, like all NLP patterns and techniques, familiarity through practice allows one to observe sequencing patterns without too much distraction.

The way children are taught to spell is symptomatic of how the educational system is stuck in old ways of thinking. Some people, it is believed, are naturally good spellers, and others are not. Of course, when I heard that, I was immediately interested in what the real distinctions were between the two.

When I was in school, they told us spelling was phonetic. You had to sound out the word, and then write it down the way it sounded. That was the only strategy the system recognized. But, of course, you also had to remember all sorts of rules, such as "i before e, except after c," and that some letters were silent, and you spelled "cat" with a "c," even though it sounded like a "k." It struck me even then that you couldn't even spell "phonetic" phonetically.

The system is also flawed in its concept that there's such a thing as a second-grade word and a third-grade word, and so on—and all that's nonsense. There are just words, and when you know how, it's possible to spell any of them.

When I modeled good spellers, I found out why. These people

didn't sound out the words, even though words are auditory; they overlapped into the visual channel. They made pictures of the words.

With that in mind, I went into schools where kids couldn't spell and taught them to make pictures of the words and copy them down. Suddenly, bad spellers became good spellers.

The same thing is true about math; the same thing is true about science; the same thing is true about learning everything. People who are said to have innate talents simply have particularly effective mental strategies.

The late Robert Anton Wilson, a prolific writer and speaker, and an old friend of mine, used to recite poetry to me for hours. When I asked him how he memorized it all, he said, "Well, I have it on a really big page, and I just read it off."

Anybody who ever saw Bob give a talk will immediately understand what he meant. As he spoke, Bob would move his head from one side to the other to "read" the sentences written there. Because the picture he created in his mind was big, twenty feet high and twenty feet across, with great big letters on it, it contained a lot of information. It was easy to read and easy to remember.

My own strategy was somewhat different. When I was in school, I tried to memorize poetry by rote. After the first line, things always got tricky. So, because I was interested in music and words are much easier to remember if there's a melody, I learned to turn them into songs. I became better and better at doing it, because it was a lot more fun.

Having the right mental strategy doesn't mean you don't have to practice a skill anymore. It means that it works and you enjoy it, and therefore you'll practice it more and more and more and more.

EXERCISE: The NLP Spelling Strategy

1. Find a word you would like to be able to spell. Make sure you have an example of the correct spelling in front of you.
2. Visualize a large whiteboard in your upper, left internal field. Imagine writing the word in large, clear letters on your whiteboard, moving your hand as you write. Make each letter a different color, if you like—or you may choose to color-code each class of word: verbs may be orange, nouns blue, and so on.
3. Check that the word is correctly spelled by comparing your internal representation with the book or dictionary in front of you. Make a special note of the feeling (kinesthetic) you get when the spellings correspond.
4. Now, close your eyes and spell the word out loud by "reading" it off your internal whiteboard. Check again against the printed word and your kinesthetic feeling that it is correct.
5. Challenge yourself by identifying the fourth letter from the left, third from the end, every second letter, all the vowels, and so on. Finally spell the word out loud forward and backward. File it away mentally, but take it out every so often to reinforce the process.

GETTING THINGS DONE

When people have problems getting things done, it's almost always because they have too much rubbish in their strategies. When there are too many steps or too much internal dialogue, there's too much fighting with yourself. You have all these excessive feelings, even when you're trying to do relatively simple tasks.

Of course, if you're going to do something complex, having a complex strategy is really practical, but if you're going to do something simple, your strategy needs to be equally simple.

It's worth looking at lazy people to see how it's done. Lazy people would never do more than they have to. Lazy people make things easy on themselves.

I'm basically quite lazy, which is how I came to recognize the value of simplicity. I do a lot of things the easy way. I have a pair of glasses that I leave on my computer so when I sit down I don't have to say, "Oh, hell, I need to get my glasses." They're a cheap, ten-dollar drugstore pair, and they save me walking back and forth across the room ninety-five times a day.

Any respectable lazy person plans for being lazy, and life just becomes easier. But if you have to do this and forget that, and worry about something else, it's just a lot of work—and if you say: "Well, I'm just not organized," the truth is that you're organized, but in a way that's not very clever. The point is, you *are* organized, because you always do—or don't do—the same thing, the same way. If you weren't organized, it would happen randomly, and that just doesn't happen.

When the plan inside your head is just too complicated and something you want isn't there, rather than saying, "From now on, before I leave the house I'm going to remember this," you're saying, "I should have remembered this," "I shouldn't have forgotten that."

Simply put: if you give yourself bad commands, bad things happen.

A bad command is not about whether it is right or ethical or not; it's about how it's phrased. Most people tell themselves what not to do and are then surprised when what they think they've planned doesn't happen. If you say to yourself, *I shouldn't forget this phone number*, your brain hears, "Forget this phone number, forget this phone number," and, of course, you will.

Almost every time I'm in a restaurant, some parent sees their kid reach for a glass or something, and they look at the kid and say, "Don't spill it!" and *pfffffft*, over it goes, simply because the unconscious doesn't process a negation.

When you give yourself commands, you have to do it in a way that works. Pick a simple challenge where you start making little visual images of carrying out a small task, such as remembering your keys or your purse. Figure out where to keep it so that it's within sight and within reach when you are ready to leave the house. Get into the habit of asking questions such as, "When am I going to use this next?" That's the magic question. When you put it out where it's ready, you're not going to need to be concerned about it until you're ready to go out.

The quick way of installing a simple strategy such as this is to *see yourself carrying out the action, then step into it.* Then—*bang!*—do the thing right away, and it will rapidly become a habit.

People often go to therapists complaining about problems such as procrastination, but procrastination is not a psychological problem; it's just a matter of mental organization.

Some people rebel against approaching life this way. They think it's too easy. But the way I think of things, there's nothing wrong with easy. Life becomes simpler and more efficient if, in your imagination, you run scenarios in which you do things the easy way.

Some martial artists use a similar approach in learning their craft. They watch the teacher do something, then make a picture of themselves doing it, step inside the picture, and become accustomed to the movements in their imagination.

Some Japanese martial arts have students go over and over the movements, criticizing them until they get it right. Chinese martial artists make a picture of themselves doing a movement as perfectly as the teacher, without even having to get on the mat.

They repeatedly make these images over and over again, and then they turn the picture around, step inside the teacher, and make the movements. In this case the teachers were instructing their students on how to plan and to be successful.

I'm asking readers of this book to do the same. Take a moment and plan. Make a plan inside your head, a decision about how to do something differently.

If you plan to make the things that you want more passionate and more appealing, here's the secret. Make vivid pictures, and put them where you already see things about which you're passionate. See what has to be done first, then what follows, and what follows that. Know where you're going—and, above all, make getting there a worthwhile undertaking.

Exercise: Getting Things Done

1. Choose a situation where you feel out of control—not because you don't have the knowledge or the skills, but because your emotions get the better of you. One example of this might be fear of success or fear of failure.
2. Understand at this point that this is simply an attitude that is stopping you from doing something you know you should do, so decide as richly as possible what you will be doing when you are back in control. Choose a specific example of this behavior, preferably one that is immediately testable.

3. Sit comfortably, then float out, imagining yourself sitting a little behind and up from your physical body. In your mind's eye, see the back of your head, the width of your shoulders. See what your clothes look like from this point of view. Make this picture as fully dimensional as possible.

4. Now, imagine that you see yourself starting to stand up, and, as that happens, actually stand, so you are in precisely the same position as your imagined image.

5. Repeat this thought and action several times, making it faster each time, until you feel yourself being pulled to your feet by the vividness of your image.

6. Imagine you are standing a little behind and up from an image of yourself about to start the activity you identified in Step 2. Ensure that it is in the same position and has the same qualities as the standing exercise.

7. Run the activity from start to finish several times. Do this faster and faster, stepping into the image each time, until you feel the same "pull" as before.

8. Test by starting the activity and following it all the way through at least three times. Then sit down quietly for a few moments and imagine how your life will be different and better as this new skill generalizes out into other, equally useful and appropriate areas of your life.

Seven

SUBMODALITY DISTINCTIONS
The Differences That Make a Difference

NOTICING REPRESENTATIONAL SYSTEM predicates was a big door opener for me, especially as I began to listen more. As soon as you list all the visual, auditory, and kinesthetic predicates that people come up with, you start to hear something else. People start to talk about the modalities as having certain qualities. A picture can be "bright" or "dim" or "unclear," for example, while a sound might be "sharp" or "high-pitched," or it might seem to come from one side of the head or the other. Feelings also have distinctions: "dull," "throbbing," "pulsing," "surging," and so on.

The more I listened, the more I heard people saying they had "big" and "bright" ideas, or they couldn't "focus" on things. They had "heavy" problems and "overwhelming" memories and "needed to get some distance" from their troubles.

I watched as I listened, and I noticed that people actually moved their bodies in ways that matched these experiences *as if they were real*.

If they couldn't "get distance" from a problem, or it was "too heavy," they shifted back as if they needed to move back or slumped in the chair under the weight of their experiences. When they remembered some terrible past experience and looked up and to the left, their pupils would actually dilate in fear. Whenever they created pictures that really upset them, they seemed to be actually looking at images that were life-size, or even bigger.

They also made significant gestures. If they had tension or churning or a knot in their stomachs, they'd move their hands in a particular direction. If you asked them directly what was happening, they were able to describe it in detail. Their pictures might be "big and in color and moving"; their fear could be "cold and clammy" and sit in the pit of the stomach, "heavy and unmoving."

Often there was internal talk going on. At that time, many psychiatrists refused to accept that everyone naturally has internal voices. It used to be considered one of the markers of severe psychiatric disorder. Neuroscientists now accept that self-talk is one of the ways we think and try out actions before actually making certain physical moves. What makes us sane is that we know we are generating the self-talk. People suffering auditory hallucinations have lost the ability to code the difference between inside and outside. More than once, I've been able to help someone diagnosed as schizophrenic recover his sanity by helping him find a way of distinguishing between what comes from outside and what is within.

I knew that internal dialogue was a natural phenomenon long before the psychology world accepted the fact. Once again, it was a lesson learned by personal experience.

A man came to me complaining that his internal dialogue was driving him crazy and he wanted it all to stop. The more I tried to discourage him, the more he insisted I do something to make it stop. More to teach him a lesson than anything, I put him into deep trance and told him to shut down his auditory digital channel. He did that—and became completely unable to move. To any observer he would have appeared completely catatonic. I left him like that for a little while and then gave him back his ability to talk to himself—with some amendments.

The problem he had was a common one. The voice that controls many people is also usually highly critical. Not only does it say nasty things, but its tonality is particularly harsh and unpleasant. Naturally, having a voice that sounds harsh and critical nagging away inside your head is going to have an adverse effect on the way you feel—more, probably, than what is actually being said.

Working on the assumption that it might be difficult to change whatever his internal voice was saying to him, I tried a different tack.

I told him to look for the volume control inside his head, and turn the sound all the way down. Then I had him find the control that changed the tone of the sound and told him to change it so that when it came back, the voice was saying all the same things, but in an incredibly mellow and seductive voice, like Sean Connery in an early Bond movie.

He did exactly that, and his problem disappeared.

Sometimes when I tell that story, someone asks, "Do we really have controls for volume and tone inside our heads?"

My response is, "If you want to, you do."

The key point here is that while we know the sensory modalities the subject uses and the sequence in which he arranges his experience are both important, there is another way of making rapid and effective change. When we alter the qualities of the sensory modalities—the submodalities—we alter the nature of the experience itself.

If you return to some of the earlier exercises in this book, you will see how you have already learned to change your subjective experience by manipulating the submodalities. Recalling something as associated or dissociated is a submodality distinction, for example. Moving an image nearer or farther away is another. A more extensive list may be found in Resource File 3 (see page 310).

All this is perfectly logical, since each of the input channels is known to contain a number of specialized receptors. Vision, for example, includes the capacity to distinguish color, movement, light, and dark, while a feeling (both touch and internal sensations) can include pressure, temperature, direction, and so on. The quality of sound cannot only be distinguished but so can the direction from which it comes, its volume, and so on.

It follows, then, that we have the capacity to build highly complex combinations of the sensory modalities and their subcomponents in response to different inputs. It also means that we have the ability to rearrange these patterns in highly specific sequences to change our responses.

There are probably an infinite number of submodalities that people use, although some recur more frequently than others. Visually, the qualities that make a difference for many people are the size and brightness of the internal image, its distance from the subject, whether it's in color, and if it's still or moving. Auditorally, tonality is often more important than the actual meaning of the words. Think of how many ways someone can say "I love you"— with sincerity and passion or with sarcasm and rejection. Kinesthetically, people tend to be most strongly aware of location of the feeling, its intensity, and especially its direction.

Two particularly important submodality distinctions are analog and digital. Analog distinctions change along a continuum, like a dimmer switch, whereas digital distinctions exist in only one state or another, like an on-off switch. Making an image brighter or darker is analog change; being either associated into an image or dissociated from it is digital change.

I consider the model of submodalities to be probably the most significant thing I've done so far. It allows us to create maps that show with tremendous precision how consciousness functions to produce wanted and unwanted results. The strategy model shows us how to work sequentially; the model of submodalities explains how things work simultaneously.

LITERALNESS IN DESCRIPTION

When my books came out in the 1970s I wrote about the fact that, when people spoke about the representations they built in their minds, they tended to be very literal. This was the first time in the history of psychology that anyone had made that observation. It's incredibly easy to test, and yet there are professionals who still regard it as too easy.

For example, when somebody comes in and tells me they have difficulties with a problem that's "blown all out of proportion" I don't need to know what the problem is. I know they are making pictures that are far too big. When people say they have a problem that they're "just too close to" or about which they "need to get some perspective," typically they will benefit if their internal imagery is moved away, or slewed in some way or another.

Some people keep procrastinating and say, "Well, it's just too far off." Pulling the pictures up makes them more immediate and gets the subject to act faster and more decisively.

We all have to have ways of propelling our behavior, but it's not the strategy alone that gets the job done. The submodalities trigger change, so when you write out strategies, the little arrows in between each modality represent the shifts the subject makes from, say, thinking in pictures to talking in words to having a feeling. As the submodalities of each system change, the strategy moves to the next step and the one after that.

Outside of NLP, thinking is very misunderstood. Psychologists talk about thoughts as if they are objects, rather like marbles inside a sack. But it's not that you have thoughts, it's that you *think*. You think in pictures, words, feelings, tastes, and smells. This process is dynamic and in constant transition, driven by the changes we make in size, distance, location, direction, and so on. Moving through these transitions produces altered states, to some degree or other.

Between the two models—strategies and submodality changes— lies the means of building new states of consciousness in the waking and altered states. By giving people practical, immediately applicable lessons in how to think differently, you help them feel and act differently. These models allow us to elicit with great accuracy how they create their models, what holds them together, and what drives them forward.

What I want for everyone is the ability to learn to optimize their brains. This means learning new strategies and skills on a regular and systematic basis. We want to help produce people who live in an age where the rate at which information is evolving is geometric, not linear. We need to develop ways to make this possible so we will be learning and relearning our jobs every two or three years instead of doing things the way they've been done for decades.

This change is already happening to some degree. We already have to buy a new computer every three years, and it's a chore to learn how to make the new one work. I think back to the first generation of remote controls, and you had to memorize all the buttons. Now you have one remote that controls five different things. If you press the wrong button, you can't hear the sound because there are no buttons on the TV anymore. You can't simply turn it off and start over again. You have to make sure everything is done in the proper order. Sequence, sequence, sequence.

The same thing is true not just with the devices in your life and the devices in the educational system but the devices in your mind as well. These internal systems have to be as sophisticated as the ones on the outside. You can't pay attention if you don't know how.

Before you learn to give people the right suggestions, you have to know how to ask the right questions, and the right questions are those that tell you how the problem functions, rather than why the person or his or her therapist believes it occurred.

Really pervasive change is only going to happen when you know how to take inventory of a human being. Taking inventory requires knowing how people are creating their realities, which submodalities they are using, where they locate their strong beliefs, and so on.

There's a certain amount of preparation that has to be done. I don't just have people walk in the door and pop them into trance. I take inventory to find out where their assets and liabilities are so that I can move things from being liabilities to being assets, and I can move the things they consider to be assets, but which are just stupid, into liabilities.

I am methodical about this. I've reformatted the menu model of asking questions so I don't need so much detail, but I need detail of a different kind. I ask the questions that tell me about what's going on in their heads. I ask them how they know things, where images are located, whether they have borders or not, whether they are life-size or smaller, close or far away. I want to know if there's a voice, and if it's at the front, the back, left, or right. Does the voice sound like it's going out, or is it coming in? Whose voice is it? Does it sound nervous, angry, loud, or soft? Which way are the feelings moving? Where do they start? Where do they move to? The more detail I gather, the easier it is for me to map out what I am going to do.

I often think about it as if I'm applying for a job as a temp and I need to know precisely how they have their problems, so I can work out what to do to help them.

Most change techniques are metaphoric or anthropomorphic. For example, they talk about people's "parts"—the "part that's upset" or the "part that's angry." There's no real "part," just as there's no real ego or id or unconscious. They're simply ways of talking about abstract concepts. But as soon as you stop anthropomorphizing internal processes and start taking them literally—that is, in terms of submodalities—then it becomes obvious that you need to take inventory. It's particularly important to uncover the difference between what the person believes and what she doesn't believe, because an important part of changing people's lives is building beliefs that change is possible. When you discover what someone is determined to do versus what she's not determined to do, you can then make her very determined to get it, and she'll be more apt to be successful.

The process of creating reality is very idiosyncratic, so you need to learn a lot about each person and how they represent things to themselves. However, there are some big generalizations we can pretty much count on while taking inventory, too. The most common is: if people are traumatized by past experiences and constantly reliving them, their images will almost certainly be life-size . . . and they shouldn't be. You can't be terrorized by the past if you don't relive it life-size. I've worked with many trauma victims—Holocaust survivors, people who have been raped or beaten, people who've been violently mugged—and they're all running their internal imagery the same way.

Yet the things in their past that are worth remembering aren't remembered life-size. When you find out where these things in their past are in their mind, how big they are, whether they are still pictures or movies, what kind of sound quality they have, and so on, you snap those things over to where they are today.

The purpose of taking inventory, then, is also to find out how to structure your approach to helping someone change.

People are always being told to let go of the past, but nobody says how they can do it. If somebody says you should have more confidence, it's no help at all if you aren't told exactly what to do mentally to become more confident. However, everybody has confidence in some context, about some things, even though they might not in others. So, discovering how they do it idiosyncratically and teaching them what to shift into that space and what to shift out of it is the fundamental structure of change. Some people are absolutely certain that they're unlovable. They avoid going out to meet people, and even if they do—they're always wracked with doubt. It's interesting how certain people can be about their doubt. As soon as you understand that even to have doubt, they have to have certainty, then you can find out what they're certain about and start to give them doubt about their limitations and certainty about the things they want.

When people tell me they're depressed, I don't ask, "About what?" I ask, "How do you know? Maybe you're really happy?"

They say things like, "No, I wake up in the morning with a heavy weight on my chest and there's a gray cloud hanging over my head, and I say to myself: 'I feel really depressed . . .'"

From a statement like that, we have really useful information about the sequence of the speaker's behavior as well as the submodalities he uses to code the experience he labels as "depression."

I met one person who put a blue tone over everything he did. He'd really enjoy himself, but when he thought back to it, it was dark and cloudy with this bluish tint, and he'd say things like, "Well, at the time I thought I was happy, but when I think about it now, I really wasn't."

He did this systematically with every memory, and it made him feel really bad.

It emerged that his mother always said she was "in the pink" when she felt good, so, to him, images that felt happy had to be pink. If she felt bad, she "had the blues." It was just the way people of her generation spoke, but after years of training as a child, he simply took on the behavior unconsciously and automatically.

Problems arose because he didn't realize he was doing this, and he had a tendency to convert all his good memories into bad ones by changing everything pink into blue. He was running his own "Swish Pattern" (see Chapter 8) and making everything that was good and happy feel depressing and sad.

When you look closely at his pattern, you realize that he wasn't really depressed during the day when he was actually doing whatever it was he did. But when he thought about the day, when he remembered what he was doing, he made everything pink look blue.

He could have spent the next twenty years talking to a psychiatrist about why his mother made him feel the way he did, or he could learn how to swish things back the other way—which is precisely what we did.

More importantly, he learned something about how his own mind worked so he could use it for the rest of his life. Give a man a fish, he has dinner; teach him how to fish and he eats for life. The man went away not only able to remember feeling good about certain things but with the knowledge that, if he could get over one fear, he could get over any fear.

The minute I discovered that the way these people were talking was literal, my life changed. I just started having them make pictures that were pinker, or better in some other way, and sure enough, they were thrilled.

One client felt like he was encased in cement all the time. So I bopped him on the head, cracked the cement off, and chipped away at it until it was gone—and the whole time I was doing it, he thought it was as idiotic as I did. But that didn't change the fact that he felt that way. In fact, he felt that way because he had pictures way too close to him and wrapped around him; everything would go out of focus, and it would feel like real stuff. But it was only a picture, and once we knocked a little of the concrete away, it started to move off into the distance.

Knowing how submodalities work and learning how to manipulate them makes change simple. It also allows us to make profound differences in people's lives without even knowing the details of the problem. This allows us to make change content-free.

When working on the exercises that follow, refer often to the list of submodalities in Resource File 3 (see page 310), but also keep notes of your own.

Exercise: Submodality Change 1

1. Choose a pleasant experience from the past and pay special attention to how you remember it. Focus less on *what* happened than on whether you're making a picture, what the submodalities of that picture are (refer to Resource File 3), making sure you also pay attention to the sounds and feelings that make up the entire memory. Notice how you feel when you intensely reexperience a pleasant memory.

2. Begin to push the image away from you toward the horizon, making it smaller and less distinct, and draining any colors out of it as you go. When it is just a dot in the distance, notice how your feelings have changed. Most people find that the intensity of their pleasure diminishes significantly.

3. Bring the memory back into its previous position, restoring all its original submodalities until you feel the same about the memory as you did when you began.

4. Bring the picture toward you. Increase the size; make it bigger, brighter, and more detailed. Step right into the picture and experience everything through all your senses. The experience should feel more real, more intense.

5. Return the memory to its original place, once again restoring all its original submodalities.

Exercise: Submodality Change 2

Not everyone responds to the same submodality changes, so it's important for you and your clients to identify the most impactful changes you can make. Often, one or two submodality changes precipitate a systemwide shift.

1. Return to the memory above, and using your list of submodalities from Resource File 3, change them one at a time. Note the effect, and then change the submodality back to its original state before moving on to the next. Continue until the entire memory changes. Remember to restore its original submodalities.

Note: After some practice, you will find certain submodality changes appear more frequently—particularly association/dissociation, position, size, distance, color, and movement. After even more practice, you will begin to be able to read your subjects' submodalities without having to ask them questions. For example, a person associated into a memory speaks and acts very differently from someone dissociated from it.

Eight

THE POWER OF BELIEF
Pink Poodles and the Placebo Effect

ONE OF THE THINGS I found out a long time ago is that many of the people in my workshops would be able to do hypnosis and do it really well—and then, suddenly, there would be a point at which they couldn't do certain things. Somehow, they or their partners just couldn't do certain deep trance phenomena, such as amnesia, positive or negative hallucination, or pain control.

Milton Erickson believed that most people could be hypnotized. He said that if you spent hundreds of hours with your clients, eventually they'd learn to do any hypnotic phenomenon.

The problem for me—and I suspect for most people—is that I don't have that kind of time. So I started to approach it another way.

One day, somebody I was working with told me he could achieve most of the hypnotic effects in trance with the exception of positive hallucination. Positive hallucination is the ability to create full, realistic representations of things that aren't actually there.

I believed this person had been hallucinating most of his life. Most people do, without realizing it. Under the right conditions, we are capable of producing every formal "deep trance phenomenon" in the normal waking state. For example, how many times are you certain you see a friend across the street, and when you look again, it doesn't resemble him at all? Has there ever been a time when you looked at your partner's expression and "just knew" they were angry—and then it just turned out they were preoccupied with something else? This is hallucination in the waking state.

So I told him to look at the table, close his eyes, and count to four, and when he opened his eyes he'd see something that surprised him—a very vivid picture in front of him on the table.

He closed his eyes and started counting. As he was doing that, I slid across a picture of the cover of one of my books that I happened to have with me. He opened his eyes, saw the picture, and I immediately told him to close them again.

I slipped the picture back under the table, then told him to open his eyes, look to his side, and see the six-foot pink French poodle.

He opened his eyes—and there it was: a giant, pink poodle. He was fascinated, closed his eyes, and dropped into an even deeper trance. After that, his problems creating positive hallucinations completely disappeared.

Of course, I tricked him. But what fascinated me was that a trick as simple as that could change an entire belief about his capabilities. He'd gone from thinking of himself as a failure to being able to do something that is widely considered to be a function of deep, somnambulistic trance—and in that split second, he became a really confident person.

To me, the wonderful thing about that experience was that he found he could do a whole lot more after that, simply because now he had changed his belief from one about being a person with limitations to one who could do exceptional things. That's how quickly the brain learns if we learn to communicate with it in a language we understand.

The belief that he was bad at learning something specific gave way to a belief that "if I can learn that, I can learn anything." In the language of NLP, it "generalized" out into other areas of his life. He became a good learner because he abandoned the belief that he couldn't learn.

Of course, when somebody makes an unexpected recovery from a problem, there's always someone who says something like, "Oh, it's just because he believes he's better."

I say, "Exactly."

Belief is an enormous power in all cultures. Placebos show us that. All active pharmacological agents—drugs—are tested against a placebo. To some degree or other, the placebo always works, whereas the drug sometimes doesn't.

Scientists tell us this is because the placebo somehow deceives the person, but it's much more a question of belief. Interestingly, if people believe that the placebo somehow triggers a natural healing response in the body, they respond, even knowing it is a placebo. In fact, in many cases their responsiveness actually increases.

Some years ago I decided to make use of this phenomenon. Together with a colleague, I set out to market bottles of empty capsules, along with printed booklets of the research showing how placebos worked. If the patient looked up the index and found placebos worked with, say, five out of six of other people with his complaint, he could take seven, just to be sure. Our idea was to clean up with the first wave, then market "new, improved placebo—with 40 percent more inert ingredients."

Then a certain government agency stepped in. One of their representatives said we couldn't do it because it wouldn't work. We showed them their own research that showed it did. Then they said it was illegal. We didn't agree. How could selling empty capsules to people who knew they were empty be illegal? Finally, they told us they couldn't permit it because it was "immoral."

When I work with clients who need extra help, I give them placebos. They not only know they're placebos, they have the belief—which I also give them—that knowing they are placebos will make them more effective. Actually, these days, I don't bother with actual placebos. I'll use whatever's available—usually grapes. They work just as well.

So, if belief can be so powerful, just stop for a moment and think of the most overwhelmingly wonderful things *you* could have or do if you take the belief that stops you from learning anything new quickly and easily, faster than you could ever suspect, and simply change it. How would you be if you could harness more of your brain's ability to alter its state, so that when you opened your eyes you'd created something absolutely wonderful—more so even than a six-foot poodle?

> *If you want to make the most of this book, pause here and write down the beliefs you would like to abandon and the changes you would like to have in their place. Put these in two adjacent columns. In a third column, write down in some detail how your life would be better for making these changes. Be sure your list is sensory-specific—that is, clarify what you will be seeing, hearing, feeling, even smelling and tasting, when you have made these changes in your beliefs.*

The questions for me, after the poodle incident, were these: What precisely was this person doing inside of himself that made it possible for him to change his belief? How specifically did he make something happen just moments after it had been "impossible"?

Like everything else, I was sure this was a learnable skill and that everyone should be able to learn it and do it in far less time than the hundreds of hours Erickson believed were necessary.

I understood that changing a belief could only be possible if the way that beliefs were stored in the brain changed. The ways in which we coded the belief that something was possible and something else was impossible had to differ from each other in some way. It made sense that if we changed the structure of a nonbelief to the same structure as we used to store a strong, positive belief, our experience would have to change.

I found this out simply enough—by watching and listening to the people in front of me. Helping people change by getting them to manipulate beliefs is now an important part of what I do.

Part of the reason people can't make significant changes in their lives or do things like go into trances is that they don't believe they can. It's not that they can't. What they're actually doing is carrying out a posthypnotic suggestion. Somehow, they've come to believe that something is "too difficult," or, like so many people, that they're unhypnotizable. The belief can come from almost anywhere; maybe a stage hypnotist had attempted to hypnotize them and failed, or a therapist couldn't get them to go into trance, and they felt somehow to blame for it.

I've helped people change beliefs like these many times. Once, two psychiatrists brought a woman who scored zero on the Hilgard Hypnotic Susceptibility Scale to a hypnosis seminar I did in Wichita, Kansas. They said: "This woman is completely unhypnotizable."

I looked at her and said, "You can't be hypnotized?" and her pupils dilated and she literally said, in a monotone, "I-cannot-be-hypnotized," in exactly the manner and tone of voice of someone carrying out a posthypnotic suggestion. I brought her on the stage and demonstrated every hypnotic phenomenon I could think of with her. I had her do positive hallucinations; I had her negatively hallucinate the whole audience. I had her do all the major deep trance phenomena—and then I turned to the psychiatrists and said, "Well, I guess you were wrong."

They said, "Uh . . . it's probably contextual."

I said, "Do you mean the fact that she was in front of seven hundred people made it easier?" and they replied, "Yes."

The truth was, they started out by saying it was impossible to put her into trance. They said they had "proved" it was impossible. After all, they had a hypnotizability scale that was supposed to be scientifically valid.

I said, "Maybe you guys should have seven hundred people in the audience and then it would be a lot easier, because if people are scared, they retreat into deep trances. Sometimes, for some people, that's difficult to do when they're alone with a therapist in an office."

What I was really saying was that people respond differently in different contexts, and that means you have to develop the flexibility to switch contexts, or sometimes just to have them hallucinate the one that works.

MEMORY AND SUBMODALITY CHANGES

Changing an experience is just as simple. Too many therapies make people go back into their past and reexperience traumatic events, not realizing that the submodalities change when they reenter that state. At some level, for the person doing the remembering, it's as real as if he's going through that experience again.

I get very angry when I hear of these things happening. People put things into the past and forget them for a very good reason: they've done it already. It's over. It needs to be coded as the past.

Sometimes, if the experience is very traumatic and a person

becomes amnesiac, she falls into the hands of therapists who insist she should remember every detail. This is nonsense: people's unconscious minds are very protective; sometimes they make us amnesiac for a very good reason. The events that happened are just too terrible to have to recall.

However, sometimes people are bothered by memories and past experiences as if they're continuing to happen—and this is where they can benefit from changing their submodalities.

To do this well, you need to make sure that the people you're working with become determined to succeed. Often they aren't, simply because they don't know enough; they don't know that they have choices, and they don't know how to be determined in pursuing those choices.

But, of course, they can be determined to do other things in other areas of their lives, and I often get the submodalities of the things they're determined to do and of what they want to achieve, and then make their desires the same as their determination. Sometimes you have to pick the state that would best meet their needs. I often do that, simply because if they knew what to do and how to do it, they wouldn't need me in the first place.

The other important thing you need to remember when making this sort of change is speed. The brain learns quickly; learning doesn't have to be slow—in fact, if the information is presented too slowly, the brain won't learn because it can't detect a pattern. Patterns only make sense when they run quickly.

One of the earlier patterns I developed used these two abilities of the brain: to change its experience by changing submodalities and to make changes rapidly. This was the Swish Pattern, and it was developed mainly to move people from their present state to a desired state, with economy and precision.

Exercise: Swish Pattern

1. Think of a feeling, response, or behavior that you would like to change. This format is particularly useful in dealing with feelings that seem to compel people to act in ways that do not match their self-image.
2. Close your eyes and see what happens from an associated point of view. If it is a behavior, identify the trigger point of the sequence. Put a border around it and make it bright and intense.
3. Now see yourself (dissociated) as if you have already made the change. See how you will be acting, hear what you will be hearing. Ensure that this representation is preferable to the one in Step 2.
4. Shrink the image of your desired state down to a small, dark square, and place it in the corner of the first image you made.
5. Now, darken and shrink the large image down as you simultaneously brighten and enlarge the second image until it completely covers the first one. Hear or make the sound *s-w-i-i-s-h* as you do so. Open your eyes to "break state."

Repeat five times, and then test your response to the original trigger. Most frequently people find it difficult to recapture the original image and feeling and simply shift into the second state.

As soon as you begin to understand the mechanics of change, you can start to understand how the person I spoke about earlier could move in a matter of minutes from not being able to create a positive hallucination, even in deep trance, to being able to hallucinate a six-foot-high pink poodle. His beliefs—and the submodalities of his beliefs—changed spontaneously.

Just because you believe something doesn't make it true. NLP—and particularly the manipulation of your submodalities—gives you the means of reviewing your beliefs, deciding which of them are useful and worth keeping, and which would benefit your life by being changed.

Once you realize that things you believe are structured differently from things you don't believe, you have the means, literally, of changing your mind. One of the most useful belief changes you can make right now is that you can learn new things—particularly the patterns in this book—quickly and easily.

Most people believe they have to struggle, or take a lot of time, to learn something new. How different would your life be if you were a naturally good learner—someone who could easily become good at NLP, good at trance, good at anything you were prepared to put your mind to?

You will still need to practice the new material, but this pattern will help you feel that it's well within your capabilities, and therefore enjoyable to practice.

Exercise: Belief-Change Pattern— Becoming an Excellent Learner

1. Find the belief that stands in your way of learning new things easily. See, hear, and feel yourself trying, but not accomplishing, your objective. You will probably be able to find many examples from when you were in school. Notice all the submodalities of underperformance, writing down your observations so you can be systematic in your work.
2. Find a strong and useful belief about something in which you already excel. It need not fall into the same

category as learning the kind of skills referred to in this book; simply find something that you *know* you do really well. Examine its qualities, the same way as above.

3. Compare the two, noting the differences. Pay particular attention to the size of each image, their positions in your mental space, and whether or not either involves movement.

4. Push the image of the limiting belief off into the distance until it is little more than a pinprick, shift it across to line it up with your positive belief, and then snap it back toward you into its new position, shifting all the original submodalities to match those of supreme confidence and proficiency. See yourself dropping into a profoundly relaxed state in which you absorb information easily and are prepared to explore and practice your new skills with deep commitment.

5. Deepen the state by manipulating the submodalities, then step into that state of deep trance and pay particular attention to the feelings associated with being an excellent learner. When you have identified a particularly strong feeling, anchor it by firmly pressing a particular spot on your body, such as an earlobe or a knuckle, so that you can easily access the state at a later date by pressing or "firing" your anchor and remembering as fully as possible the experience you created in Step 4 (see Resource File 1 (page 305)).

6. Slowly come back into the room, bringing all the learnings you've made with you, and in the knowledge that you can repeat this exercise as many times as you like, doubling the intensity of the experience each time.

The tools in this book allow people to think and feel differently and better, giving them the means of changing themselves and moving toward getting what they want. I don't want people to just desire things; I want them to be *driven* toward them, into new behaviors.

Successful people in all fields, whether they are physicists, chemists, violinists, rock and roll musicians, or inventors of wonderful things, are all driven. People who make a mark in medicine or education are all driven. I'm not talking about driven in the way Type A personalities are, but driven with curiosity. They are driven to do what they do better each time.

PART 2

Patterns of Induction

Hypnosis and the Art
of Creating Powerful
Learning States

Nine

DEVELOPING YOUR SKILLS
Altered States, Hypnosis, and the Power to Learn

BECOMING A COMPETENT HYPNOTIST is an important skill to develop. Whether you call it "hypnosis," "meditation," or "altered state" doesn't really matter. The important part is that you learn to control your state of consciousness—and the states of those people who come to you for help—so you can apply a powerful tool to harness the ability to learn.

We have the power to develop our skills. The better we learn to use our hands, for example, the more exquisite things we can create. Some artists have such precise control they can carve entire scenes on the head of a pin. I can't do that, because I haven't developed that particular degree of control. There are musicians who have extraordinary control over their fingers on the keyboard. I can play to a certain degree, and if I paid more attention to doing scales and practicing, I would be a better musician.

The same thing is true about your state of consciousness. Being able to put yourself into a state of relaxation, a state of deep meditation, should become a skill as natural as breathing.

People are sometimes confused about the difference between hypnosis and meditation. I would say they are very similar states, the exception being that hypnosis has a direction to it, an outcome you have decided before you begin, while meditation is more formless. Speaking personally, when I go into an altered state I want to do something. I want to know when I'm going in, when I'm coming out, and I want to know what I'm doing while I'm there. Meditation, for me, is not directed enough—but it really is a matter of individual taste.

If you want to achieve anything with self-hypnosis, you plan it out before you begin. When you're hypnotizing other people—in fact, whenever you're communicating with someone else, even if you're simply trying to share a good memory—you're trying to induce in them a specific state. You're using images and feelings and word pictures, and, if you're sufficiently effective as a communicator, you induce an altered state in them. Knowing exactly how that's done and doing it with precision is what makes someone a good hypnotist.

Of course, not all people who set themselves up as hypnotists are necessarily good at hypnosis. That's one of the first things I learned when I set out to study the field.

For example, I came across that item I mentioned called a "hypnosis susceptibility scale," which was designed to measure how "hypnotizable" someone is. In my opinion, it functions as a measure of the hypnotist's incompetence, rather than the susceptibility of the person one is trying to hypnotize.

I went to Ernest Hilgard's laboratory years ago, and I was told that some people could score a zero, meaning they were totally unhypnotizable, while others could score really high, which meant they could do positive hallucinations and other "advanced" hypnotic phenomena.

We know that all the so-called hypnotic phenomena—amnesia, anesthesia, arm catalepsy, positive and negative hallucination, and so on—can be seen in the normal waking state, so that makes nonsense out of that criterion. Think about how many times you've negatively hallucinated your car keys; you left them on the table, but they just weren't there when you went to find them—until someone else pointed to them in plain sight.

The hypnosis tests themselves went something like this: the researchers played a tape recording while people sat there and listened. The degree to which they could go into an apparently altered state and do hypnotic phenomena became the measure of their susceptibility.

The problem was, it wasn't even a good hypnotic induction on the tape. It was monotonous and uncreative, and the way I saw it, it proved only that a certain minority of people could escape into trance out of sheer boredom.

I was able to put a hypnotic induction on the same tape recorder and hypnotize many more people—and yet, officially, the Hilgard Scale is still given considerable credence as scientifically valid.

The belief that you need to speak in a monotone to put someone in trance is central to this approach to hypnosis. The researchers thought of this as congruent with inducing an altered state—but the truth is, you speak in a monotone if you're going to speak *incongruently*. If you speak congruently and slowly and inflect your voice downward where you give commands, people will respond much more intensely.

Those kinds of beliefs have created a situation in which a limited number of people were believed to be capable of achieving a limited number of things. That's why hypnosis was primarily used for simple things, such as getting people to lose weight and quit smoking. Therapists really didn't have tools for more complex problems.

In contrast, if you trained as a psychiatrist, you learned how to give drugs to deal with emotional problems. If you were a psychologist, you might have learned a little about conditioning or aversion therapy, so that you could expose your clients to cigarettes and give them electric shocks in an effort to get them to stop smoking. You might have been trained in getting people to challenge their thinking to change their behavior.

The problem was, you simply weren't taught how to actually help your clients to think differently, change the way they felt, get over physiological addictions, or to do really practical things, such as developing amnesia for traumatic experiences so they didn't have to keep reliving the past, over and over again, until they became functionally disabled. Psychologists were never even taught that these things were possible.

Since the model didn't exist, I had to develop tools from scratch to accomplish this. I did it by the simple and logical process of finding people who had already done what I wanted to study. I found people who had "spontaneously" recovered from certain bad experiences and then looked carefully at what they had done that was different from those who hadn't overcome their traumas.

Hypnosis turned out to be a useful tool. As I developed newer and better strategies, it turned out to be a good idea to induce hypnosis and then install these strategies in an altered state. The fact is, we learn better when we're in an altered state than we do when we're in our normal state of consciousness. If that weren't true, we'd all be learning to solve our problems all the time simply by thinking about them.

Hypnosis, therefore, can be thought of as a learning state in which we can optimize our thinking and refine our strategies. Of course, that sometimes happens automatically. Many people have found that brilliant ideas and solutions to problems came to them when they were asleep, or when they drifted into deep states of relaxation or meditation.

Albert Einstein, for one, did thought experiments—simply another way of describing hallucination. He went into deeply altered states and imagined riding on a photon of light. That's not the normal waking state. Linus Pauling described riding around on the inside of molecules and won a Nobel Prize. That's not the normal waking state. Quite clearly, we have the potential to enter profoundly altered states of great creativity. These are simply alternative ways of thinking from our default "normal" waking state.

Despite the possibilities this approach suggests, and the hundreds of years of experience we've had actually applying the technology of trance, many people are still deeply fearful of hypnosis.

One reason is that an unfortunate number of incompetent people are practicing it. Another is that sometimes people don't carry out the suggestions you give them when they are in hypnosis. Most people in the therapy business don't like the idea that they can fail. If you just have people free associate, and every time they say something you say, "And how do you feel about that?" you don't run that risk.

The problem with that approach is that you also don't help people change. It's an amorphous approach; it's long-winded and doesn't have any outcome orientation.

Some of us who are openly and deeply committed to using hypnosis, on the other hand, are prepared to accept the risks. We actually want to get people to lose weight or quit smoking, to be unafraid to cross the bridge or get in the plane. We're less interested in problems and more interested in new ways of behaving.

Some therapists are widening their horizons. The better ones, at least, are prepared to try out new tools, because they're starting to think of the end result.

Even the word "hypnosis" still causes some mainstream "experts" great anxiety, which is an unfortunate and wasteful response. I believe it's time for us to stop looking at the bugaboo about hypnosis. This is a new millennium, and people are smarter than ever before. They're developing new ways of doing things better, growing up using computers and playing video games that are impossible to play in a normal waking state. These games create powerful altered states in which people are able to change even their relationship with space and time. To play, they have to become adept at the incredibly advanced hypnotic skill of time distortion just to be able to keep up with the speed of the game.

This makes for greater motor-eye coordination. But even more significantly, these games are based on technology that is going to be used to make us smarter and faster, whether by teaching people how to do microsurgery or fly the space shuttle. Our electronic tools are literally changing the way we think.

One of the major steps forward in hypnosis was the field of Design Human Engineering (DHE). When I developed this, I began to take machines that existed on the outside and put them on the inside, getting them to function with equal precision and effectiveness. So if, for example, you had a particularly accurate measuring tool that existed in the outside world and learned how to build one exactly like it on the inside, you could dramatically improve your abilities. If I have a synthesizer that can create and record sixteen tracks of music, there's no reason that I can't build the same machine inside my head. Then I can do the same thing mentally and, in a state of time distortion, "play" until I like what I'm hearing, then sit down with a real machine and record it externally.

Even though I have to travel thousands of miles by air for my work, I don't particularly enjoy flying. So, the moment I board an airplane, I go into a deep trance, go inside, and play in the playground in my head.

This is a place that's full of all the things I own on the outside world, as well as a lot more wonderful creations. For example, I have a TV set that lets me play back old programs when I feel like seeing those again. I have the world's best stereo system inside my mind. I also have a spare orchestra and a choir, and I can have them sing and play anything I want.

I never used to have these things—or even imagined having them—until I learned to go into altered states and install strategies I learned from other people.

It's sad, then, that hypnosis is regarded with suspicion by some people simply because of the unfounded belief that "it's bad, and it doesn't work." Of course, those people don't explain how anything can be bad if it doesn't work, but that doesn't stop them putting their objections across.

Milton Erickson fought for years trying to make hypnosis legitimate, and he believed the way to do this was to have it restricted to doctors and dentists.

Unfortunately, these aren't the people who are necessarily in the best position to use it. They simply don't have the time. I would prefer them to work with other people—experts in trance-induction—who prepare their patients for them, so they can get on with their work.

Some years ago, I taught a group of dental patients to be able to go into deep trance and get absolute control over pain and then sent them in to have molars pulled. On the basis of this alone, one official of the American Dental Association said at the time that the only effective approach available to deal with dental phobia was Neuro-Linguistic Programming.

Doctors can also learn a lot from NLP, because when hypnosis is looked at through the eyes of Neuro-Linguistic Programming, it becomes a powerful tool to achieve results impossible in an "ordinary" waking state. What makes NLP powerful is that it teaches people *how* to have more freedom, *how* to be smarter, *how* to be more talented.

It's also about doing these things more easily, because you don't have to go through hours and hours of preparation and hard work.

NLP developed out of our study of hypnosis, but while Erickson was prepared to take one thousand hours to get someone to make an effective change, I wanted to get the same results in much less time.

Now I can do that—and I can teach others to do it—because, having done hypnosis for so many years, I know exactly how to adjust my behavior to make it easy for the person I'm with to go into the appropriate state.

This is an important ability to develop: to get people to change, you have to be able to change your behavior. If you want someone to go into a different state—say, a state of trance—you must be able to go there first.

One of the ways people learn is by emulating others. We call this "entrainment." There are certain distinct signs of developing trance that people unconsciously pick up on and follow, until they, too, go into trance.

So, before that is possible, it's important for anyone who wants to become competent in NLP and hypnosis to become familiar with the hypnotic state themselves—and then learn to control it. Ideally, you want to be able to enter a trance state, but not lose yourself in it. When working with other people, you need to be leading by example, and you also need to be able to maintain contact with them.

When I first started to study hypnosis, I found there were entire courses on how to hypnotize people without going into trance yourself—and that's just ridiculous. If it's good enough for your client, it's good enough for you. You just have to make sure when you learn to go into trance that you can still speak and see and hear and act and respond—and that only comes from practice.

In using hypnosis, it's extremely important to keep your eye on what you want to achieve, which is to put people into wonderful, relaxed states, and then have them face their problems with all the resources they didn't know they had. That way, you help them change their beliefs about what is possible.

Then, when you bring them back, the waking state will never be the same, and that's what it's all about. That's called learning.

Later in this book, you will learn some powerful and sophisticated language patterns that effortlessly guide people into trance. I studied language patterns for many years. I wrote down hundreds of different versions of each pattern, so now I can automatically and unconsciously generate them. I don't need to think about them any more, nor will you if you learn the language of persuasion, know what trance looks and feels like, and get your client looking and feeling just like that.

LEARNING TO GO INTO TRANCE

If you are new to hypnosis, it is important to gain the experience of going in and out of trance as soon as possible.

One possibility is to seek out a highly skilled, reputable hypnotist, and explain exactly what you want. Have him take you into trance and give you the posthypnotic suggestion that whenever you touch yourself on the back of the hand, in a particular way, in a specific place, you will go back into trance, easily and effortlessly. This is what we call "anchoring," and it's a core skill of Neuro-

Linguistic Programming (see Resource File 1 [page 305]).

Practice touching the back of your other hand (firing the anchor) repeatedly, going in and coming out of trance until it is familiar and easy.

Once you are comfortable with the experience and the transitions are smooth, practice keeping your eyes open while remaining in trance. Then, sit down with another person, start to pace him by breathing at the same rate, and reenter trance by firing your anchor.

Continue talking to them as you do this, preferably about times and experiences of comfort, peace, and relaxation, noticing the changes that take place in both of you as you go into a shared trance.

Even as you go into trance, the quality of your voice changes. Your breathing changes, and you will display certain physical cues—the signs of developing trance—that, together, will powerfully influence the person you are with.

THE SIGNS OF DEVELOPING TRANCE

The more hypnosis you do, the more easily you will recognize the signs of developing trance. People look different when they're in trance. It's quite easy to see when people are relaxing. By further tuning yourself to the subtleties, you can increase your ability to deepen their trance states quite informally and conversationally.

Various experts have listed more than one hundred signs of trance, which is making things too complicated. You need focus on only a few of the more obvious ones.

Look out for:

• Slowed breathing rate
• Dilated pupils
• Lower lip engorging with blood
• Slowing and slurring of speech
• Increasing flaccidity of facial muscles and skin tone
• Altered blink rate (slower or faster)
• Increasing immobility of limbs
• Eyelids fluttering, or closing naturally

Now notice what you can achieve when you apply these tools systematically.

Exercise: Using Signs of Developing Trance

1. Sit opposite your partner, take a deep breath, let it out, and allow yourself to begin to relax. Watch your partner without speaking and with soft, slightly defocused vision.
2. Each time you notice your partner developing a sign of developing trance, simply nod, amplify the signal you observe (feed it back in a slightly exaggerated form), then switch to another signal, noticing whether your partner copies the sign. For example, if your partner's blink rate slows, slow your own blink rate and defocus your vision further.
3. Repeat the steps until your partner naturally closes his or her eyes.
4. When that happens, reinforce other signs of developing trance with gentle phrases such as "Very good" or "That's right."
5. Allow your partner to rest comfortably in trance, and then suggest they return to waking consciousness, feeling relaxed and wide awake. Change places and repeat.

6. If you have a third practice partner, have him or her sit and observe the responses of both hypnotist and subject. When each of you has had a turn, all three of you should then share your experiences.

Most commonly, the hypnotist and the subject both experience a shift in their consciousness. The observer will also often enter a trance state.

This is a powerful skill-building exercise, but also a strong indication of how easily we can entrain to another's changing state of consciousness. Simply observing trance developing in one person is often enough to cause an observer to alter his state of consciousness to match.

HOW STAGE HYPNOSIS WORKS

Many people get their ideas about hypnosis from watching hypnotists on stage and television. There are both differences and similarities between what the stage hypnotist does and the actions of a person who wants to help other people optimize their minds and achieve their goals.

The first thing to notice is that most hypnotists start out with thirty or forty volunteers from the audience. You may not see this part on television, since some governing bodies ban showing actual inductions on screen. This is a joke, of course, because when you know what to look for, hypnosis is everywhere. The evangelical preacher urging viewers to send money to him to reserve their place in heaven, the late-night infomercial shows

selling cheap jewelry to insomniacs, the politicians urging voters
to action are all using hypnotic methods.

Like the compulsive late-night shopper, the people who vol-
unteer to come up on to the hypnotist's stage are already predisposed to having an "experience." Some of them have even been
hypnotized by that hypnotist at another time on another show.
They want to be part of this group experience.

The hypnotist goes through a series of "tests"—commands to
lift one arm, clasp the hands and be unable to pull them apart, and
so on. This is not hypnosis. This is simply to see which people
will follow orders.

One at a time, people are sent back to their seats, so the
remaining volunteers are watching and learning at an unconscious level what is required of them. They are literally being conditioned. When a select few are left, the hypnotist can be sure
that he will be working with people who want to cooperate and
more or less know what is required of them. All the rest of his
induction tends to be showmanship, since most of the work has
already been done.

In the kind of hypnosis I do, expectation plays a part as well, but
it is by no means everything. I have a letter framed and hanging on
the wall of my office that says I'm "the best hypnotist in the world."
I don't keep it there to feed my own ego; I know that every person
who comes in to make some changes will read the letter. Some of
them just sit down after that and go straight down into trance
before I say anything.

One of the main differences between stage hypnosis and my
kind of work is that stage hypnotists give credence to the idea that
some people are not hypnotizable, whereas I have never met anyone who can't be hypnotized—as long as I am prepared to take

enough time, pay sufficient attention to their responses, and modify my own behavior accordingly.

Of course, you will always get people who go into deep, somnambulistic trance, then come out and say: "I wasn't hypnotized. I could hear everything and think and feel things." My reply is always that there is, indeed, a state of consciousness in which we hear and feel nothing. It's called death, and it's our job to avoid it as long as possible.

Ten

HYPNOSIS AND CONTROL
Success Is an Altered State

PART OF THE MISUNDERSTANDING that surrounds hypnosis comes from the word itself. Hypnosis to me is an ill-defined term. Hypnosis and hypnotic procedures are really simply about controlling altered states. There are as many types of altered states as there are people to imagine them. The possibilities are limitless.

Great athletes go into altered states to do what they do. If you ask any one of them how they get ready to perform, they will say things like, "I wait for the green to shrink and the hole I'm driving for to get really big," and "When I'm running, it's as if I'm in a long tunnel. I'm aware of the other runners and the crowd, but they're on the outside. All I have to do is stay in my tunnel and keep running."

You have to go into a slightly altered state just to be able to correctly spell a word.

When hypnotists talk about trance, they're really talking about "deep" or "somnambulistic" trance, and the way they define that is according to the hypnotic phenomena the subject is able to produce.

The biggest misconception is that hypnotic states are rare and under somebody else's control. The truth is you actually have more control over yourself in an altered state than you do in the waking state.

Somebody in a seminar once challenged me to make someone squawk like a chicken in trance. When I said I didn't need to get someone in trance to have him do that, the person was skeptical. So I said, "Okay, but first show me how you'd know what a squawking chicken sounds like."

My challenger said, "Sure—it's like this: *puk–puk-puk* . . ."

I said, "Okay . . . any other questions?"

The thing is, people will often do what you want them to do if you simply ask. I don't bother with trying to influence people to close their eyes when I'm hypnotizing them. I just ask them to. It saves a lot of time.

Trance should be used in more challenging situations than making people act like farmyard animals, because when people go into altered states, they suspend not just their inhibitions but their beliefs about what's possible—and that can have extraordinary results. They'll probably need to think it through, to make whatever changes need to be made inside, but when they do, they can control heart rate, blood pressure, body temperature, experience of pain . . . and, probably more important, they can control their ideas and beliefs. When people change what they believe in, they can change their lives.

It is entirely possible, for example, for almost any hypnotist to put someone who is terrified of snakes into a trance and have them look at any number of snakes without any fear whatsoever. If you're a good hypnotist, you can make it possible for them to bring that change with them, out of trance, so their lack of fear lasts forever.

As I have said many times, Neuro-Linguistic Programming was born out of studying hypnotic processes and asking the question, how is it possible that somebody can do this in deep trance?

Some years ago, Gregory Bateson came over to my house to watch me work with a deep trance subject. He observed closely for a while and then whispered to me, "Get him to talk backward."

I said, "Wha-a-t?" because it seemed so outrageous, but Gregory insisted. I lifted this eighteen-year-old kid's arm and said: "Now, you're going to go inside to make all the necessary mental and physical adjustments so that when you speak, you'll speak backward. A sound will come out just as it would if you recorded a tape and then played it backward. Make all the adjustments, and when you're ready, I want you to lift one finger to let me know . . ."

Two or three minutes went by, and the finger came up. I brought him out of trance, and he began to talk—and, it sounded exactly like a tape recorder running backward. He spoke a couple of sentences and then Gregory talked back. He was speaking backward, too.

The two of them sat there for ages, going back and forth, until I put the boy back in trance. I remember thinking to myself, *How in the world could anyone possibly do this?* I told him that when he came out of trance he would explain to me in every detail how it was possible to speak backward.

He came out of trance and explained that he thought of what he wanted to say, typed it up in his mind, spelled it phonetically, and then simply pulled the letters off, put them in reverse order, and sounded them out. Now, as soon as he explained it to me, it seemed simple. His strategy was to go first from normally spelled English to phonetic English, reverse the letters, and then sound them out.

This demonstrates very clearly that as soon as you have a mental strategy to do something, the "impossible" becomes not only possible, but easy. The fact that he could make that up in a trance was because he didn't have the limitation of believing that it couldn't be done. On the other hand, I was sitting there in the

waking state, thinking it couldn't be done, and yet I got somebody else to do it.

Of course, I wanted to know how Gregory did the same thing,
apparently out of hypnosis. He explained that when he and his
colleagues were studying films of Adolf Hitler, trying to figure out
how he was able to influence such large numbers of people, they
played the soundtracks backward on wire recorders to see if there
were any hidden messages.

It turned out that Gregory had adopted a similar mental strategy to learn how to speak backward. He became so good at it
after a while that he could hear a sentence forward, then play it
backward. He'd done this trying to communicate with schizophrenics. It didn't actually work, but at least he gave it a try. Gregory tried lots of different things, which was admirable. It just so
happens that talking backward to people doesn't really help them
much.

I was always interested in how people did certain things, and
how knowing that could help others achieve their goals. Finding
out how somebody successfully completes a mental task is the
foundation of Neuro-Linguistic Programming. The part I particularly like is exploring the apparently bottomless depths of creativity. When I teach hypnosis, I call it "experimental hypnosis,"
not because I question whether it exists or not, but to locate that
moment of creativity where people find solutions to what appear
to be impossible situations.

Over the past forty years, I've come to understand much more
about how it's possible to use altered states for people to produce
profound change. I happen, also, to have come to think that an
important part of achieving change is humor.

Not everybody has a sense of humor, so not everybody can use

humor. But I use it all the time, because I think it's very important that people learn to laugh at their own beliefs and their own
difficulties, because exactly at the moment they start, they create
a chemical foundation on which to create change.

As we know, everyone ever influenced by Freud still believes
that insight produces change, that understanding gives freedom
from suffering and pain. The truth is, though, it just doesn't work
that way, no matter how hard and how long people try.

I've had many clients who came to me knowing exactly where
their fears came from. One might have almost drowned and has
developed a terrible fear of water. Or maybe they'd been in relationships with untrustworthy people, and now they can't trust
others. Perhaps their father had molested them, so now they think
all men are bad.

The fact that they understand something doesn't mean they
then behave differently. Changed behavior can only come from
changing belief systems and from the way we generalize our experience.

As children, we learn not to stick our hands into fire because
just before we do it, our parents yell at us. That triggers fear, and
we pull away. Loud noise, fear, fire, fear. Pretty soon we're smart
enough not to stick our hand in the fire; we don't have to get
burned to learn. We generalize from one event to another.

PROBLEMS AS OVERGENERALIZATIONS

Sometimes, though, we overgeneralize, and this is where we
need to redirect our thinking. People who have panic attacks randomly are responding to things they don't actually need to fear.
People with Obsessive-Compulsive Disorder are building rituals

of comfort where they don't need them. We all know that locking the door eight times isn't going to make it any more locked than locking it once. But by engaging in this ritual, they create a false sense of comfort, because they've built into their model the belief that their fears will go away if they carry out the ritual.

Now, to some extent, everybody is in this situation. We've all built some generalizations that work very well for us, and some that don't. Being able to test our world and to expand it is best done in an altered state, because, by definition, our waking state has all of our beliefs in it, including the limiting ones. It becomes important that we extend the range of human consciousness by going into a state of relaxation and considering fears, doubts, desires, motivations, and all the other things we need either more of or less of to extend our capabilities.

When I started studying psychotherapists, I focused on the details of what they were doing. Quite early on, it became obvious that they were all using hypnosis without realizing it. Fritz Perls had clients hallucinate other people in empty furniture while denying he was inducing hypnosis, even though positive hallucination is the product of a profound altered state. Virginia Satir had her "centering" and meditative processes that were deeply hypnotic. Only Milton Erickson used hypnosis and knew it.

My purpose was not only to study these people and their hypnotic processes, even if they didn't acknowledge them, but to be able to go beyond what they did. Over the four years I modeled exceptional people, I was able to take the things I'd learned and do things with hypnosis that none of the people I modeled would ever dream of being able to do.

This was possible because they *all* had belief systems that, in some way or other, limited them. Even the best hypnotists I met believed that some people couldn't be hypnotized, whereas I have yet to meet one. The only people I find who can't be hypnotized are the ones who aren't in the room.

Of course, someone could put their hands over their ears, close their eyes, and refuse to listen, and then they are unlikely to be hypnotizable. But, for the most part, all of us, when we talk to each other, use the same processes that are used in the hypnotic exchange. The only difference is that a hypnotist is more precise.

Some hypnotists can only hypnotize certain people, but this is almost always because they have one particular induction that they've mastered.

I've always tried to teach people to be flexible enough to respond to exactly who's in front of them. Look for the subject's uniqueness and respond to that. Learn to be able to alter everything, from the tone and tempo of your voice to your physical appearance. In fact, you need to be able to alter even your own state of consciousness at will. Then, as you start to enter their world, you can influence them deeply—even at the level of their early childhood cognitive structures.

When you are able to do that, you can easily encourage and influence people to move beyond whatever their limitations happen to be.

Some strategies require an altered state not only to install them but to put them into effect. Those great golfers I modeled were getting ready to tee off, taking a mini swing, then looking down to the green, taking another mini swing, and looking back down to the green, waiting for that moment where the green begins to "shrink." That's not going to be done in the waking state.

Some strategies require a profoundly altered state, and some require minimal shifts. Highly accurate pistol shooting might

require a comparatively deep trance, whereas good memory strategies require only very light trance states.

One of the best memory strategies I ever encountered was a
woman from India. She came to a seminar along with eighty other
people, and when I asked if anybody had an unusual skill, she
raised her hand and said, "I can remember the name of absolutely
everybody I meet."

I brought her to the front of the group and had all eighty
people say their names, one by one, then sent them all outside. A
little later, when I brought them back in, I had them sit in different places. She went around the room and identified every single
person perfectly.

Her strategy was as follows: when someone said his or her name,
the woman repeated it inside her head, while looking to find some
unusual physical characteristic. Then she'd create a large cartoon
figure out of what she saw, and say the name again while writing
it under the image. Finally, she'd open her eyes, look at the person
and ask, "Is your name X?" and make sure that it matched. When
they said "yes," she'd shrink the picture back to the size of his face,
and then move on to the next person. Whenever she saw the person again, the unusual characteristic would pop up in her mind,
together with both the sound of the name and its written form. No
matter how much time lapsed between being introduced to people
and meeting them again, she never forgot their names.

Looking closely at her strategy, we can see the image was richly
encoded, and since the encoding was so thorough, decoding it
was easy.

Of course, some scientists might argue against calling any of it
"trance"—but whether you call it a trance or an altered state, or
just "remembering," it's only a description.

We have to keep in mind that words like "hypnosis" and "trance" are really processes, verbs, that have been turned into nouns. They're not real "things"; they're what we call "normalizations" (see Resource Files 4 and 5 on pages 311 and 316).

When I set out to learn hypnosis, many people I knew tried to discourage me. It was bad, didn't work, only suppressed the symptom, and so on. But knowing how to use hypnosis is to make yourself a better communicator, whether you're a salesperson, a psychotherapist, a teacher, a receptionist, or a dentist. It's a skill that helps you interact better with other people and makes your job more efficient and your life easier.

The irony is, many states, and even countries, have laws prohibiting the use of hypnosis. In the United States, there were laws that said it couldn't be used with the military. You can't use it at school or show inductions on some television channels. Yet all of the people involved are encouraged to visualize, to use their imagination, to pretend. I remember going into a chemistry class where the professor told us to imagine a mirror that was reflecting a helix molecule that we were then to spin backward, looking just at the reflection and not at the "real" one in front.

Some people could do it and some couldn't, because, for some people, the waking state doesn't allow for this kind of image making, whereas for others, it does. That's a profoundly altered state.

There was a time when the phrase "altered state" was used hypothetically, but with the advances in neural scanning we can demonstrate that measurable changes take place in the brain. The research I've been involved in takes readings from sixteen locations in each hemisphere.

What I did was to get people to meditate, or engage in other, really interesting, mental activities, and I was able to see the

changes taking place. We could see the brain moving from beta to
alpha and sometimes epsilon. Those people who had really creative moments showed very low alpha with theta spikes in a very
consistent pattern. Altered states are thus not amorphous; they
can be shown to be very precise.

We already have devices that cause the brain to entrain to various patterns, ranging from deep rest to high alertness, and soon
we'll be able to get direct, real-time feedback from our clients so
we'll be able to monitor their brain functions even more accurately than we can currently with an MRI or a PET scan.

When I started out, many years ago, I got to use one of the
early MRI machines on—of all people—claustrophobics. I had
to duct-tape them down to get them to go inside, but when they
did, we saw that they all had certain things in common. For
example, one hemisphere almost totally shut down, while the
other went into overdrive, accompanied by accelerated heart rate
and breathing.

But then, when I took them through the original treatment
that I developed many years ago and put them back in the
machine, every single one of them was calm, while their scans
showed that both hemispheres of their brains had become active.
This finding told me that they made physiological, neurological,
chemical, and mental changes that could stay with them for the
rest of their lives, simply because they'd learned to use their brains
differently.

This is the way I've thought about producing change ever since.
Being able to make enduring change means it has to occur at a
neurochemical level, rather than just as some vague psychological
concept. "Control" shouldn't be a question of willpower or effort.
It should emerge from new ways of thinking. By doing what we

do in NLP and hypnosis, we are literally repatterning our brains, and, if we do that correctly, if we run the correct sequences, we gain the kind of control that means we can move away from the sequences that produce pain and fear, and toward those that give us freedom, opportunity, and choice.

Eleven

INSIDE AND DOWN
The Patterns of Trance-formations

WHEN I PUBLISHED *Trance-formations* more than a quarter of a century ago, it almost immediately became the benchmark for books about hypnosis. Even now, long after it is out of print, copies are trading at dozens of times the cover price.

Before then, hypnosis was seen as a rather mysterious and inaccessible subject. Most hypnotherapists adopted an extremely directive approach. It was widely believed that the hypnotist had to dominate his subject's will and drive him into hypnosis with repetitive, monotonous commands.

Predictably, only a relatively small number of people responded. There was absolutely no suggestion that this might be the hypnotist's fault. Everyone, it was suggested, was hypnotizable to a greater or lesser degree. It was considered to be an innate trait, rather like the size of your feet or the color of your eyes. If you had difficulties going into trance or were unable to perform complex, deep-trance phenomena, it demonstrated your shortcomings, rather than your hypnotist's.

Even Milton Erickson believed that subjects had to be "trained" to become good hypnotic subjects. Most of his followers still see him as a kind of instant miracle-maker, but he made no secret of the fact that he sometimes took between one hundred and one thousand hours to prepare his patients for therapy. The idea that hypnosis was something that anyone could experience, or do to another person, was inconceivable at the time.

Trance-formations changed all that. It demonstrated that hypnosis was a natural phenomenon, open to everyone to experience, and that getting people into trance—even really deep trance—was an easily learnable skill, and that hypnosis could be a tool that therapists and teachers in all fields could apply to help their clients and students to learn.

It was the first book ever to demonstrate that hypnosis had a structure, and the structure could be modeled, learned, and taught.

In that book, I outlined several hypnotic patterns, all of which could be immediately applied. These patterns had either been modeled or refined from the work of Milton Erickson or were developed from my own work in the field. The purpose of revealing the "inner structure" of several patterns was to encourage hypnotists to be systematic. It was never intended to suggest that any of these patterns represented "the" way to do hypnosis, nor that the hypnotist was expected to favor one over the other.

However, within a very short time, these patterns were copied and reproduced many, many times. Each new book that came out, each new "creator" of these techniques, presented them as if carved in stone.

What people need to understand is that no one induction is automatically better than another. The most powerful factors that decide whether your subject goes into trance are your rate of speech, tonality, breathing, and your own overall ability to alter your state as an unconscious way of guiding her into an altered state.

The specific patterns and exercises that follow, therefore, are intended both as a guide and a means of developing flexibility. My experience is that the failure of someone to go into hypnosis has nothing to do with "hypnotizability" and everything with the hypnotist's ability to respond creatively to the person being hypnotized.

If you are new to hypnosis, I suggest you take each pattern and practice it until it feels easy and natural. It is not necessary that you have a subject to practice, but the important thing is to do it as if you do. Speak out loud, listen to your own tonality, and alter your performance as you go along.

It can be useful to record your early efforts, then listen to them later to find out whether they have any kind of effect on you. If you cannot put yourself into trance, it's unlikely that you'll be able to do so for others.

RHYTHM AND TONALITY

One of the characteristics of trance-inducing speech is its use of transitional, or linking, words and phrases.

A competent hypnotist speaks smoothly and effortlessly, with few discernible ends to his sentences. Even though linking phrase with phrase and sentence with sentence may not be grammatical or even logical, the effect is soothing and reassuring to the listener.

Even though his voice was deep and gruff, Milton Erickson was the master of rhythm. He achieved this in a number of ways, including the way he rocked his body from side to side to mark out certain phrases to the listener's unconscious. In compiling the Milton Model, we identified a number of linkages, some stronger than others. As with all the language patterns, I strongly suggest you not only closely study the Resource Files at the end of the book but that you create and write down as many of your own versions as possible.

Possibly the easiest, but also the weakest, way of connecting phrases is to use simple conjunctions, such as "and" and "so." *And . . . as you do so . . . learn to listen to your own voice . . . so you can develop your own sense of rhythm and confidence . . . and become confident enough . . . so you can expand your capabilities far beyond anything you . . . and anyone else . . . might have thought possible . . .*

The second, somewhat stronger, linkage is created by what, in the Milton Model, we call "implied causative." Simply put, this kind of pattern suggests a cause without actually stating it. The fact that a direct claim of causation is not made makes it extremely difficult to resist. *If you learn to incorporate the implied causative in both your normal speech and your hypnotic inductions, then you will dramatically increase your ability to influence others, and while you consider what that could mean to your career and your personal life, your unconscious is already thinking of new ways to apply these learnings.*

Even stronger is the Cause-Effect pattern, which suggests that one event triggers another. The second exists *because* of the first. The word "because" itself may or may not be in the sentence. *These patterns are laid out in the Resource Files section, which means you have a reference easily at hand. The more you practice these patterns, the more spontaneously you will generate them, because simple repetition will ensure that you remember them both consciously and unconsciously.*

Exercise: Creating Inductions

Decide on the state you would like to induce in a subject, and write out at least three ten-minute inductions using three examples of each of the following patterns in turn:

1. Simple conjunctions
2. Implied causatives
3. Examples of the Cause-Effect pattern

This will give you nine statements for each trance to refine and develop.

Note: This is not a suggestion that you use prepared scripts with clients. The end-point of this and most other exercises in this book is to help you learn how to spontaneously generate inductions in any form you choose.

A pleasant tonality is extremely important to effective change work. It is not simply what you are saying to the person that carries the message. You bathe his entire body with your voice; every cell resonates to the waveforms you generate. I can't recall how many hypnosis workshops I've attended and how often I've heard someone say in the screechiest, most annoying tone possible: *"Relax, now . . . you are feeling more relaxed . . ."* You know from the very start that it isn't going to work.

A "good voice" isn't necessarily something you're born with, but it's certainly something you must acquire. Over the years, I've trained myself to be able to shift accents from New Joisey to the Deep South, via any state you care to name. I can take on Erickson's voice, his rhythm and tonality, as easily as I can use my own.

In workshops, I often take people through the following steps:

1. Put your finger on your forehead, and say in a high-pitched, strident voice: "This is my forehead!"
2. Now, touch your nose, and, speaking as nasally as you can, say: "This is my nose."
3. Touch your mouth, and in a somewhat deeper voice, say: "This is my mouth."
4. Now touch your chest, deepen the voice a little further, and say: "This is my chest."
5. Finally, touch your stomach area and say as if you really mean it: "This is my stomach, and if I speak from here I can influence everyone I meet, make millions, and get all the sex I want . . ."

The other important pattern to develop is that of authority and credibility. This is simply a matter of learning to drop your voice in the right place in the sentences you use.

- As a general rule, when you ask a question, you inflect upward at the end of the sentence.
- When you make a neutral statement, the sentence is uninflected.
- When you make a statement or issue a command, the sentence ends on a downward inflection.

Knowing and applying these simple rules can markedly increase your flexibility, and therefore your effectiveness, as a hypnotist. For example, by downwardly inflecting what superficially seems like a question, you can deliver a command to the listener's unconscious.

Repeat the sentence "Would you like to relax now?" out loud, first inflecting upward at the end as usual, then downward. Notice the difference, both in the way it sounds and how it feels viscerally. My students often report feeling a lot more confident, grounded, and in command when they learn to manage their own tonality. Women, especially, can gain considerable authority in this way.

Exercise: Toning Inflection

Choose a section from this, or any other, book and read it out loud, in turn:

1. Inflecting upward at the end of every sentence
2. Uninflected throughout every sentence
3. Inflecting downward at the end of every sentence.

Now, set aside a whole day during which you attempt to downwardly inflect every sentence you speak. It is unlikely you will achieve this, but with practice it becomes easy and natural, and will considerably increase your authority without challenging the status and power of the people you meet.

DIRECTING THE SUBJECT'S ATTENTION

Erickson once defined trance as "reduction of the multiplicity of the foci of attention." What he was saying in a very ponderous way is that hypnosis allows us to narrow our attention until we are focused just on a specific area of our subjective experience.

Another way of thinking about trance is as a shifting of the subject's outer awareness to his inner experience. Whenever our attention moves inward, we begin to alter our state . . . or go into hypnosis. Whenever the "foci of attention" move outward, the subject returns to his normal waking state.

Knowing this can act as a systematic guide to the new hypnotist, informing both the overall "shape" of her induction and the language she uses.

PACING THE SUBJECT

Combining this outer-to-inner direction with "pacing," the subject's experience provides an easily remembered model for doing hypnosis that is both naturalistic and effective.

Pacing is a behavior that both tells subjects you are aware of, and respect, their experience and acts as a feedback mechanism to guide them further into trance.

The effectiveness of this particular technique depends almost entirely on creating and stacking agreement upon agreement, then linking that with a specific command. Compliance increases more or less to the degree we can get the subject to agree, even if agreement is about issues unrelated to issues other than the one at hand.

Putting it more simply: if we can get someone to agree with two or three irrefutable facts (that is, verifiable through their senses), they are likely to comply with any non-sensory-specific suggestions we might make.

Example: "You're sitting back in the chair, your feet are on the ground, your hands in your lap . . . and you can start to feel more relaxed."

The first three statements are irrefutable truisms, the fourth is an injunction or command.

It is extremely important for this model to work that the

hypnotist avoids any form of opinion or judgment in the three pacing statements. You may not say, "You're sitting *comfortably* on your chair . . . ," simply because "comfort" is potentially deniable. Perhaps the subject has a sore back, or a headache, or the seat is too soft.

The formula is to pace the subject (preferably three times), then lead him with a suggestion that corresponds with the outcome you've decided.

The induction is built out of successive pacing/leading statements and, as the subject relaxes more, becomes increasingly internally directed.

You can increase your flexibility and effectiveness as a hypnotist by learning to make artfully vague statements that are nevertheless still undeniably true: "feeling the temperature of the sun on your skin" is preferable to "feeling the warmth of the sun." This ability will prove especially useful in the models for doing hypnosis that follow. Remember: the less content you presuppose, the less likelihood there will be of you being wrong. The more process-oriented you are, the greater your chances are of pacing your subject's inner experience.

Exercise: Using Truisms to Induce Hypnosis

Write out an induction using the following model:

1. Three statements that are inarguably true, followed by one suggestion of increasing comfort and relaxation. Repeat this step three times, giving you nine pacing statements and three suggestions. Now, add . . .

2. Two "truisms" and two "comfort" suggestions. Repeat three times. Add . . .

3. One truism and three comfort or trance-deepening statements. Repeat three times.
4. Add several suggestions that the subject enjoy three or four minutes of deep and refreshing rest, then return to full, waking consciousness.

Test your induction on a partner.

OVERLAPPING

Achieving rapport by matching the subject's behavior and sensory preferences is important, but not as important as some NLP "experts" would have us believe. You don't need phenomenal amounts of rapport, simply enough that people understand what you're doing.

If somebody is talking to you in pictures, you talk back to them in pictures so they can understand better. But of course, understanding is not the most important outcome. Changing is the important outcome; learning is the important outcome.

I am constantly amazed to meet self-styled experts in Neuro-Linguistic Programming who want to tell me what I really meant. These are usually people who have certified themselves, who woke up one day and said, "Hmm. I remember now—I invented NLP." Even though I created this field and have been in it for forty years, I still have people come up and argue with me about the right way to do NLP.

One of the things I hear a lot about is the importance of getting rapport. Out there in the field of NLP, there are entire books about how to establish rapport. In fact, all I ever said was, if you *need* rapport—which I don't think is necessary, most of the time—you could establish it by matching behaviors.

But there are times when you don't want it. You don't want to have rapport with paranoid schizophrenics, for example. I certainly don't. I scare the hell out of them so they want to change.

One of my favorite paranoid schizophrenics, Andy, had the following bizarre complaint: he said people came out of the TV and followed him around. Just the thought of it gave me the willies, but when I heard about it, I just couldn't pass it up.

The psychiatrists were very reluctant to take him off his drugs "in case he got out of control." I pointed out that they were both over six feet tall and he only came up to their chests.

So they dragged him over to this place where it had been decided to film the entire process of my meeting with him. When he arrived, there were lights and cameras and technicians and people staring at us—exactly the sort of situation to reassure a paranoid schizophrenic.

His brother, whom he was very close to, came with him and told me that his ambition was to go on a trip together, something they had planned when they were young but had never done. But, he said they could never do it because his brother kept having violent arguments with people who weren't there.

I asked, "Like whom?" which is not the kind of question most people would ask, but it seemed entirely relevant. He said characters from television shows would come out and have arguments with his brother—especially Mary from *The Little House on the Prairie*, a show that was very popular at the time. Other things that upset him, his brother said, were being touched and people with long hair (which, considering the length of my own hair at the time, promised to be interesting).

When Andy arrived, he turned out to be the cutest schizophrenic I had ever met, because he was so sincere about everything he did. He told me at great length how Mary would step out of the TV set and follow him around, nagging at him and driving him crazy. On one occasion a preacher got out of the set and followed him around, shouting at him and telling him everything he did was a sin.

Andy gave me a very penetrating look and said, "He also told me to watch out for people with long hair."

I leaned over, touched him on the knee, and yelled, *"Don't worry about it!"*

Andy yelped and scooted back. I scooted forward and said, "Andy, they tell me you're a schizophrenic." Andy agreed and then went on to give me a very detailed, official-sounding account of his diagnosis.

When he'd finished, I said, "Andy, you're not schizophrenic." The two psychiatrists who had brought him looked outraged; after all, it was their diagnosis, and even Andy looked confused. I continued, "The problem is not one of schizophrenia. It's one of bad taste."

He said, "What do you mean?"

I said, "Andy, have you ever heard of the Playboy Channel?"

There was a pause as Andy thought about this, and suddenly the Red Sea of schizophrenia parted in front of us. The two psychiatrists suddenly looked at Andy with envy in their eyes.

I said, "Andy, this is a multimillion-dollar disorder you've got. How many people would pay big bucks to be able to do what you're doing? Think of all those traveling salesmen who're away from home and can still have fun without getting into trouble with their wives."

Andy looked at me and said, "You think?"

I replied, "Here's another thing. You've also been watching the wrong cartoons. Have you ever seen those Bugs Bunny shows where the artist's pencil comes into the frame and erases Bugs's legs? And when he starts to complain, he erases his mouth?"

Andy responded, "Oh, yeah, I've seen that one," so I made a very expansive gesture as if I was handing him a giant pencil, and I said, "Well, I want you to take this and erase Mary's mouth."

Andy took the "pencil" with a very determined expression on his face, turned, and obeyed without a single question. Then he sat back and started to laugh with a sense of power.

I said, "Don't stop there. Now erase her whole head and put a giraffe's head in its place." The thing is, it's not so bad when people hallucinate. It's when the hallucinations get the better of them.

Even after I had worked with Andy, the psychiatrists took him back and pumped him full of drugs again "just in case." Since the drugs acted as a powerful anchor, Andy went back into a schizophrenic state. So I sent the videotape of the session over to him and got him to watch what had happened while he was on the drugs.

After a while, he was able to do this new thing I'd taught him with or without Thorazine, because it was just a mental skill.

The way I look at it, Andy's hallucinations were no worse than the person who comes up to me and says, "I can't be happy" or "I can't really experience love." My answer is: not while you're thinking like that, you won't—because the more you think about what you're not doing, the more you won't do it.

As I mentioned earlier, it's important to match primary representational systems at first, and then to overlap into all the other systems. This way, you expand the person's ability to take in and process information. You open up new avenues in his brain. One of the ways of looking at my work is as extending people's representational systems with great precision, to get a specific result.

Neurologically, all the systems overlap in the brain. The distinction between feeling and pictures and feeling and sound is tenuous at best. There's a tremendous blending of these things.

Of course, people are often completely unaware of one or another representational system, and it's here that their problems usually lie. When someone says, "My job's just getting on top of me" or "I have a problem I need to get some distance from," it tells us *how* they are structuring their experience, not that the person knows *what* they are doing. The truth is, just because somebody doesn't see images or is unaware of his internal dialogue doesn't mean he doesn't have them.

It's easy enough to establish where people's problems really lie by asking Meta Model questions (see Resource File 4 on page 311). For example, they might say, "I'm depressed." The response to that is, "How do you know that?" I always go for the biggest chunk question—the one that will give me most information. "How do you know?" and "What does that mean?" are two examples of big-chunk questions.

Usually, they'll say, "I don't know, I just feel it," and then you respond, "Well, how do you know you're depressed? How do you know when to be depressed? How do you know you're not really happy?"

You're listening for sensory-based information—and you're also paying attention to what *isn't* there. The fact that someone might have every sensory system in place but is not using them all in consciousness will answer a lot of questions about where their problems come from. If someone doesn't see the images he's responding to, he doesn't stand a chance of altering them. It's that simple.

It's easy, then, to see that problems exist within the "hidden" representational system. But we should also be aware that when we help people extend their awareness of their representational systems, we also open up resources that have previously been shut out of their conscious awareness. In doing this, it soon becomes obvious that the person who is shifting awareness from one representational system to another is also profoundly altering his consciousness.

"Normal" waking consciousness usually corresponds with the individual's functioning within her preferred—and, by definition, most familiar—sensory system. Overlapping systems rapidly alter states. When a very visual person starts to pay attention to her feelings, she will go into trance. When a predominantly auditory person makes pictures, she will go into trance. A kinesthetic person who learns to make vivid images goes into trance.

Extending sensory systems is most easily achieved by the process of overlapping. As the word suggests, the subject moves from one system to another, enriching her experience and capabilities in the process.

Exercise: Overlapping to Increase Skills

1. Think of a physical activity you enjoy—running, dancing, or riding a bike, for example. Create as vivid an internal experience as possible, using the representational system that comes easiest to you. For example, you might visualize the road slipping past under the wheels of your bicycle, seeing your legs pumping rhythmically, and your hands gripping the handlebars.
2. Now, add an example of one of the two absent sensory modalities. For example, as you look down at the road beneath your wheels, imagine, then intensify, the sound of the tires on the ground.

3. When you have successfully added a second modality, think of a third and include that—perhaps the feeling of your knees pumping as you drive the pedals down.
4. Continue the process, systematically adding another layer of modalities, until you have at least three examples of each.
5. Notice how this alters the reality of this experience.
6. If possible, try out the activity for real, and notice how using overlapping improves your performance.

It is necessary to overlap systems to achieve learning and change. This, by definition, is an altered state. Overlapping, therefore, is not only a powerful hypnotic technique but an educational tool with infinite potential.

Exercise: Overlapping to Induce Trance

1. Working with a partner, ask him to tell you about a place that's special to him. Note his preferred sensory system.
2. Invite him to close his eyes and join you in a visit to his special place, starting: "And, as you imagine being there now, you can . . . ," and then begin to develop the experience with a succession of statements pacing his preferred system, and then overlapping into another system. Pay close attention to his nonverbal response. If he appears comfortable, continue.
3. Make several more pacing statements, then overlap to another system.
4. Continue in this way until you have overlapped into three (or possibly five) sensory systems.
5. Allow the subject a few moments to reflect, and then suggest he return to normal waking consciousness as soon as he is ready.

Avoid being too specific. Refer to "the color of the sky" rather than "the clear, blue sky," "the temperature of the air on your skin," rather than "the warm breeze." This is a challenging, but extremely rewarding, route to deep trance. Being artfully vague was a significant characteristic of Erickson's work and is codified in the Milton Model (see Resource File 5 on page 316).

Note: It is perfectly permissible to use phrases such as: "I don't know if/whether . . ." to facilitate content-free instruction. Example: *"Now, I don't know whether there are any clouds or not, but you can pay special attention to the color of the sky . . . especially . . . the difference at the horizon between the sky and the water . . . And the colors and tones and light on the water itself . . . And exactly how the air feels on your face . . . Or, if there is anyone else around and you can hear voices or not . . . or, are enjoying being alone . . ."*

Twelve

DEEPER, AND FASTER, STILL
Rapid Induction and
Trance-Deepening Techniques

WITH ALL THE TOOLS AT your disposal now, hypnosis should be a rapid process. People are still teaching outdated methods, like progressive relaxation, or the Staircase Induction, in which the subject has first to be able to create an imaginary staircase, and then walk down it into trance. My feeling is, if they can hallucinate a staircase, they're already in trance.

Nowadays, I don't spend the hours and hours that I used to do inducing trance. I have discovered that most people are flipping in and out of altered states all the time, and if I can just observe them, catch them at the right time, and reinforce what they're already doing, it's the quick road there.

However, even though I no longer use protracted hypnotic inductions and would like you, the reader, to develop rapid methods, I believe spending time on the fundamentals, as outlined in this book, like the hours I spent experimenting when I started out, will pay dividends. The benefits to me include learning how to organize my language so that I can use ambiguity, creating multiple levels as I speak and talking to people consciously and unconsciously at the same time. Very importantly, I learned how to analog mark, so I can deliver direct orders without people detecting them. When they tell me they're too nervous, and I say, "So what you're telling me is you can't . . ." [then I analog mark, by speaking slightly louder, and use the downward inflection of a command] *". . . relax and let go."* I repeat this pattern over and over, and by the time I get to the point of actually starting a hypnotic induction, people are typically already there.

Another extremely important quality of rapid hypnosis is timing—timing your words, the rhythm of your voice, which words you mark out. People typically don't process grammar formally, especially when they're moving into trance. That's why I spend a lot of time focusing on the two-word utterances that are characteristic of early speech development. These patterns are still embedded in the nondominant hemisphere, and when you use them, you can elicit a very powerful response. *Relax now. Feel good. Comfortable rest. Learn new. Feel safe. . . .*

I've already said that, simply by observing the client, you can see when he is moving into an altered state. However, this degree of observation takes practice and experience. This is why I used to place a lot of emphasis on verbal pacing, and I recommend that you become adept at pacing verbally before moving on to other ways of gaining access to the patient's model of the world.

I tend to observe more now than I used to. I look at the client's pupils, his lower lip, the tonic quality of his muscles, his skin coloration. I know how these things change as people go into trance. For example, as people begin to alter their state, their lower lips fill up with blood, the pores become smaller, and the pupils dilate.

I watch for these things, and I align myself with them. I begin to breathe at the same rate as the client, in through my mouth and slowly out through my nostrils, to begin to relax myself. Even though they'll be breathing differently—perhaps through mouth and nostrils simultaneously—if I breathe in through my mouth and lean slightly forward and breathe out through my nose and lean back, pretty soon they'll follow the pattern and start to relax, too. The more you can get them to follow you non-verbally, the better.

But this doesn't mean I work entirely indirectly. The fact is, I give as many direct commands as are needed. This notion of nondirective hypnosis among Ericksonian hypnotists is not really accurate. He used a lot of ambiguity, and because other people, especially in his day, couldn't follow him, they called it nondirective. It was only nondirective in the sense that he prompted transderivational searches in his clients—that is to say, he would tell them something unspecified was going to happen that would let them know they were relaxing, and leave them to decide what it was.

Of course, they would scan their bodies, and say, "Oh my God, I can feel something. It must be that." He was unspecified, but in many ways Milton was one of the most directive hypnotists you would ever want to meet. He only had five goals for people to get well: get out of the hospital, get a job, get married, have children, and send him presents. That was his definition of a cure.

Mine is a little broader than that. Not everybody starts out in hospital. I don't really want their presents, so we can scratch that one off. I don't necessarily think they have to be married or have children. I think it is good for people to have work that satisfies them, to have relationships that make them happy, and I think it is important for them to have fun—and lots of it. The reason people get so miserable is because they spend so many hours doing it and they get to the point where they master being miserable. It's beyond a habit; it's become expert behavior.

Whether I go about this conversationally or not isn't impor-tant. Either I embed the suggestions, or I look at them directly and say, "Relax." Then, when they respond, I'll say, "Relax more."

Then I'll look even more deeply into their eyes, almost as if I'm looking through them, and say: "More . . . more . . . more . . . more," leaning forward with each word, and ending each word with a downward inflection. If they're responding, why make it more complicated than that?

I've become closely attuned to the way people blink. There's a conscious blink and an unconscious blink. The eyelids close a little more slowly with an unconscious blink and stay closed just a little longer than a conscious blink. I know then that the subject's attention is moving inward, and he's starting to relax, so I'll reinforce it, by nodding and saying, "That's right." Then I start to blink slowly in exactly the same way, and as the subject does the same thing, I'll say, "Close your eyes."

I watch as the eyelids come down. If he shuts his eyes too quickly, I'll tell him to open them again, then close them again "only as you're sleeping." It's a confusing statement to the conscious mind, but when the unconscious understands, the subject responds with fluttering, double blinks. When I see those double blinks I know my subject is headed toward trance, so I look closely and say reassuringly, "That's right, that's right," lowering my tone and reinforcing any other signs of developing trance.

One of my more rapid and powerful inductions involves leaning over and taking hold of someone's hand, with finger and thumb circling the wrist. If necessary, I turn the hand so the back of the wrist is uppermost, and I lift it to about shoulder-height and push it back slightly toward the subject's body.

Now, if this were done very strongly, it would be a wristlock characteristic of some martial arts. The particular combination of moves makes the arm feel out of control, and by doing that, and pushing the arm back, it comes near to triggering catalepsy.

At that moment, I say, "Hold it for a minute," but I'm ambiguous about what "it" really is. Is it the thought of relaxing he has to hold, or the arm itself? Is it the thought of

> *going really deep down and knowing that you don't know where you're going to go but it's going to feel good. So the question is always: how much pleasure you can stand? Can you relax your forehead and your knee at the same time? Can you relax the front and the back of you at the same time? How about both ears and only one nostril? The truth is where we relax isn't important, it's only important that we do it . . . now . . .*

Consciously, people are able to handle only a few suggestions at a time, so when you stack suggestions like that, it's too much to process, so it passes into slipstream of unconscious communication for processing. Since their hand is up, and I've let go, and it stays there, it's already cataleptic. There is no need for lengthy suggestions to get the arm up in the air and have it become cataleptic. Because it's a lot harder to lift your hand than it is to put it down, I lift it for them—then tell them to "let it come down only at the same rate that they relax and go into a deep trance . . ." Notice the dissociative effect of the words. The presupposition is that they're no longer in control of the arm, so, therefore, something else must be: their "unconscious."

As an alternative to lifting the arm, I'll sometimes grab the wrist, shake the hand, feeling for whether their muscles are relaxed, then throw the arm down as I tell them to "drop your consciousness and your arm." The effect is almost instantaneous, and people relax all at once.

LEVERAGING AND DEEPENING TRANCE

One way of explaining these phenomena is by the principle of leveraging. People in our society have certain ideas about what marks real hypnosis. Arm catalepsy—sitting motionless with one arm extended—is one such marker. It's not something people do in their normal waking state. So, once it occurs, it increases your credibility as a hypnotist.

But since no particularly useful purpose is served by having a subject sitting for an entire session with a cataleptic arm, we can use leveraging to deepen the trance even more. Simply tell the person: "And your hand can begin to go down, in honest unconscious movements . . . but no more quickly that you are ready to . . . go even deeper into trance . . ."

Many newcomers to hypnosis worry unnecessarily about whether they can induce trances that are "deep enough." Of course, the question then is, deep enough for what?

I don't necessarily think that everybody needs to be in deep, somnambulistic states to make changes. In fact, often I find it's too dissociative, and people are inclined to forget what is required of them if they are now given proper posthypnotic suggestions.

I mostly put people into states that are altered just enough to allow them to engage in new behaviors that I can then reconnect with the conscious state.

I really want people to have control. Milton wanted them to just respond. If people were depressed he wanted them to go into a state where they were more optimistic. He didn't really want them to have the conscious control.

I want them to be able to turn depression on and turn it off. I want them to be able to turn happiness on and turn it off. As

Virginia said to me, "If people have choices, they'll always make the best one." Our job, as I see it, is to give them choices.

Deepening the hypnotic state just enough to be able to work effectively with it while maintaining control over how deep the subject goes is a relatively simple and easy matter with the technique known as "fractionation."

This works by leading the subject into trance, then, just as he's settling in, bringing him out again, and repeating the process. Each time you do this, he will lapse into a deeper trance.

Beware of doing this too much, however. If taken too far, the subject may respond by refusing to come out of trance, in which case you have lost your role as leader of the experience, and you will need to back up to regain rapport.

There are many different ways that trance can be induced and deepened, and we're developing them all the time. The key point to remember is that the hypnotist functions as a feedback mechanism for the subject's state, and as your abilities improve to demonstrate and reinforce trance nonverbally, you will introduce the subject to richer and more productive experiences.

Neural scanning lets us know that when people go into hypnotic trance, real changes take place in their brains. Brainwave entrainment technologies, such as the Mindspa, for which I've developed a number of programs, also allow us to induce specific altered states using lights and tones.

To realize that we're only scratching the surface of what is possible is truly exciting. Even though I am best known for my work in NLP and hypnosis, I've never stopped being a physicist, and that allows me to look at even more advanced technologies than the ones we already have.

At the time of writing, I'm working with leading scientists to develop technologies that will profoundly increase our ability to see, measure, and change the way the brain works.

As technology and self-development come together, we will find new ways that will allow us to speed up our own evolution even more rapidly. But until this happens, the best means to accomplish all this is your sensory system—especially your ability to observe.

Even if you've never done hypnosis, that doesn't mean you haven't seen it before. Remember those times when people are standing in the elevator and the door opens and they don't step out, or the times someone is at a stoplight and the light changes but she doesn't move? Think of that expression on your child's face when he's being nagged, and his eyes begin to defocus and his skin becomes flaccid and he loses the swallow reflex. These are all mini trances, and the more you notice how people go quite naturally into these mini trances, the more familiar you'll become with the signs, allowing you to set up a feedback loop to reinforce and direct their changing state.

The purpose of trance is to get people into a state where their brain is more flexible, more able to tolerate their problems and to develop solutions. All of our beliefs, all of our fears, all of our limitations reside in specific states of consciousness. You cannot be afraid if you're genuinely amused; you cannot be anxious at the same time your muscles are relaxed or your breathing is slow and regular.

State-conditioned learning is something we've all experienced many times. For example, you might have studied hard at home, then taken a test at school or college and found you can't remember anything, but when you get back to where you did the original studying, all the knowledge comes flooding back.

What this tells us is that we need to be in the right state to do the right thing. Many activities are conditioned this way. Athletes know this; often they'll follow elaborate rituals to get into the right state, because they know from experience that their performance will be significantly better.

On the other hand, when people are agitated, they can't perform optimally. If the level of stress is high enough, they can't even add or subtract or read the safety instructions on the back of their hotel room doors in the event of fire.

This book has been designed to help you know how to shift the submodalities of your unwanted experience, to do Swish Patterns, to create new sequences so you have new strategies you can run at will. In short, you can optimize your performance as a human being.

Since we know that stress does not help one perform well, it follows that to be able to go into deep states of relaxation, to change our beliefs, to change how we look at things also changes our understanding, our feelings, and our behavior.

In even the oldest cultures in the world, it's been known that people can enhance their performance and improve their quality of life—and the first step is always to be able to go into some kind of relaxed, altered state.

I've studied many different kinds of meditation in many different countries. I've been to hundreds of sacred temples and spoken to every guru I could find. Their methods might have differed, but they all said more or less the same thing: learn to meditate and practice it regularly and your problems would float away. You'd become more enlightened as a person, more functional as a businessperson. You'd be better for your family, a better spouse and parent, a better partner and friend.

I don't think this is unrealistic, however far-fetched some people might think it is. People who meditate are simply more evenly balanced. Instead of letting the stress of everyday life snowball into chaos, they have a place to go that brings them peace, comfort, and regeneration.

People need these benefits as much today as they did in ancient India—even more, perhaps. But time is at a premium. Not everyone can go off and meditate for hours at a time. To help people experience and benefit from peace and comfort now, we need to be able to induce deep trance quickly.

Where I used to spend an hour hypnotizing people, I now spend three minutes. That's because I've become very familiar with the process. I don't have that expectation of people just starting out, but I do have the expectation that they can learn to do the same, and I certainly have that expectation of people who have done hypnosis for a long time.

Unfortunately, many people in the field don't have that expectation of themselves. They found a way that works for them and stayed with it, but if they are not prepared to challenge their own limitations, they will never improve beyond their present point.

The better you get at hypnosis, the faster you should be able to get people into trance. The faster you can do that, the more people you should be able to work with, and the greater the variety of difficulties you should be able to resolve.

These technologies are designed to help people to think more creatively and constructively, to have a greater depth of feeling, and to develop more flexibility in their behavior. Above all, they make it possible for people to learn faster than ever before.

Thirteen

REMEMBERED PEACE
Accessing Previous Trance

THE PREVIOUS TRANCE INDUCTION is easy and universal, for the reason that every human being has at some time experienced an altered state and reentering that experience triggers a near-identical neurochemical and behavioral response. Another way of putting it is that the more senses we use in recalling a particular experience, the more real that memory will be.

Previous Trance inductions may refer to a specific incident (with which the hypnotist will, of necessity, need to be very familiar) or they may make use of universal experiences, such as the example below.

To become adept at this and other forms of induction, you will need to study and practice. The Milton Model (see Resource File 5 on page 316) lines up the language patterns that induce altered states. You can practice by creating your own inductions, writing them out, and testing them on other people, or even on yourself (you'll need to record them first, of course).

When I began studying hypnosis, I copied out hundreds and hundreds of inductions by experts, such as Milton Erickson, not so that I would become a carbon copy, but so that the patterns I had identified could become embedded in my unconscious, to surface whenever I needed them.

That is how I am able to create inductions such as the example below. I've done it a few times before. . . .

PREVIOUS TRANCE: EXAMPLE

As you begin to go back and remember that original experience . . . which might have been when you were hypnotized before, or even . . . when you went to the dentist, and maybe . . . he gave you nitrous oxide . . . you know, that gas that makes you . . . feel really good . . . or some other experience where you began to feel really comfortable and relaxed . . . and notice . . . the very first thing you heard . . . and the first thing you felt . . . and then what you remember hearing next . . . and the next thing you felt . . . so . . . off you go . . . as you sit here, looking at me, just close your eyes for a minute and recall what it felt like to be there, in that place . . .

And . . . maybe if you meditate, you can go and think about what you feel like when you're in deep meditation . . . where you feel it first in your body? And which way it moves . . . as you become more relaxed? And then, literally, take that feeling and extend it so that it spins faster . . . and I have a tendency really . . . to just breathe at the same rate as the person in front of me . . . and just relax myself . . . and I'll tell them that as I relax . . . you relax, and you'll sit there . . . and you'll wonder what's going to happen . . .

And you may find you have a tendency to talk to yourself, and . . . if you must . . . talk to yourself slower . . . and in a lower voice, or just count . . . 20 . . . 19 . . . 17 . . . and with each count . . . keep counting down and . . . put in some yawns, s-l-o-w yawns . . . and, if you feel relaxed, just say aaah *. . . and feel even more relaxed . . .*

And if you feel yourself float up a little bit, don't worry about it . . . just float back down . . . because, you know the difference between relaxation and nonrelaxation . . . it's like being in water and floating . . . and you know the difference between down and up, so just let yourself . . . go down . . .

And the more you try to make yourself stop . . . and worry and wonder if you're doing it right . . . if you're worried about whether you're relaxing . . . that's not right, so what's left is . . . to go deeper and deeper still . . . learning, still . . . understanding still . . . remembering relaxation, whenever you breathe . . . in and out . . . and think about the word . . . soften *. . . and I love that word because . . . if you soften* sum-ptuous-ly *. . . you can soften your muscles . . . you can soften the focus of the images in your mind . . . you can soften even your internal dialogue and you can yawn more . . . and go deeper and deeper still, into . . . what it is you do not know yet in the depths and the depths of a very relaxed state . . . things in the back of your mind can come forward, and things that used to worry, and things you used to fret about can simply disappear . . .*

And, if you make an image in your mind, dissolve it, push it off into the distance, and . . . if you have a voice talking, let it move away from you and . . . just float down . . . into a state of comfort, and as you listen to my voice, each and every word has its own meaning . . . because it's a miracle of language that you understand things . . . before you really know what they mean, so when I say the word soft, *your body knows what soft is . . . and, when I say the word* sleep now *you know what it is . . .*

And when I say your unconscious now wants to help you . . . your unconscious now needs to do certain things . . . your unconscious has always protected you . . . if something begins to fly toward you, you blink . . . if somebody begins to move toward you, your peripheral vision notifies you and . . . you go into the state that's alert, and . . . when you're done, you relax, really relaxed, with a growing sense of comfort . . . and the deeper you go, the more comfort you have . . . and remember to smile, because it should feel good to know . . . your unconscious now is helping you to do things, which otherwise you would be unable to . . . it's as if you're in a dream, because when you have a dream, you don't always know you're dreaming . . . so the dream you should have now . . . is the one where your desires bubble up, where your hopes bubble up, and where your worries and your fears move backward, because . . . when you move backward, deep down, down deep, inside out . . . what happens is, your unconscious now . . . will help you be able to move these thoughts from a state of comfort, to one of perpetual delight . . . because in this state . . . the only thing you need to know is that . . . there is delight at the end of the tunnel.

Exercise: Previous Trance Induction

1. Decide on three real-world universal examples of times when people relax deeply.
2. Using the Milton Model (Resource File 5 on page 316) as a guide, create three ten-minute inductions designed to create and deepen the experience of comfort, peace, and relaxation by linking "artfully vague" references to each other with conjunctions, temporal phrases, and other devices discussed earlier. Keep your language nonspecific—that is, do not presume to tell the subject how to feel, but create options and possibilities from which the subject can choose.
3. Overlap from each sensory modality to the next to deepen and enrich the experience.
4. Test the induction, either on a partner or record it and experience it for yourself.

Note: Make sure you give clear instructions for the subject to end the trance and return, fully awake and alert.

Fourteen

CREATIVITY OUT OF CONFUSION
Pattern Interrupts, Stacked Realities,
and Nested Loops

INTERRUPTING SOMEONE'S PSYCHOMOTOR PATTERNS can be extremely disorienting. When people are disorientated, there is a tendency for them to grab hold of the next statement that seems to make sense. Linguistically, I often stack negation or presuppositions one on top of the other to overload the conscious, dominant hemisphere and gain access to the listener's unconscious, nondominant hemisphere.

Pattern interrupts can take many forms and be extremely effective. One of the first ones I ever did was with a feminist named Phyllis. She wanted to be emancipated, but she kept complaining to the group she was in about how everyone walked all over her and took advantage of her. Her roommates always make her do the dishes, nobody ever tidied up, they didn't appreciate her, *blah blah blah.*

Eventually, I turned to her and said, "What's the matter? Can't you just say no?"

She looked at me and went pale. She said, "No, I can't say no to people."

I asked, "What do you mean?"

She replied, "If I say no to people, they'll die."

She accepted this as the literal truth. She understood it because she'd been through psychoanalysis and had discovered that when she was young, her mother had decided to leave her father, who was a severe alcoholic. The father begged them to stay, but they went out—and when they came home, they found him dead with his head three inches from the telephone. Blood was running out of his mouth from a perforated ulcer.

Of course, Phyllis came to the conclusion that if only she and her mother hadn't refused to stay, she could have called an ambulance and saved his life. And it went on from there.

But the fact was, living her life, letting people treat her like a doormat, and never saying no to their demands was just crazy. So I looked at her, straight in the eye, and I said, "Okay—tell me NO!"

She looked at me and said, "No, I can't do that." I fell right out of my chair on to the floor.

Phyllis finally had to look at me, and I'd say, "Tell me no! Tell me no again. Tell me no. Tell me no now!" and she kept saying, "No, no, no, no, I won't," and the more she did that, the more she had to laugh, because there was no way out. None whatsoever. It's a complete double bind.

The thing about verbal double binds is that if you can do it in a way that makes people laugh, they start to get fed up with the way they've been behaving. I do this by teasing people. I call it "chiding," because it's not done mean-spiritedly. It's getting people to laugh at their silliness.

I use the Universal Quantifier (see Resource File 4 on page 311) behaviorally. I say, "Okay, Phyllis, I'll tell you what I want you to do. I want you to lay in front of my front door so people can wipe their feet on you."

She'd say, "There's no way. I'm not going to do that."

I'd say: "So you're saying no then? You're trying to kill me. You hate me. You want to murder me. Please lay in front of my door now . . ."

What happened after that was that the next time somebody asked her to do something and she started to say no, the giggling would start to spiral up. Instead of the fear of killing somebody being in the unconscious, it became both a conscious and an unconscious response. The trouble is, someone might consciously want to say no, but if, unconsciously, they feel in danger, that conflict immobilizes them. It's only when you line up conscious and unconscious desires in the same direction that people really engage in behaviors wholeheartedly.

I remember seeing Phyllis some years later, and she wasn't dressed like a feminist of that time anymore. She was dressed like a corporate executive, and it turned out she was.

She was still a feminist, but in a new way. Rather than being the feminist who couldn't say no, she was now the boss. My guess is she was saying no to a lot of people—especially when they asked for things like raises.

For some time I focused a lot on pattern interrupts because I realized that all these strong beliefs loop back on themselves at some point. People who claim they're unsure about everything are really sure about that. People who procrastinate never wait to do it. These patterns all have that paradoxical element to them.

The thing about pushing paradox is that you get people to laugh.

THE HANDSHAKE INTERRUPT

Milton Erickson used pattern interrupt and confusion on many occasions. Almost everywhere I go to teach hypnosis, I'm asked to demonstrate his Handshake Interrupt induction. However, I have to admit that he never used the Handshake Interrupt pattern exactly the way I've always demonstrated it. Since he was paralyzed, he couldn't have carried out the movements as smoothly and as rapidly as is required.

But I do credit him with giving me the idea. I saw him being introduced to a rather self-important young man once, and pomposity was something Milton loved to puncture. The man was certain he knew everything there was to know about hypnosis and made it clear Milton had nothing to teach him.

But as he was introduced, Milton picked up his paralyzed hand with his good hand and flopped it out at the visitor at just the point where a normal handshake would have occurred. The effect of this paralyzed limb being thrust at him was so unexpected that the man became momentarily confused. Milton loved confusion and often deliberately created it to induce trance, and as the young man opened and closed his mouth without saying anything, Milton leaned forward and uttered his classic line:

"Now . . . speaking to you as a child . . ."

The shock of Milton's gesture and the ambiguity of his statement were such that the young man dropped straight into deep trance, and began to age-regress as Milton proceeded to chastise him severely for his lack of manners.

The reason the man was confused was simple. In all cultures we have certain psychomotor patterns—we call some of them "traditions"—that we follow automatically. The handshake is the one best known in the West.

It exists as a pure stimulus-response. If someone extends a hand to us, we automatically respond by clasping it. There is nothing in the program between the hand extending and the hand being shaken. We, and many millions of other people, have made a generalization like this by which we all function quite happily.

As long as the program is completed, there's no particular problem. But if it is suddenly interrupted, confusion follows—and wherever confusion occurs, trance can be induced, simply because the brain is groping around for instructions as to what to do next.

The Handshake Interrupt, as it was later developed, deliberately breaks into the stimulus-response, inserting other, unexpected suggestions and instructions before closing it off again by completing the handshake. The subject is almost always amnesiac for what happened in between.

Even if you never use the Handshake Interrupt as laid out here, I suggest you practice it with a partner until you are completely proficient. This will increase your ability to induce or recognize mild confusion, then use it creatively to induce trance.

EXERCISE: The Handshake Interrupt

1. Extend your right hand toward your partner as if to shake hands. Do this confidently, making eye contact at the time.
2. As his hand comes up to grasp yours, slide your left hand forward and take his extended hand, your thumb along the back of his hand and your fingers around his wrist.
3. Immediately rotate his hand counterclockwise and bring his palm toward his face until it is only a few inches away.
4. Simultaneously point with your right index finger at his palm and say, "Look!" in a commanding tone of voice.
5. As he tries to focus on his palm, move it slightly backward and forward, and continue, "at your hand, and notice the changing focus of your eyes . . . and as you continue to look closely at the details of your palm, your hand can begin to come down . . ."

6. At this point, move the hand in small, ambiguous movements until you feel the subject's muscles tighten, then let go, and continue:

7. ". . . in honest, unconscious movements . . . and notice, as that happens, how your eyelids begin to close . . . and your hand can drift down and your eyes close completely, but only as quickly or as slowly as you're ready to go into a deep, relaxed, and comfortable state . . ."

8. Continue with the hypnotic language, reinforcing the downward drift of his hand and deepening his state by reinforcing even the smallest sign of developing trance. Ensure that the movements are truly unconscious. These are small and jerky, rather than rapid and smooth. If his hand moves down too quickly, catch it with your forefinger and say, "Not so fast. I said honest, unconscious movements . . ." as you jiggle his hand. When you feel a cataleptic response, reinforce it by saying, "That's right," then continue with your instructions. At any point, you may have him pause the downward movement of his arm while you insert whatever suggestions or commands are relevant, then simply tell him to allow the downward drift to continue "until it touches mine, and we can shake hands as if nothing has happened."

9. When his hand reaches waist level, catch it in a firm grip, shake it, and tell him to open his eyes ". . . now!"

At the time, the Handshake Interrupt was thought to be the most rapid induction ever. Since then, I've developed even faster methods, all of which depend on being able to recognize trance as it develops naturally and altering my own verbal and nonverbal behavior in response.

Some methods of confusion can be disturbing and disorientating. Others, however, are gentler and just as effective.

STACKING REALITIES

One of the patterns I wrote about in *Trance-formations* was called Stacking Realities. This process embeds one story inside of another, so that the listener becomes unsure of what fact belongs to which level of story. The effect is mildly confusing and, depending on the nature of the stories, very soothing.

The easiest way to stack realities is to begin by saying:

> *I had a client once, rather like you . . . [this tends to relax the listener, since the story is about someone else] . . . who had a similar problem . . . [pacing] . . . which had also been causing her many sleepless nights . . . [more pacing] . . . until she met a friend. And she said: "You know, worrying about it is not going to solve the problem" [suggestion]. My mother always said: "Decide what you can change and change it. Accept what you can't change, relax and get on with your life" [suggestion], and she realized that she had been focusing on what she didn't want, and said: "It's more important to decide what you* do *want" [suggestion], and so she said . . .*

By this time, the listener has lost track of which reality we are talking about. The effect is a state of gentle confusion.

Once you have moved through several levels of realities, you can begin to embed process instructions about what you want the client to do. Any of the relevant language patterns, particularly the Milton Model "Quotes Pattern" (see Resource File 5 on page 316) may be used, as can the various techniques outlined in this book. The client is likely to be especially compliant—and will also, almost certainly, have amnesia for precisely what the instructions were. But, expect his experience and behavior to change, apparently spontaneously.

EXERCISE: Stacking Realities

1. Decide in advance the outcome you want to achieve. Ensure that it meets all the conditions of well-formedness.
2. Construct a succession of stories or anecdotes, each leading into the other, as demonstrated above. Use the Milton Model "Quotes Pattern," as well as any other patterns that meet your requirements.
3. Embed process instructions inside one or more stories. The easiest way to do this is simply to say: "And he said, "'Do X . . .'"
4. Test your stacked realities on a partner.

NESTED LOOPS

Since learning is at the heart of the work I do, I am always looking for faster ways to install information in the people who come to me. I pioneered the process of unconscious installation, which, among all the other techniques of multilevel communication too numerous to go into here, makes use of the technique of nested loops. Loops are powerful techniques for rapidly inducing altered states, and when information or instructions are properly delivered inside nested loops, the subject is often unaware of receiving them and surprised to discover at a later date how her thoughts, feelings, or behavior have changed.

Nested loops may be as simple or as complex as you like. As you begin to learn how to manage this powerful mode of communication, you will need to do some careful planning. However, like every other skill you acquire, regular practice makes the process easier.

The principles on which nested loops rely are the conscious mind's compulsion to make sense of the information it receives, as well as the unconscious mind's ability to track multiple strands of input and its need to seek closure to any unfinished business or loop.

Opening and closing loops is at the heart of storytelling. Children are automatically caught up by suspense stories. The classic way to open a learning loop with a child is to start, "Once upon a time . . ." It seems to me that this is another area in which education is missing out. Just because we're trying to teach people something doesn't mean we shouldn't entertain them—thus, the term "edutainment."

Nested loops can have a number of purposes.

- The first, of course, is to capture the listener's attention and prevent premature closure. The moment someone says something like, "Oh, yes, I know that," no further information will be taken in. "Uh-huh . . ." is the sound of the human mind shutting down.
- Nested loops can also connect or "chain" different states in the listener. By eliciting a different emotional response at each stage, you can lead a subject in whatever direction you choose.
- Information or process instructions are embedded inside the loops, so that, as each loop is closed off, the information collapses into the listener's unconscious and he becomes amnesiac for the actual "installation" that has taken place.

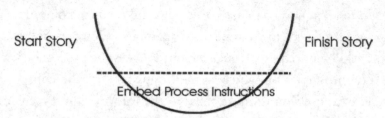

Figure 14.1. Simple loop pattern.

This figure represents a simple loop in which a story or statement is begun, broken off to allow information or process instructions to be delivered, and then completed.

Nested loops, as the name suggests, are more complex and use multiple stories. The first story is interrupted part of the way through and the next story begun. That, in turn, is left unfinished, and the next one begun. The listener may become increasingly curious and a little frustrated, not knowing how one or more of the stories end. Information or instructions are embedded at each level throughout the process or just before you start to close off the loops *in reverse order*.

So the procedure (using three loops) is: Start Story 1 (optional: embed information), interrupt to start Story 2 (optional: embed information), interrupt to start Story 3 (embed information). Then finish Story 3, finish Story 2, finish Story 1.

The exercise below uses five loops, but with experience, this can be increased. All my trainings use many, many loops, each with a different outcome in mind. Loops may be closed in the same conversation, or hours, days, or, as in the case of some of my trainings, even weeks later.

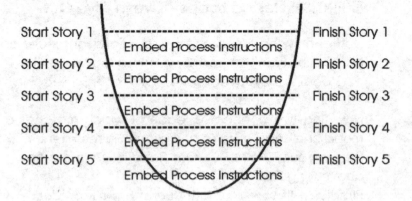

Figure 14.2. Five In, Five Out Nested Loop Pattern.

This figure represents a Five In, Five Out Nested Loop Pattern. At each stage, a story is begun, interrupted to allow information or process instructions to be delivered, and then the next story is begun. The process repeats for all five stories, 1, 2, 3, 4, 5, which are then completed in reverse order: 5, 4, 3, 2, 1.

EXERCISE: Nested Loops—Five In, Five Out

1. First identify the five process instructions, or pieces of information, you wish to impart. These may be embedded commands, overt instructions, or, in a teaching environment, exercises.
2. Now find five anecdotes, each of which matches a mood or elicits a state (e.g., curiosity) in the listener.
3. Design your Five In, Five Out Pattern, using the figure above for guidance.
4. Practice, either with a partner or a voice recorder.

Note 1: Remember that if several layers of process instructions have been set, they, too, will be installed in reverse order—from the last to the first.

Note 2: Beginners often have trouble making the transition from one story to the next. You might use phrases like "Oh that reminds me . . . ," or, pick a word or phrase from your last sentence and use that as a starting point for your next statement. When practicing, experiment with different transitions to build in flexibility and confidence.

Fifteen

ADVANCED SUBMODALITIES
Freedom, Fun, and Fuzzy Function

OUR ABILITY TO OVERLAP from one sense to another can be a powerful, creative tool. It can also cause massive problems if we don't learn how it works and how to manage it.

Overlapping occurs to different degrees, with different effects, with different people. Psychologists have identified what they regard as a rare ability that some people have to change one sense into another. This phenomenon, called synesthesia, describes how some people can hear colors, and others can taste sounds. Often those people who are regarded as particularly gifted—savants, psychologists call them—use synesthesia, together with more usual ways of processing information, to achieve extraordinary results. However, if the senses are hopelessly muddled without a strategy to sort them appropriately, immense suffering can result.

Even though some developmental experts believe all babies are synesthetic when they're born and gradually learn to separate their sensory modalities into different channels, synesthesia is generally assumed to be rare and exotic among adults.

That isn't to say we can't—or don't—use synesthesia. To some degree or other, most people are able, when pressed, to allocate a shape to a sound, or a color to a taste.

Earlier, when you were practicing the simple Previous Trance induction, you, or the person hypnotizing you, deepened the experience by mapping over from one sense to another, enriching the subjective experience. As you felt your eyelids begin to close, you could notice the shifting focus of your eyes; when you felt the rise

179

and fall of your chest, you could also hear the gentle sound of the air moving in and out of your lungs. Being able to move from one sensory modality to another creates a fuller and richer experience, as well as providing you with more tools to generate new and wonderful skills that are limited only by your imagination.

Quite early on, I found that overlapping from one sense to another was not only possible but was also the source of creativity and, for some people, confusion and fear. Although the experience of having wonderful internal body sensations while listening to music is very different from feeling bad when we hear a nagging tone in our partner's voice, the process is the same. This is a function of "fuzzy logic"—when the representational system used as an input channel is different from the system used by the output channel. Some people follow a hear-feel pattern, others a see-feel pattern.

Whenever you are communicating with other people, be aware that words are power, and the way in which you use words has to be as precise as the results that you desire. When I'm giving hypnotic suggestions, I build in fuzzy logic. For example, I may have somebody in a trance, knowing they have memories that terrify them. I tell them:

> In a moment [which is a way of saying "not right now"]
> I'm going to tell you to go back and look at that memory,
> but I don't want you to do it in the same way as before.
> From now on, the more you feel fear when you look at that
> memory, the more the image will shake and shrink, and
> the more you look at it, the more it will fade off into the
> distance. The more painful it is, the farther away it will
> be . . .

DEALING WITH ABREACTION

When I initially started doing hypnosis I was warned about abreactions. These are sudden eruptions of emotion that happen to some people as they go into a relaxed state. Instead of quieting down, they start freaking out. Sometimes abreaction is so intense that the person literally has convulsions.

I believe this abreaction happens because some people have never had the experience of truly relaxing, and the experience is so unfamiliar it scares them. The minute I see any sign of abreaction, rather than bringing the person out of trance as I was told you should do, I take an entirely different approach. I got my inspiration from an old John Wayne movie. In this movie he was badly hurt and in great pain, but he said: "Well, at least the pain lets me know I'm alive." I remember saying to my first abreacting client: "Well, you know, feeling this fear lets you know you're alive, and the more you become aware of the fear, the more it will disappear, and the more you're sure you're alive the better you'll feel." The abreaction just disappeared.

On another occasion, a trance subject went into a very unpleasant state. I said, "This is unpleasant, and the more unpleasant it is, the sillier it will seem." This person suddenly burst out laughing, just like babies do when they start to cry, and you pretend to cry, and then you giggle and they giggle. This works because people can jump from one state to another, from one sensory system to another.

Linking the start of the problem—or even something before the start—to a new and more resourceful response is a useful approach. I like to get that shift as early as possible in the sequence. Some people make the mistake of calling this a pattern interrupt, but it's really a function of punctuation ambiguity (see Resource File 5 on page 316).

I'm a mathematician and a computer scientist, and math to me is not a pure science; it's a behavioral science. Math and computer programming are models of human behavior and the way humans think. Humans have "and" gates and "or" gates, which means when they get to a certain point, they could go either this way or that. This fact is particularly useful when you want to help people with problems such as asthma or anxiety attacks—with a lot of physiological activity.

One of the approaches I've used for many years is to put the person into a superdeep relaxed state, then give a posthypnotic suggestion that when he or she comes out of that trance, they'll drop back the moment I tap the knee. Then I bring the subject out and trigger the panic attack, and at that precise moment I fire the relaxation anchor. I trigger an asthma attack, trigger relaxation, trigger high blood pressure, trigger relaxation, and I do it over and over and over again, until it starts to happen by itself.

The only way you can really panic is by being physically tense and holding your breath. You can't panic if you're really relaxed. You can't have an epileptic seizure or a fit or an anger attack while you're in a state of deep relaxation.

One of my clients—a really lovely person—was sent to me by the court because he attacked somebody in public in a blind rage. He said, "I don't even remember it. The guy stepped on my foot, and I just started hitting him."

He went to therapy, and the therapist told him he had a "hot button." The therapist explained that once you had a hot button, there was nothing you could do about it. I love the optimism of that statement—the belief that if you're a person who instantly goes into rage, you can't be helped. Of course, my subject knew he was going to end up in prison.

When he told me all about it, I asked, "So if you have a button, it won't go away?"

He said, "Yeah."

I said, "You're saying you have a hot button?"

"Yes," he said.

I thought, *"Cool!"* At that moment, I knew exactly what I had to do.

I put him in a deep trance, made him feel totally relaxed and comfortable, and then gave him a posthypnotic suggestion. As I brought him out, I attached his hot button to my cool button. Once I'd attached the two buttons, I pushed the hot button and the cool button triggered. And then I stomped on his foot. He just smiled and laughed and relaxed.

It's very important that you keep backing up to find out where the difficulty starts, and then put the resources in *before* the difficulty arises. Once you're in a state of rage, it's hard to get out of it; once you're stressed, it's difficult to relax.

Back in the days when we still used audiotapes, every company in the field of psychology products contacted me at one time or another to ask me to make a stress-reduction tape. I'd say, "Can't we make one so that people don't go into a stress state in the first place?" and the response every time was, "No, everybody has to go into stress."

That turns out not to be true. If you find out the things that trigger stress, you can make them trigger relaxation or a state in which you don't really care much about the pressure—a state in which you just get the job done without any unpleasant feelings.

Each of these problems is, in fact, an altered state. Anger is an altered state. So are rage and depression and anxiety and fear. Any state of consciousness can be triggered by pretty much anything else. Therefore, we can set things up so that one altered state immediately triggers another, more desirable, altered state. Posthypnotic suggestion is a powerful way of doing this, and anchoring (see Resource File 1 [page 305]) makes it work that much better.

EXERCISE: Hot Button/Cool Button

1. Think of a response you have that you would like to change—for example, irritation, depression, anger, worry. Just for a few moments, fully immerse yourself in the last time you experienced this. See what you saw, hear what you heard, and feel exactly what you felt at the time.
2. Now, step out of the experience and slowly run it backward as a movie, until you find the very first moment the response begins to develop. Shift the movie just one frame further back than that, and imagine this as a big red button—your "hot button"—on your left knee.
3. Open your eyes, shift your position, then close your eyes again.
4. Now, take three to five breaths, allowing the out-breath to be a little longer than the in-breath. Fire your "trance anchor," or simply instruct your unconscious to float you down to a deeply relaxed and enjoyable state. Spin the feeling of comfort and relaxation so it begins to spread throughout your body.
5. As this state begins to peak, imagine a large green "cool" button on your right knee. Keep pushing the button several times, going twice as deep each time.
6. Open your eyes and fire your hot button. Immediately fire your cool button and hold both for a moment. Release your hot button and hold your cool button as

you run through how your response would have been different if you had it instead of the hot button response. Make sure you shift representational systems as you do this: if the earliest reaction was an image, ensure that you end with a strong, desirable feeling; if the earliest response was a feeling, end with a picture of your discomfort flying away into the distance, and so on.

7. Repeat steps four through six several times, until firing your hot button automatically triggers a cool response.

Synesthesia or fuzzy logic can also be used to increase creativity. The key to really unusual experiences lies not only in changing representational systems but also in manipulating submodalities.

By now, you have been developing the ability to create increasingly complex and detailed subjective experiences with relative ease—for example, imagine standing or sitting near a crackling fire on a cold winter's day. As you do so, watch the dancing flames, notice the subtly changing colors, smell the pungent wood smoke, and feel the side of your body closest to the source of heat becoming warmer than the other side. And as you allow the warmth to spread, speed up the process more and more, faster and faster, and let the warmth spread throughout your body, realizing that you're actually on the very edge of a new and wonderful experience, because you're about to use just some of the skills you've been learning to create an entirely new technique, and as you consider that, I want you to begin to wonder, as you warm yourself comfortably, what would happen, and how strange it would be, if the submodalities of one system affected the submodalities of another whenever you wished it to be so. What would happen, and how could that be?

When Milton Erickson was experimenting with hypnotic phenomena, he did some curious things, such as inducing temporary color blindness. But when he induced hypnotic color blindness, something strange happened. Some of the people became tone deaf. That and other, similar, occurrences were spontaneous demonstrations of the overlapping from one sensory system to another.

Now, what you're going to do—either with a partner, or maybe even as you're reading these words—is to consider, for example, right now, if you decided to drift into a trance, and that was to allow you to go deep enough, that your unconscious mind would begin to make all the necessary changes such that pain control, for you, can be accomplished by saying that everything that you felt in one arm took every single degree of pressure and turned it into a volume, with a particular location, so that where you were touched determined what sound you heard, so if somebody rubbed your arm, you wouldn't feel a thing, but you'd hear the sound of something wonderful. It's a lot more of a fun way to deal with pain control. . . .

See, very often it's done differently, and your unconscious mind understands this perfectly. So, now, or in a few moments, on your other arm, you can begin to feel an ice cube, and that ice cube could become colder and colder and spread all the way down to the point where if you put ice on something long enough, if you were to touch it with a pinprick, you don't feel anything at all.

Now, let that ice cube go away, and let your attention go back to your other arm, and let your unconscious imagine what it would be like if, even more thoroughly, you took any sensory system and chose to have parts of that system go into another. And, for the purposes here, I want your unconscious mind to take a moment to review the list of submodalities in this book (see Resource File 3 on page 310), and I want you to just randomly, for no particular reason, realize there's no need to hesitate and there is no need to wait. Just choose a few submodalities and move them from one system to the other. Imagine the ways in which you can do this, so that, like the last time I did this, I ended up playing songs on someone's arm by making the pitch higher up the arm, and lower down the arm, the more I pressed, the louder the volume became, and while I played a song, somebody operated on that arm and the subject didn't feel anything in that arm at all. However, they did notice that the song they were listening to had some strange static in the background.

Now, another thing you might do would be to take auditory external, and turn its pitch into a feeling; its volume can become the pressure of that feeling, and so on.

As soon as it's practical, I want you to go into a profoundly altered state with a partner and begin to experiment with any kinesthetic sensations you have by turning them into sounds or pictures.

Be creative, and think of applications. For example, if certain people crave certain illicit substances, you might change their cravings into a picture, and set it up so that the more intense the feeling becomes the farther that picture goes away.

Exercise: Advanced Synesthesia Change Pattern

This exercise is designed to increase your flexibility and to provide a template for creating techniques that are new and appropriate to whatever situation you are working with.

1. Decide on a desired outcome. Review in all sensory modalities how you or your subject will behave, feel, look, and so on, when fully experiencing that outcome.

2. Identify whatever stands in the way of the outcome being achieved. As an example, say being confident in meeting people and enjoying new situations is your outcome; constructed images of "making a fool of myself" accompanied by an internal voice saying, "Don't even try," accompanied by a feeling of "dread," stand in the way of accomplishing this outcome.

3. Refer to a comprehensive list of submodalities (see Resource File 3 on page 310) and choose three at random. These might be color/black-and-white, sound/silence (both digital), and location of a kinesthetic feeling.

4. Experiment with turning the feeling of dread into a sound (say, the screeching of a buzz saw—switching it off and on and off again, noting the response), or turning the sound of critical self-talk into a cascade of colors. Adjust the colors so they are bright and attractive. Keep experimenting with each submodality until you find one or more synesthetic shifts that change the entire experience.

5. Attach a trigger to the shift so you or your partner can enter the state at will.

Synesthesia patterns open up many choices. If you incorporate finger signals, you greatly increase your flexibility. As your subject drifts deeper into trance, and deeper still, set up finger signals, and then ask his unconscious to agree to a period that you define, maybe five or ten minutes, in which he makes all the necessary adjustments, at an unconscious level, to all the submodalities you choose.

PART 3

Patterns of Utilization

Using the Tools of Trance-formation

Sixteen

BACK TO THE FUTURE

Changing Personal History

ONE OF THE BEST WAYS of getting over an unhappy past and guaranteeing a happy and successful future is to practice making yourself feel better for no particular reason. If you wake up in the mornings and feel good, you'll make better decisions about what to do with your life.

People are making problems for themselves all the time. Some break up with a partner and then they go out and get drunk to meet other people, and a couple of hours and a lot of beer or whiskey later they're telling someone they only met a little while ago how much they love them. Then they wake up in the morning and find they're in bed with a piece of wood.

Sometimes people do stupid things and say later they acted like that because they were "confused," but one of the things I have discovered over the years is that confusion is not a state that should lead to stupidity. It's a doorway to new understanding.

If you begin to think of things as difficult, they will be. If you begin to study what makes things impossible, you'll find out. But if you adopt the attitude that that's only true in the state of consciousness you're in, you won't get stuck. So if you begin to learn how to make yourself feel differently, it will change your future once and for all.

After a while, you may start feeling better and you won't know why. But, you see, you don't need to know that; you just need to know how to get good feelings to replace the old ones—or, even better, to drop them in to what happens just before you feel bad, so you start to go down a new pathway.

Exercise: How Much Pleasure Can You Stand?

1. I would like to invite you to think of a time and place where you felt extraordinary pleasure. When a smile begins to spread across your face you will know when you have found a significant event.

2. Notice how you are remembering the event: see exactly what you saw at the time, hear what you heard, and notice how feelings come back to you.

3. Now, using the list in Resource File 3 (see page 310), begin to change the submodalities one by one. If there is no significant change, put it back the way it was. If the experience intensifies and becomes more appealing, make the maximum shift possible. When you have made all the changes that seem possible, make a circle in the center of that experience and open it up rapidly, like the iris of a camera, so you can see yourself experiencing *twice* as much pleasure. Make the colors twice as bright, twice as intense, and make the sound of supreme satisfaction resonate through your mind, then every cell in your body . . . *Aa-a-h!*

4. Do this two or three more times, pushing the feelings of pleasure as far as they will go, and then anchor them to make the feelings available to you any time you choose (see Resource File 1 on page 302).

5. Notice which way the feeling of intense pleasure moves, and connect up the start and finish points. Begin to spin it as you think of some areas in your present and future life where you could benefit with these changes in place.

6. Step into that future memory, fire your anchor, and see, hear, and feel as fully as possible how you will benefit from this much pleasure flooding into that experience . . . *now.*

7. Do this twice more with two other scenarios, and then pause to allow your mind to begin to generalize the process out into areas that you might not yet have thought of consciously, but which would be useful and appropriate.

People struggling with problems often say things like, "If only I had my life over, I'd do things differently." Or, my favorite: "I've got all these problems now because of all the terrible things that happened to me when I was a kid."

My response is: "Well, change it. It's never too late to have a happy childhood."

People are either shocked because I'm not "empathetic" enough, or they laugh, because intuitively they understand that it's true.

Of course, we can't change what happened to us. But we can change the way we respond to it—either consciously or unconsciously. The idea that we are all victims of past experiences is an attractive one to many psychoanalysts and counselors. But as far as I know, there is not a single shred of evidence that this always has to be the case. If it were, we wouldn't have the situation where two people go through an identical trauma, and one is devastated while the other is apparently unscathed.

The reality is, since the past is over and done with, the victims must be responding to the memory of it in a way that causes problems for them now. It's not that trauma has made them dysfunctional as much as they're responding in a dysfunctional way.

Over the years, I've approached the problem in a number of different ways, creating patterns to release people from the tyranny of outdated beliefs. "Changing history" describes a group of techniques I developed to help the subject respond differently to the generalizations they've formed as a result of some traumatic past experience. This is not the same thing as going into someone's past, time after time. We need minimum information—or, often, no information at all—to be able to help people change their responses to the past.

THE FAST PHOBIA CURE

The first and best known approach is almost certainly the Visual-Kinesthetic Dissociation Pattern, or Fast Phobia Cure. As mentioned in the first part of this book, the Phobia Cure works by dissociation. Instead of constantly reaccessing the cause of the phobia as if it is actually happening now, the subject learns to dissociate—step out of the first-person viewpoint, so she can replay it without becoming overwhelmed.

Psychologists know that people's problems are often caused by their history, but their belief is that understanding that history is going to miraculously make the problems disappear. It would be a nice idea, if only it worked. But it doesn't.

Old-school psychoanalysts then go on to blame the patient for being resistant or not ready to change. I think that's nonsense. Their choice should be either to send them away until they're ready, or *make* them ready to change. People are sometimes hesitant about accepting a new choice, either because they're not engaging the right strategy of going for it, or they haven't yet gone over the threshold of the problem. When they think about being afraid of elevators, or being abused in a violent relationship, they don't string together enough experiences to make the feeling intolerable. It has nothing with being a resistant client, but it may have everything to do with the therapist's inflexibility or limitation.

Insight alone isn't going to do it. I know somebody who had a phobia of water because he fell in when he was five and drowned. He didn't *almost* drown; he drowned and had to be dragged out, clinically dead, and resuscitated. From that day on, he was terrified of water and remembered the entire experience vividly. When he went into therapy, the therapist had him go back and relive it . . . and he was still afraid of water.

This wasn't a mild fear. This was a person who couldn't take a shower or step into a bathtub, or wash his hair, and who had to wipe his body down with a damp cloth to get clean. He had taken the idea of water and overgeneralized it to the point where his life was becoming unmanageable.

Now, knowing all the details in the world isn't going to change these responses. What is going to change them is deciding he's had enough—and knowing what he needs to do differently in his mind from what he's been doing so far. He needs to dissociate from that experience. He needs to start with somebody resuscitating him, and then move backward through the whole experience. When he does that, he's going to feel differently, because his brain is processing the experience differently. And when he feels differently, he can start to do the things that scared him and that he avoided before.

My interest in the content of an experience extends only to how it affects the way the subject maintains his fear. I don't want to go too deeply into the past because I don't want to increase the fear. I'm not a psychologist, and therefore I'm not interested in giving my clients insight. I want to give them personal freedom instead.

Some people accuse me of putting people into denial—and

they're right. I want people to have the means of denying the need to have bad feelings for the rest of their lives.

By now, it is clear that changing the submodalities of our representation of an experience is one of the quickest and easiest ways to change our feelings. Association and dissociation are important distinctions to apply. Most people find a dramatic difference in the way they feel about something they experience associated and the same thing dissociated. For example, if you see yourself in the front seat of a roller coaster as it goes up and down, it's a totally different set of feelings from seeing what you'd see if you were there right now. That's a great caffeine-free way to wake up in the morning. Imagine being cranked all the way to the top of a roller coaster, seeing things exactly the way you'd see them if they were happening now, then . . . just . . . *let go* . . . !

Some people would love that experience; others would hate it. What causes fear in one person can be exciting to another. But I believe that people with phobias—in fact, everyone with fear or depression or some similar state—are, in essence, carrying out some kind of posthypnotic suggestion, whether it came from somebody in their childhood or from something they created themselves.

I'm very fond of telling people that I'm one of the best hypnotists on the face of the earth (I have a letter to prove it), and therefore any suggestions they've received from other people can be countermanded by my voice. It just sounds so logical, but I think everybody should say it.

One of the ways I challenge other people's posthypnotic suggestions is to put the subjects into deep trance and then give them a posthypnotic suggestion that their head will come out of the trance, but the rest will stay inside. When they open their eyes, they can't move anything but their head. Then I say to them, "Now, let me ask you head to head—this belief you have, where exactly does it comes from?"

Many conditions, including psychosomatic pain, rashes, high blood pressure, and stress-related disorders, function hypnotically. Some very weird things can happen as a result.

I met this kid—about twenty-two, very bright, could take any engine apart, and put it together in no time flat . . . but he just couldn't read. He went to every available remedial class, but he just kept going: "I can't. I can't."

So I put him into trance and said, "I want to ask your unconscious if something is stopping you from reading?" I got an acknowledgment, so I said, "I want you to bring it into his conscious mind and have him jump up and tell me about it."

A few seconds later, he jumped up and told how, when he was in elementary school, a teacher snapped a pencil in front of his face in frustration and said, "You'll never learn to read!"

His unconscious mind took it as a command and blocked any attempt from then on to get him to read. It stuck somewhere in the back of his mind, and he struggled his whole life with reading. He was a bright kid, but fear can induce a very altered and suggestible state.

I simply told him, "Everything the teacher said to you is now no longer true, and the reason it's no longer true is that she did it accidentally and I'm doing it on purpose. Now you will start reading, and it will be fun, and you'll learn quickly."

I got a call from that remedial department a week later to say that he was reading perfectly. The fact is, he'd been reading his whole life. He just hadn't allowed himself to know it.

Where problems come from doesn't matter much to me. What

matters is the altered state they're in and what needs to be done to get them out. The minute a phobic starts a phobia, he's in an altered state, carrying out a posthypnotic suggestion. The same is true when depressives feel depressed. To me, their behavior functions in the same way as a posthypnotic suggestion works, and therefore it can be canceled the same way a posthypnotic suggestion can be canceled.

The Fast Phobia Cure is one of the first and probably the best known of the patterns I created. It proved that because someone had experienced a fear for twenty years, it didn't mean they had to experience it for their rest of their lives.

Exercise: Fast Phobia Cure
(Visual-Kinesthetic Dissociation)

1. Seat the subject comfortably in a small, imaginary movie theater, and have him visualize a small white screen, a little above eye level. Explain that he will soon be able to watch his traumatizing experience safely and comfortably, starting a moment before the event occurred (Safe Place 1) and ending when the movie of his experience fades out to white (Safe Place 2).

2. Reassure the subject that he can return to his normal state of awareness, free of any anxiety, at any stage he chooses.

3. Relax the subject and anchor his state of relaxation (see Resource File 1 on page 305), then have him dissociate by stepping out of his body and into a projection booth, from which he can both control the running of the movie and watch himself sitting comfortably watching the screen. If the subject is particularly anxious, it is desirable to dissociate him again (instructing him to "watch

yourself watching yourself watching the movie"). This allows him to be at sufficient emotional remove to be able to complete the exercise.

4. Hold the comfort anchor, and have the subject run the movie of his traumatic experience from Safe Place 1 to Safe Place 2, very rapidly, in black-and-white, ensuring that he stays dissociated from the experience of the trauma.

5. When he has completed this stage, have him float down and reassociate into his body, sitting watching the screen, then instruct him to float out into the end of the movie (the white screen), associating into the experience, restoring the color and preparing to run the entire experience backward, from Safe Place 2 to Safe Place 1. Add in some lively circus music as a soundtrack to the experience.

6. At Safe Place 1, the subject is returned to his seat, to watch the screen, to which the small black and white image of Safe Place 1 has been restored.

7. Instruct him to float up out of his body back into the projection booth, and repeat the process from Step 3 to Step 6.

8. Repeat the Visual-Kinesthetic Dissociation Pattern three to five times, and then test the subject by having him think about the trigger of his phobia and notice his response. If necessary, repeat the pattern as often as required.

Most people can get the Phobia Cure to work, but when they don't, it's usually because they haven't done it fast enough. They'll do a bit this week and another the week after, and then complain that it doesn't work.

When we want to produce really powerful change, we reformat the brain in much the way information is reformatted in a computer. Years ago we had all this information on big Kennedy tape drives you could literally load into a computer and reformat it into something else. You might take a lot of data and put it in three dimensional matrices and then load it on to floppy disks the size of a table. If you needed to use the information in a particular program, you had to reformat it through that program.

People's memories are all mixed up together, full of fear and humiliation, to the point where they can't even make it all the way through the memory without becoming overwhelmed. They get to the source of their fear—say, an elevator—and the fear triggers automatically.

To help them reformat, I first have them step outside of the memory. Separating themselves from the memory helps them look at what happened without becoming engulfed. Now they're looking at themselves, so they're much smaller than before; they're watching themselves inside of another small frame (the screen), so they've changed both location and size.

Then I have them turn the movie on, dissociated, and then have them run through it faster than normal, maybe with a little circus music, so it's reformatted. When they get to the end, I have them step inside, make it life-size again, and run it backward so the analog runs in reverse. Running it backward isn't actually necessary since the subjective experience will change anyway. It just changes better that way.

But if they dissociate from and leave the image life-size, it isn't going to work. I've tried it every other way, and that's the way that works best.

Over the years I've had many clients who have been traumatized and diagnosed as suffering from Post-Traumatic Stress Disorder. These are people constantly reliving every conceivable nightmarish event, from kidnapping and shooting to torture and rape. I've worked with Holocaust victims from World War II who were living and reliving horrible experiences, over and over again. The thing they all had in common was that they all represented their experience life-size.

If you are able to get people like this to step outside of the memories and look at their suffering from a different point of view and shrink it down, you can make it so they never feel the same fear again.

We can't change what happened, of course, but we can change the way we feel about things. Our job is to take charge of our own thinking processes and help others to do the same. We want it so they don't put themselves in situations of danger, but also so that they don't live in fear for the rest of their lives simply because something bad happened to them randomly.

It's very important to me that people understand that fear doesn't come from outside. It comes from inside. I think I've probably discovered more than any other living person how to get rid of fear. I doubt whether there's anybody who has rid people of as much fear on this planet as I have.

Not only have I developed techniques I use with people myself, but I've also taught them to hundreds of thousands of people all over the world, so they are using them to help even more people. I've spent a tremendous amount of effort finding things that work, and then refining them so that other people can easily do them for themselves.

I don't much care how people get the way they do. I don't want to know how they got broken or stuck. All I want is to help them operate optimally. I want them to understand that if they replay terrible things life-size, these events will continue to disrupt their lives, as if they're actually happening all over again. That's why they have massive screens in movie houses: the bigger the screen, the more intense your feelings.

The Fast Phobia Cure was extremely effective. It worked with everybody who came along, but I started thinking: "It can take thirty minutes to do. We should be able to do it in three." Of course, everybody thought that concept was crazy, but that didn't bother me too much. Most of what I've accomplished I've done by acting crazy.

I was crazy enough to believe that it was possible to get clients out of their difficulties in a single session. I believe it's easier to do it in one session than in ten or one hundred, because, as I've said several times before, human beings learn better when they learn fast. When those pages flip by, you see the pattern of the movement; when you take a series of still images and show them at thirty-five frames a second you have a movie. The brain understands this. Also, the faster we can get a pattern to run, the quicker it moves into the unconscious.

We know now how this works in the cortex. First it takes large areas of the brain to sort out a pattern of, say, learning to roller-skate or ride a bike; then suddenly it recodes and occupies a comparatively tiny part of the brain. It's the difference between short-term memory and long-term memory. It's the difference between a conscious behavior that you struggle with and an unconscious, automated response.

Problems occur because we have unconscious, automated responses that are not the ones we want. But we are infinitely programmable, and we can recode our responses in ways that support and enhance our lives—but only if we become completely intolerant of staying the way we are.

THE DIFFERENCE BETWEEN PHOBIAS AND ANXIETY

When working with people suffering from fear-based disorders, we need to distinguish between phobias and anxiety. Phobias are straight stimulus-response. Anxiety is the result of a longer process—a build-up to the anxiety attack. The approaches to dealing with these conditions are therefore different.

By helping subjects change the way they respond to their past, we are effectively teaching them how to change their personal history.

Not long ago, a woman who had been kidnapped by terrorists in Peru was brought to me almost incapacitated by fear that was triggered by almost any situation she couldn't easily leave. She became terrified in cars, elevators, trains, and so on. She even had to keep the windows of her own house open because of what had been labeled as claustrophobia.

But, strangely, even though she was supposed to be claustrophobic, she could fly in planes, as long as she could sit near a door.

Everybody knew exactly why she had her problem. During her very first vacation, she was mugged on the way from the airport to the hotel, there was a bomb incident at the hotel, and then, soon after she boarded a light aircraft to fly to another destination, it was taken over by terrorists with ski masks and Uzis, and she had such a bad panic attack that they got such a fright they stopped the plane on the runway and opened the door to calm her down.

Now I thought that was funny, and when I laughed she looked at me terribly upset. She said, "I don't think that's funny."

I replied, "You don't? You don't find it funny that you had such a panic attack that you scared a plane full of terrorists, and they didn't just shoot you, and throw you out of the plane? I'm sorry. To me, that's funny." Then I said to her, "But unless you can laugh about it, you have to suffer for the rest of your life."

Humor is a valuable aid to making significant changes. If we can genuinely laugh at the same time that we try to hold the problem in place, we alter and weaken the neurological structure of what was worrying or scaring us. People often come up to me and say, "I know that one day I'm going to laugh about this, but . . . ," and before they can get any further, I say, "So why wait?"

This woman didn't really have a phobia but was suffering from a habituated pattern. What I had to do was, first, make sure she was fed up with responding that way. She'd had this problem for twenty-five years, and even after years of therapy, she was still anxious. She was also embarrassed by the problem—but not embarrassed enough.

As part of her treatment, I dragged her to movie theaters and seminars in front of the cameras and audiences of hundreds and hundreds of people. I pushed her into an elevator, and all the time she kept saying, "Oh, I'm getting worse. I'm the worst patient ever."

But she didn't realize I was making her worse on purpose, because I wanted her to become so intolerant that she would start trying to change, asking herself questions such as, "How far can I get into the movie theater by myself?" "How comfortable can I be?" and she started becoming really excited about each little bit of progress she made.

Some time later now, she flies everywhere, rides in elevators and cars, and would have never believed it was possible. But first she had to be fed up, and then she had to get good feelings to reinforce every little step forward. She needed to learn to notice to what degree she was better than the day before.

She sent me an e-mail recently that I found quite funny because she listed all the problems she no longer had and then said, "I think it's related to what you did."

But it wasn't. It's related to what she did. She had become intolerant of the biggest problem in her life, and when she solved it, all the other problems didn't seem so insurmountable, so she started chipping away at those, too.

That's what good learning is. Learning is about looking at things differently, making your life a little bit better every day, noticing the progress you make, however small in the beginning. The truth is, people don't stay the same. People either get better or they get worse. Those are the only two choices.

We know that people who have ongoing problems have, at some time in their lives, built generalizations that no longer serve them well. Most therapies try to find ways of getting people to replace their thoughts, feelings, and memories with new and more appropriate patterns. The problem with this approach is that it's not exactly how the human brain works.

What I try to do is to get people back to a point before they built the generalizations that didn't work, and then put in new generalizations to override the old ones. This works because the human brain operates by a kind of push-down storage, rather like the sort you see in cafeterias, where plates are stored by pushing them down into a spring-loaded compartment. As each one is taken off the stack, another comes up to take its place.

We've all had the experience of getting a new telephone number, and for the first couple of weeks, we keep calling the old number when we try to phone home. Eventually you put the new number on top of the old one, which gets pushed back into the recesses of your mind. The human brain archives information; it never forgets anything.

This is a powerful and dramatic phenomenon. I can age-regress people with hypnosis, so they'll remember every phone number they ever had—and they do it in reverse order.

My approach now is to recognize this archival system and put in a new resource, a new "memory," so that it's accessed *before* the memory responsible for the unwanted generalization kicks in.

What I usually try to do is to go back before people built a specific bad learning, put in a new resource, and prompt it to generalize out, so that when they go back, it doesn't feel quite as it did before. That sense of, "Yes, I know I did this but it's not really me anymore," is a very important part of the process. Since discovering this, I don't use formal age regression as much as I used to. I focus much more on the future at this point in time. We could use the old NLP term "future pacing" to describe this, or, in hypnosis-talk, "posthypnotic suggestion." Whatever we call it, I want to make sure that the new state of consciousness comes out at just the right moment.

People don't need to have confidence every moment of the day. But if they have been having trouble crossing bridges or driving on the freeway, they need to have confidence that everything will be fine when they get to that situation. This needs practice.

Exercise: Putting a New Spin on the Past

1. Think of a specific, habituated response you would like to change—for example, nervousness in front of large groups, or short-temper while driving.
2. Replay a vivid example of the response, paying particular attention to the feeling it triggers. Notice how it moves in a particular direction.
3. Now, follow that feeling back to the first significant time it occurred. You may or may not be able to remember this consciously. If you cannot recall a specific incident, simply move slowly back until you come to a halt.
4. Once again, notice the feeling, and this time, connect the endpoint with the start, and spin it *in the opposite direction*. This will significantly change the feeling. Continue spinning it in reverse as you move on to the next phase.
5. Now, take a step back in time to a moment just before the original sensitizing incident, continuing to run the feeling in reverse, spinning it faster and faster, spreading the feeling through your entire body. Then, begin to move forward, through each subsequent experience in turn, allowing it to recode in relation to the reverse-spin of the feeling it was first associated with. Do this rapidly until you come up into the present moment.
6. Check to see how you feel about your unwanted response. If it still feels a significant part of you, repeat the exercise from Step 5 to Step 6. Keep testing, and stop when you approach a sense that it doesn't seem to matter that much anymore.
7. Now, recall the exercise at the beginning of this chapter, where you learned to have intense, good feelings for no particular reason. Reaccess a strong, joyful, optimistic state; start it spinning strongly; and see yourself

moving along the future in front of you. Notice how you respond differently and better, especially in those situations where you might previously have had problems, with these new resources in place.

8. Repeat three to five times—and resolve to notice every day or so for twenty-one days what improvements, large or small, have occurred.

Seventeen

PUSHING PAST LIMITATIONS
Hesitation, Threshold, and the
Freedom Beyond

HOW MANY TIMES HAVE YOU missed out on something good, simply because you hesitated? In my opinion, hesitation is the disease of our age, and I think it's time we stopped putting off getting over it. How much better would your life—or the lives of your clients—be if it were possible to enter a state of wanton desire at will, and to just go for it, knowing that nothing can stand in the way?

This is a problem that all life planners and coaches try to overcome by helping their clients set great, big, juicy goals, then pushing them to go for it. But, as most people have found out for themselves, there's a massive gap between hesitation and a go-for-it attitude. There's an even bigger gap between hesitation and actually taking action.

Also, goals, as we've already discussed, are not nearly as important as setting and maintaining direction. Setting up a direction for action is something on which both hypnosis and NLP prefer to concentrate. Once the format has been set up, the content can be filled in later. By setting direction and moving someone through a series of familiar states they've experienced many times in the past, it becomes a simple matter to turn hesitation into dynamic action.

As you move through this section, you will also have the opportunity to learn and practice several patterns, including anchoring, chaining, or sequencing (setting a particular order for events to occur), finger signals or ideomotor responses, age regression, and posthypnotic suggestion. Age regression was a favorite tool of Milton Erickson's. Quite simply, it's a way to tap into experiences and resources you have already experienced and mastered and recycling them to achieve a new outcome.

There's a very well-known tape of Erickson working with a woman named Mondy. As he very slowly goes along, he elicits five different experiences from her past. He regresses her step by step, getting her to recall a spanking, breaking a window, and then to a time when she was chasing ducks "with abandonment." He called her "Duckchasing Mondy." The exercise in this chapter is similar to Erickson's procedure, but much faster and easier.

Before we begin, though, you need to set up unconscious finger signals.

Setting up finger signals is a lot simpler than it looks or sounds. When your subject is in trance, simply reach over, lift one finger, and tell him that moving that finger will unconsciously communicate agreement. That is his "Yes Finger." You can do the same thing to communicate disagreement—a "No Finger"—although I prefer not to have my clients argue with me.

Now, with finger signals set up, instruct your subject to answer your questions "with honest, unconscious movements." You are now in a position to do a number of interesting things, including playing a kind of twenty questions.

The state we begin with is, of course, hesitation, and it's a pretty radical jump from there to go-for-it, so we need to find a graceful way to do this. Like Milton, you'll be eliciting five states in all.

These states are:

Hesitation
Frustration
Impatience
Wanton Desire
Go-for-it

Why these particular states? Well, think about what would happen if *hesitating* makes you become really *frustrated*, to the point where you start to think about alternatives. You begin to become *impatient* at your inertia; you want to *do something different*, and the more you think about what that is, the juicier and more attractive the alternative becomes . . . to the point where you start to lust for it, until not having it becomes unbearable, and you simply have to . . . let go and *go for it*. . . .

In NLP, we value what we call elegance. This is another way of saying we attach importance to, and always pursue, the most efficient and effective way to accomplish an outcome. It is far more elegant to move seamlessly from hesitation to go-for-it in smooth and well-established steps than it is either to give up before you start, or to try without enough forward impetus and fail.

Where would a pattern like this be useful?

How about trying it out with the lessons contained in this book? The patterns presented here are, as the title suggests, among the most transformative ever created. They have been tested over more than four decades in virtually every country in the world, and their mastery will open more doors for you than any number of gurus or therapists.

So, if you have been hesitating about bringing together trying out what you've learned so far, here is where hesitation ends.

OPTIMIZING THE SUBJECT'S RESPONSE

When setting up finger signals, ask your subject's "unconscious mind" whether it has made "all the necessary exchanges for you to be able to take [your subject] all the way back in time . . . honestly."

The word "honestly" has semantic density. This semantic packing means the experience will be full-blooded; you achieve much fuller age regression. In effect, the subject *becomes* younger.

Be somewhat more creative than simply asking the person to remember a past experience. You might suggest looking at "The Book of Time," turning the pages a year at a time, each time becoming one year younger. Your subject can do this until finding the strongest example of a target state—and when that's done, have your subject use the finger signals to communicate the fact.

Follow the instructions closely. Be systematic and make sure that each step is in place before you move on to the next.

Exercise: Overcoming Hesitation

1. Have your subject go into trance and set up finger signals. Have her think of what "hesitation" really means to her. As soon as her expression changes, anchor it kinesthetically (with a touch) and auditorally (give it a name, such as "Hesitating Jane"). Have her move back in time to some of her key moments of hesitation and regret, and indicate arrival at these memories by finger signaling. Amplify the anchor each time. When you have a strong hesitation anchor, move on to the next state and repeat the process. Do this five times, once for each state.

2. When you access and anchor the go-for-it state, use submodalities to amplify your subject's response. Make the final state of action highly specific. It must literally involve "getting up and going" for an objective.

3. The third step involves "chaining"—connecting the five anchors so that firing the first sets off the others, ending in the strong go-for-it directionalized state:

   a. As you fire the first anchor, have your subject think of all the times and places where she stopped herself, where she held back.

   b. As soon as you see changes in her expression, skin coloration, and so on, fire the second anchor. Hold both for a moment, then release the first anchor.

   c. As the response automatically changes from Number 1 to Number 2, fire off Number 3, then test again. Fire Number 1, and when it triggers 2 and then 3, fire Number 4. Repeat until firing the first anchor automatically drives the subject's experience through to the go-for-it-state.

4. Give your subject the posthypnotic suggestion (see below) that she can bring this ability to move from hesitation to going-for-it at any time she chooses. She should review her present situation and the direction and outcomes she would like to achieve, then identify the intervening steps, especially the initial one that precipitates action. Then she should fire the first anchor.

POSTHYPNOTIC SUGGESTION

Learning, especially in trance, is state-specific, which means that the new response or behavior will stay in that particular altered psychoneurological state, unless we ensure it generalizes out into the appropriate area of the subject's life. This is a common mistake among many hypnotherapists. They achieve remarkable responses while the client is sitting in front of them, but when he resumes his daily life, the effect just seems to wear off.

To avoid that occurrence, give your subject (and yourself) posthypnotic suggestions that the desired action will be carried out as and when required. Whenever you find yourself starting to hesitate about learning to do something new, fire off the first anchor and experience yourself moving quickly and smoothly through all five states.

A posthypnotic suggestion is easy to give: simply state specifically what to do and where and when to do it. To lock it in even tighter, think of three to five situations in the future where moving from hesitation to go-for-it would be a useful response, and mentally rehearse the details until comfortable with the prospect of coping with these new resources.

Acting without hesitation should, of course, occur only within an acceptable context. Hesitation is an appropriate response when you come to the edge of a busy highway, for example, so you need to be specific. The unconscious mind is quite literal, so to reinforce and optimize everything you've done, you can bring your partner out of trance by saying something like this:

> *Now I am going to lift your hand [lift the hand, turning it so that the wrist is uppermost, as described earlier] and leave it here . . . and that hand can begin to come down . . . in honest and unconscious movements . . . only as quickly as your unconscious is ready to . . . make all the appropriate internal arrangements to ensure that each of the three [or five] examples you've been rehearsing for the future . . . can represent three more . . . and each of those*

*three, three more . . . and each of those . . . and so on, and
so forth . . . so that you can really . . . go for it . . . in situations you may not even have thought of consciously yet
. . . wherever it's useful to and appropriate for you . . .
now . . .*

Make sure your subject comes fully out of trance, have him
change position, or talk about something else for a few moments
(called "breaking state," in NLP), and then have him think of a
project or undertaking he would like to get started on, but has
been hesitating over, and test the pattern by having him firing the
first anchor.

Note: whenever you are undertaking a venture of any kind,
ensure that you know what the first step is and the key steps that
need to be taken after that.

GOING OVER THRESHOLD

The more I can get people to know how to process, how to
think on purpose, the more able they will be to cope without me
in the future. I'm not trying to build dependence with NLP; I'm
trying to build *independence.* I'm not trying to get people to feel
they need to come to me every time they have a problem and go
into deep trance. I want it to *be* the trance that makes it so that
when they look at the future and whenever something happens,
good or bad, they realize that when they change the way they think
and believe, they change the way they feel. When they change the
way they feel, they have the ability to change the way they
behave—for all time. I want this to be the trance that lasts forever.

I can't even count the different things that I've approached this way, and I don't have clients who come back. They don't get rid of one phobia and then come up with another. When I started out, the "experts" all said, "Hypnosis is bad and only treats the symptom," and I would say, "Isn't that a good thing? Why treat anything else if you can treat the symptom?"

Their response was, "Well, if you suppress the symptom it comes out somewhere else. If you suppress the symptom, it could come out in a place where it doesn't have to come out, somewhere bad."

I'm a mathematician, so I thought: *Cool* . . .

Now I do exactly that, but with precision—to deliberately "aim" symptoms to come out somewhere else, so, for example, the client who got rid of hysterical paralysis could have the best erections of any man alive.

By not accepting the presuppositions within the field of psychology—which included that people had to be "fixed"—and, instead, looking at how to optimize human behavior, I found greater freedom to design techniques that helped people become happier, healthier, and more effective in everything they did.

When I started out, all these people were dropping out of their jobs to "be happy." The truth is, they didn't get happier; they just wore uglier clothes. What they really needed was to be able to enjoy their families and their jobs, since it wasn't those things that were holding them back. In fact, those were the very things that were giving them freedom, money, support, and opportunity.

It wasn't a swingers' club or joining an ashram that was going to make them happy. Those were just different lifestyles they thought would bring them happiness. It didn't work, of course, because if you want to be happy, you have to practice being happy with what you have, and then move on to other things. If you can't be happy with a good job and a great family, I don't think a large medallion and a paisley shirt will work.

In Neuro-Linguistic Programming, we don't "treat" patients; we give people lessons on how to think and make better choices. As soon as you switch from the remedial model, which is about repairing someone, to the optimizing model, where you teach them and give them lessons in how to think and in how to change the way they feel, living better suddenly becomes more feasible.

It also puts the practitioner in the right frame of mind.

Unless people know they can, and are prepared to, make better choices, they are unlikely to change. A hypnotist may get a client to believe cigarettes taste awful, but that doesn't necessarily remove all problems, and it may create more.

I remember reading a book about that and tried it with a smoker who wanted to quit. I hypnotized him and made cigarettes taste like cod liver oil, that they were the most disgusting things in the world, and he'd never want to smoke one again.

He came back the next week, told me he hadn't smoked a single cigarette. Then he reached into his pocket and pulled out a bottle of cod liver oil and took a swig. I remember thinking to myself, *Well . . . that's a problem.* Cod liver oil may actually be worse for you than cigarettes if you drink it all day long. That wasn't a giant step forward, and I had to take him back into trance and find another way to do it.

The lesson is: it's not that you make something unpleasant to get people to stop doing it. It's that you make them smart enough to not do it in the first place. Once people make a decision that they've had enough, that they're never going to do something again, and you help them truly to believe that, they can make it through. This is especially true of addictions.

For example, I used to be a smoker—and one day I quit.

It happened in a hospital where I'd been very ill, and my doctor sat down next to my bed and said, "Richard, I've got something very serious to tell you."

I asked, "What's that?" Usually, not many good things follow an opening like that.

She said, "You're going to have to quit smoking. You need to take the medication you're on for the rest of your life, and you can't take it and keep smoking."

I went inside for a moment, then came out again, and said, "Okay, doc. I've quit."

She told me, "You don't understand. It's very hard to give up smoking. You're going to have a difficult time of it until you're finally free."

I said, "No, I won't. I've quit."

She persisted, "I've brought you some pamphlets to help you taper off."

I hadn't planned to taper off, but I read the pamphlets anyway. They were full of statements like: "Tobacco is one of the most addictive substances known to man" and "Giving up smoking is extremely difficult and can take a long time."

In fact, giving up smoking takes no time at all. Once you've made the decision, that's it. You're a nonsmoker. What takes time is what leads up to finally quitting—that is, if the person quits at all. Often they're too afraid to be without their cigarette to even contemplate life without it.

Before I quit myself, I remember coming across a friend of

mine, lying on a hospital gurney smoking a cigarette through a tracheotomy tube.

I asked, "Where did you get the cigarette?"

He told me, "Oh, somebody came by and I asked him if he had a cigarette and he gave one to me."

I watched him smoking through that hole in his throat for a while, and then I said to him, "Now, *that's* what addiction looks like."

But I still kept smoking then. I knew the risks. Every single smoker knows what a cancerous lung looks like, and they keep going. You can walk into hospitals and find people who've had arms or legs amputated as a result of their tobacco habit, and they're still wheeling each other out somewhere so they can light up.

The thing that stops many people from ever quitting is the fear of something called "the urge to smoke." The terror of feeling an urge and not fulfilling it is overwhelming to many smokers, and yet it never occurs to them that they have dozens of urges every day they don't act on.

That's what got me through. It wasn't that I didn't have the urge to smoke. It wasn't that I didn't sometimes feel nicotine gnawing at my soul. It was a combination of several facts. The first was that I decided in that moment that I had already quit. The second was that I recognized the urge to smoke was like any other urge. If I resisted it, if I tried not to think about cigarettes, if I tried not to want to smoke, the urge got stronger.

This seems to be a quality of resistance. The more we do it, the more it happens.

Try the following exercise: put both your hands palm to palm, then push very hard with your right hand. Push harder, and even harder than that.

Now, be honest. Were you one of the people who end up in a struggle? The harder you pushed with your right hand, the harder you pushed back with your left?

The significant thing is: I asked you to push with your right hand, and most likely, when you did, you *pushed back* with your left.

We have problems for several reasons when we try to change long-standing habits. One is that we resist the way the habitual part of our brain fights back. We hate and fear the urge to go back to what it was we were doing before. Sometimes we hate and fear the urge more even than we do dying.

The other problem is that we try to program ourselves by telling ourselves not to do whatever it is we're trying to change. We tell ourselves, "Don't smoke," "You mustn't think of cigarettes," "You have to stop smoking."

This is where one of the differences between language and brain function shows up. As I've mentioned before, negation—words such as "don't," "can't," "mustn't," "shouldn't"—exist in language, but not in the way the brain works. Linguistically, we are putting forward an idea (in this case, smoking) and then negating it with words like "stop" or "don't." As far as the brain is concerned, the command has already been given. You have to make a picture of the process, and only then can it be negated. But by this time it's too late—and the more you try to ignore or suppress the picture, the bigger and brighter it becomes.

Try this: For the next sixty seconds, *don't think of the color blue*. Try really hard. Try harder than that. No, really, I mean *don't*. . . .

All the brain really hears is, "Think of the color blue"—or, in the case of trying to suppress the nicotine habit, "Smoke!"

Around this time I started to understand that if you take a

feeling you don't want and you begin to expand it, and spin it and then expand it even more, and even more than that, one of two things happens: the feeling either turns into a different feeling, even a pleasant one, or it becomes ridiculous and simply doesn't have hold over you anymore.

Something else helped me quit smoking for life. I really enjoyed torturing all the people who came to me expecting me to suffer. They'd say to me, "Isn't it really, really difficult to quit? Don't you miss it real bad?"

Even when I missed it, I'd say, "Nope. It's really easy." It drove them all crazy, especially the medical experts who spent their time telling other patients like me how difficult it was to quit.

The lesson is: when you're making a big and challenging shift in your life, it helps to find a way to have fun with it. Then it really does get easier.

A good NLP practitioner needs to understand the importance of threshold patterns to help clients move forward. Put simply, the nervous system is capable of maintaining a certain way of functioning only up to a certain point. When you exceed this level, the pattern blows out.

People are willing to tolerate so many things. Those with obsessive-compulsive disorder go through endless hours of rituals. Smokers, heavy drinkers, and other addicts know their habit could kill them. Some people live in abusive relationships and just won't leave.

The point here is that there hasn't yet been enough of the unwanted experience to breach the threshold.

I'm not suggesting that people should go back and be even more abused, but that you, as a change agent, should help your clients change their perception.

The very first thing I try to do is get people through threshold. If you string twenty-five bad memories together back-to-back, and go through each one, making it bigger than life-size, there's a point at which the brain just goes *Phhht! Enough!* and the person pops out of the experience, looking at it in an entirely different way than before.

When people get to the point where they are sick and tired of how they are, the way they held their experience begins to change, and then you can start to get them to be determined to go in another direction.

The technique outlined below is extremely powerful and should be approached with caution. Once threshold has been fully breached, returning to the original state is virtually impossible. It is identical to the pattern often inadvertently run by people who, for no apparent reason, "fall out of love." The process is that at the start of the relationship, they associate into details they like and dissociate from those they don't. Then, as familiarity grows, they switch the pattern, focusing on what isn't working and failing to notice what is.

Being aware of how the pattern works can avoid unnecessary partnership breakdowns. On the other hand, going over threshold can be used deliberately to help people extricate themselves from abusive and dangerous relationships.

Exercise: Going over Threshold

Warning: Changing threshold patterns can be extremely powerful and permanent. Make sure you are acting in the best interests of your client or yourself.

1. Take a situation or response you wish to change and clearly identify five things you liked about it and five you disliked. For example, if you wish to move past a certain relationship, you might have liked your former partner's smile, generosity, good looks, and so on, and disliked the sudden temper, unreasonable demands, and physical abuse.
2. Starting with the things you liked, cycle through each five times (making a total of twenty-five for each category), seeing yourself in the scenario (dissociated), pushing it off into the distance, draining it of color, and so on. Do this rapidly and decisively, and notice how the intensity of the experiences changes.
3. Now, with each of the situations you don't like, very rapidly make them bigger, have them rush toward you, increasing in detail, intensity of color, and so on. Have them completely engulf you (associated) as you ratchet up the details. Spin the memories so the vividness rockets to newer and more intense levels until the entire scenario seems to pop. When you have done this successfully, you will either find it difficult to recover the original experiences in detail or your response to them will be markedly changed.
4. Now, thinking of the situation you wish to change, ask, "Do you really need to have this limitation anymore?" Then spin it out into space and explode it into the sun.

Important: Carry this process through to completion. Increasing the intensity of an experience without going over threshold risks leaving the subject in a worse state than before.

Eighteen

REPATTERNING THE PAST
The Magic of False Memories

A WHILE AGO, SOMEONE pointed out some research that said people who believed they had been able to lose weight in the past had an easy time of losing weight again—even if they hadn't really done so before.

I'm not sure how these researchers had these people believe they'd been successful in the past, but it sounds to me like some kind of false memory syndrome.

False memories were something we heard a lot about a few years ago because some therapists were actually installing in their clients memories of things that had never happened by the ignorant way they asked questions and made suggestions.

This practice caused terrible problems for the individuals and their families, especially when the therapist suggested indirectly that Uncle Fred had not just been giving them a bath when they examined some childhood photographs together. These therapists would go through the client's pictures and select perfectly innocent snaps of, say, a baby sitting on someone's knee. Then they'd ask the client questions like, "How can you be sure that was *all* that was happening? How do you know your uncle or aunt wasn't *interfering* with you?" and, of course, since they couldn't possibly be sure, it had to be true.

It's very easy to lead people in ways that get them to "remember" things that never happened, especially if they're very young or in an altered state. I remember watching those old films of a hypnotherapist regressing people who claimed to have been abducted by aliens, and they always followed a certain pattern.

The hypnotist would say things like, "So, it's a warm night on July 5, and you're asleep in your room, right? And, suddenly you hear a noise—you remember that, don't you?"

The subject would say, "Uh-huh. Yeah. I guess so . . ."

"And you become aware that whatever is making that noise is in there with you near your bed, don't you?"

The person would say with greater conviction, "Yes. That's right. Near my bed."

"That's right. Near your bed. Noises . . . *and how many aliens are there in the room?*"

This kind of language is extremely persuasive because it operates below the level of conscious awareness. We recognize these patterns from the Milton Model (see Resource File 5 on page 316): "You hear a noise," "Something is with you in the room," "You become aware that it's near, don't you?"—all these statements function as commands to do something embedded within a seemingly innocent sentence. The listener's unconscious mind hears them as injunctions rather than questions or statements, and then it experiences them as "true." If you get a subject to agree enough about other things—dates, times, locations, and so on—he is altogether more likely to perceive a statement presupposing there *are* aliens as true. This is hypnosis in its simplest but still very powerful form.

Problems are made worse because memory is extremely plastic. We create memories from moment to moment. We remember things that never happened, and sometimes we forget things that did happen. Sometimes, in the case of things we forget, it's a blessing.

Psychologists are always bringing clients to me, wanting me to get them to remember being molested as a child or some such nonsense. Even if it happened, I don't think that remembering trauma can be profoundly useful. If people have true amnesia, it's often a good thing.

These days, I find it very useful to give people amnesia for bad experiences that are still destroying their lives. If they didn't remember it happening, they can't keep going over what it was like and making themselves feel terrible.

I much prefer teaching people to remember good things and to build on their strengths rather than reinforce their weaknesses.

Our ability to remember things that happened many years ago is apparently limitless. Two clients who proved this very dramatically spring to mind.

One woman came to me because she and her husband had been fighting for years. Six months after they got married she lost her wedding ring, and he'd never let her forget it. To him it was a deliberate act. He believed she washed it down the drain or threw it away after a fight.

But she was still very upset about it after twenty-five years. She said, "The ring's lost, and there's no way I could ever find it."

I asked her a couple of Meta Model questions. I said, "Well, what would happen if you did find it? What would have to happen for you to do that?"

She said, "I guess in the back of my mind I know it's somewhere."

As soon as she said that, I said, "Good. Then let's go into the back of your mind and find out."

I put her in deep trance and told her not to come out until she had remembered where the ring had gone. I told her to sort through her memories to the moment just before the ring disappeared and said, "When you find it, let your hand go up."

She sat there for three hours while I went off and did something else. Then my dog came in and acted like I should go back in (my dog was pretty clever that way), so I did, and sure enough, her hand was floating up—completely cataleptic.

I told her to wake from trance and tell me only what I needed to know—that is, exactly where the ring was. She sat up, the way people do when they're in a trance, looking blank. Then she said, "Basement . . . water heater . . . rolled under . . . ," and then dropped back into deep trance.

I woke her up and said, "Do you still live in the same house you did when the ring was lost?"

She said, "Yes. It's my parents' house, and when we got married we moved in with them, and when they died, we stayed there. My family's been in that house for five generations. It's a very big house."

I said, "It has a basement, doesn't it?"

She answered, "Yes," so I asked her if her husband was home. She said, "No. He's outside in the car." But when we went outside, he'd already gone home. He'd thought the session was going to be shorter, especially as I'd told him I wanted him to come inside later to work on their difficulties with each other. I guessed he got in a tizzy because I left him out in the driveway for three hours.

However, when I called him at home, he was annoyed because he was convinced she'd been talking about him for three hours. I said, "Well, actually she didn't talk about anybody. She's been sitting there in trance the whole time."

He was even more annoyed. He said, "What's the point of that?"

I told him, "Get a flashlight and go downstairs. You've got some kind of a boiler down there in the basement, right?"

He said, "Yes. It's a water heater."

I said, "I want you to get all the dust bunnies from underneath and tell me what surprise you find there."

He called back about fifteen minutes later to tell me he'd found the ring. His comment was, "She must have hidden it there all these years and then told you and not me."

I said, "Actually, she doesn't know yet. I want you to bring it here—and be careful, because she might accuse *you* of having hidden it all these years."

Interestingly, when he gave her the ring, she had absolutely no memory of ever having told me. It constantly amazes me what people can do in trance—in this case, going back twenty-five years, even though she hadn't been consciously aware of the ring falling off and rolling under the heater. But somewhere in her unconscious, she was able to sort through and find that sound and know what it meant.

The brain is capable of amazing feats. Recently, a woman came to me suffering from post-traumatic stress disorder. She'd been attacked but was vague about whether she'd been raped or just beaten or robbed. I didn't push for that kind of detail, because I don't think it's always useful. But she was absolutely terrified almost all the time, because she kept reliving the attack.

When I asked, "Is it life-size?" she said, "What do you mean, 'it'?"

I told her I could tell by the way she was looking that she was making pictures, but she said, "Yes . . . but it's dark." She knew she'd feel better if she could bring the memory out of the shadows, so the first thing I did was to put in a few lights. I had a Corel Draw program that let you put lights anywhere you liked in a photograph, and that gave me the idea. The brain is very digital that way. It was possible to take a memory that was dark and out-of-focus because of fear, and illuminate it to the point where she could see the faces of the other people in the memory.

I had one case that was even more bizarre. Somebody had grabbed the victim from behind and covered the victim's eyes. The police weren't clear about what had actually happened, so I slowed the movie down, froze it just before the hands touched the victim's face, and magnified the image. Then I had the victim draw the fingerprint—and the police found the attacker. That's how precise the mind is.

Now I'm not saying that was quick by any means. That took me hours to do. The person concerned was a good hypnotic subject and could also draw pretty well. The drawing of the fingerprint was really big.

Once we had something, the police shrank it down and ran it against their database of known felons. The image wasn't perfect by any means; it was only what they call "a partial," but it was enough to get a match.

When they pulled the guy in for questioning, he confessed immediately. Not only did he confess to that, but he confessed to about ten other incidents. This was pretty helpful of him, because if it ever became known how we'd gotten the print, it would have been thrown out of court.

So, sometimes it's good to remember things, other times not. What the researchers mentioned earlier in the weight-loss study discovered is that it can be useful to remember something that may not even have happened.

What they missed was that telling people they had been good at losing weight when they were young was simply another way of giving a suggestion. It doesn't really matter whether it's true or not. If part of them remembers as true that they've already succeeded at something, doing it a second time isn't going to be that hard.

For this reason I often install false memory. I have people go in and experience being totally in command in front of an audience, and then I make it a real memory. I go through and look at their reality strategy, comparing a real memory with the one we just made up, then adjusting the new memory so it's a perfect match: same size, same location, same distance, same voices, same feelings.

What happens then is that when the person thinks about the new behavior, it's as if they're doing it for the second time.

I've done this with very some odd experiences, too. I've consulted with organizations such as NASA (and some others that shall remain nameless) whose people were expected to go into some very challenging and scary situations, and I was able to have them, for all intents and purposes, live it out so they could cope in the real situation.

Of course, people in sports make good use of this. One of my clients was a downhill skier who had been really badly hurt in an accident. He was so traumatized he couldn't get back on the slope.

I put him in trance and had him go back on the slope and ski all the way down in his mind. His memory was life-size, a fully associated revivification. I remember being fascinated watching him, because I could actually see his cheeks being forced back by the wind.

When he came out of trance, he couldn't wait to get back on the slopes because another part of the memory had been restored: the sheer enjoyment he'd had when skiing. Previously, he couldn't even think about skiing, because he couldn't get past the bad memory to the good ones. By building him one good, new memory, the old memory simply collapsed, and he was able to recall just how much he enjoyed his sport.

Sometimes it's just a function of sequence. It's not just which of your memories you access, but where they are in your mind.

Exercise: Installing Positive Memories

1. Think of a situation in your life that would be easily accomplished or improved if you had had previous experience of success. This could involve learning a new skill or enhancing one you already have. As in the example above, it could involve successfully losing weight, stopping smoking, or changing some other habit.

2. Imagine yourself as if you had been completely successful in this venture at some previous time in your life. Make a comprehensive list of the submodalities of this representation.

3. Find a strong and positive memory of something you know incontrovertibly that you accomplished in the past—perhaps learning to drive, becoming fluent in a second language, passing an important exam. List this memory's submodalities in detail.

4. Compare the submodalities, and adjust those of the new memory to match those of the real memory.

5. Now imagine floating up and back in time to where you would have most benefited from gaining these new resources and drop down into the "you" you were then.

6. Fast-forward through all the relevant points in your past, allowing your unconscious to make all the necessary adjustments, embedding the knowledge and skills where they will have most useful to you from the point in the present all the way into the future . . . now.

7. Imagine three to five situations in the future where you are fully using your new skills. Do this associated, experiencing them as richly as you can. See what you will see, hear what you will hear, and feel what you will be feeling.

8. Imagine these three to five examples generalizing out into the rest of your life, expanding all possibilities appropriately in ways that will surprise and delight you.

9. Repeat this exercise several times. Then make the decision to practice the skill or behavior you want to acquire, noticing how much easier it is when you "remember" your success.

PART 4

TRANCE-FORMATION IN ACTION:
CLIENT SESSIONS

Editor's Note: The following four examples of Richard Bandler at work are transcribed from sessions with real clients. The first two are provided to help the reader understand the structure of trances, including Milton Model language patterns, and the second two make explicit some of the processes behind the change-work. Transcripts are printed on the left side of the page and the editor's commentary on the right. It would take another book at least as long as this one to deconstruct the richness and complexity of Richard Bandler's work, so these examples should not be taken to be complete. The reader should feel free to add to the analyses.

Note that while the clients in the second part of this section both regarded their problems as "phobias," Dr. Bandler does not approach them as classic examples of this class of disorder. As he often observes, phobics respond instantaneously and without exception to the triggers of their fears; people suffering from anxiety disorders work up to it. The two people here fall into the latter category.

The second important observation is of Richard Bandler's relentless pursuit of useful information. Third is his skillful use of language patterns that indirectly, but powerfully, drive people away from their problems toward solutions that enhance self-efficacy. His tools are humor, playful irony and chiding, stories, metaphor and analogies, submodality changes, embedded commands, direct and indirect hypnotic induction, and much, much more.

GT

Nineteen

THE STRUCTURE OF
Trance-formation 1

Note: Embedded commands are *italicized*. Nominalizations are in **bold** text.

Trance-script	Language Patterns
Now, *close your eyes* and *ask yourself* if you have ever known that *you can go into a trance*, deeply? Just *lift your hands* like this and *let me put my hands here*, and when I move them this way, or that way, you follow like . . .	RB places his hands over the backs of the subject's outstretched hands and makes a series of small, ambiguous movements that the subject tries to follow. As soon as arm catalepsy occurs, he continues.
. . . that's right . . . and just *let them be there* and *allow them to drift down* involuntarily only as quickly or slowly as your eyelids begin to close . . . or resist in vain.	Hands will inevitably come down, so RB uses this to accomplish eye closure. "Resist in vain" (bind: presupposes that, even if the subject chooses to exhibit a polar response, his resistance will fail).
So, maybe you have and maybe you haven't—at least, not that *you remember it well*—but that doesn't matter. Because you didn't need to *know you've been in a trance* because *you can learn here what I'm saying*. And I want you to *go inside*, because I will, I go inside and I say to yourself, "When I was riding in the elevators, when I was riding in cars, when I lost myself in thought" . . . and you say you've never been in a trance? That's all I was asking . . .	Slightly confusional instructions include multiple embedded commands, phonological ambiguities ("here/hear") nested inside punctuation ambiguities ("you can learn here what I'm saying" = "you can learn here" or "hear what I'm saying"). Ambiguity (embedded command): "I will (you to go inside!)." Switched referential index ("and I say to yourself"). Previous trance is elicited.

Trance-script	Language Patterns
Well, at least *you know that there is such a thing as trance.* Do you realize when I teach people to go, they want to ask questions like, "What is **trance** exactly?" I ask him, "What is air exactly?"	**Mind reading.** Here RB is inoculating against undue conscious analysis, directing the subject through phonological ambiguity to focus instead on immediate experience ("what is air/here exactly?").
Now, what I like to do is something simple, and what I'd like you to do is to *start now*, because, you see, one of the things about hypnosis is it's purely a subjective experience and if *you're going to have a subjective experience*, you really should *do it yourself.*	Temporal predicate: hypnotic subjects need to be told when to begin to follow instructions. RB hands responsibility to the subject for his experience. Simple deletion.
You know, I went on stage with this hypnotist once, but do you know, I would never embarrass anyone in public, especially myself, and he said, "I want you to *go deeper and deeper into a trance* in which you will *allow your unconscious to show you the possibilities of the future,*" and I looked at him and I said, "I can *see those possibilities* . . .	Reassures subject that he will not be embarrassed. Quotes pattern delivers direct commands ("go deeper and deeper . . .") as if by someone else to increase compliance. Phonological ambiguity ("your unconscious/you're unconscious").
. . . they're, they're like when you stare at something and you look at it and you become aware of the need to attend to one's needs, it's like the weight of thoughts. The weight of thoughts as they become so heavy. Heavier and heavier I can barely hold yours up, now . . ."	Elicits the experience of attentional fixation ("when you stare at something, when you . . ."). Wordplay (near palindrome): "Need to attend to one's needs." Ambiguous statement.
So, as you go *inside*, wherever you go when you go *in there*, I often *wonder where you go* inside, you know, how far can you go, and what I want you to do is, to *remember* . . .	Embedded question prompts trans-derivational search. Phonological ambiguity ("wonder/wander") encourages both curiosity and attentional drift.

Trance-script	Language Patterns

. . . whatever you consider to be *the deepest trance experience you've ever had* . . . and I want you to see what you saw at the time, hear what you heard, until you can begin to feel what you felt. Remember where it was and who you were and go back and recall it. Notice whether or not as you recall it, is it a movie or a slide? As you look at it, as you *drift deeper into your trance*, what changes subjectively, above and beyond the way you feel about it? Is there anything else, for your pictures to move off into the distance? When you talk to yourself, does the voice sound further away? Do the sounds that you hear change in some way tonally?

Elicits previous trance.

Overlaps sensory systems to enrich subject's experience.

Elicits submodalities of previous trance experience.

Manipulates submodalities to deepen experience.

Stacked presuppositions (that the subject sees images, hears sounds, etc.).

And notice to say there is such a thing as **trance**, *something must happen.*

Presupposition prompts transderivational search ("something must happen"); therefore *whatever* the subject notices happening ratified the development of trance.

Now in order to be able to *be a hypnotist*, when you're hypnotizing people, the question is, what externally do you do that's going to influence people?

Syntactic ambiguity.

See, for example, if you make a picture of yourself right now, if you happen to make good pictures and then see yourself sitting where you are and change that picture, starting from your head, so that every muscle begins to relax and you see yourself going into an even a deeper trance than you are now.

Implied causative ("if . . . then").

Dissociates subject, changes the visual representation to one of increasing comfort and relaxation, then has the subject associate into the deepened experience in order to amplify the kinesthetic.

Trance-script

Does it change the way you feel or not because only you know how deep into a trance you are at any moment?

Now if you consider, for example, that if you take the picture you see right now, of yourself in trancing and step inside it, so that you would see from the position of that and then step back outside it. Which one feels more like a trance that you want? See, there are different trances for different purposes. Some trances are better for one thing as opposed to another because they're really, just a change of state . . .

Now, go ahead and look at that picture in which you see yourself there and, first, I want you in the lower right hand corner to make a line to the upper left hand corner and then I want you to take the upper left hand corner and the lower right hand corner and fold them back in your image until they touch and when that's done, move just that line that you see, further and further but still hearing the same sound that you would, except that you move it. I want you to hear it further away and then I want it to start moving not just further away, whether you're just talking to yourself or there's sound in your image, then I want it to start moving so then it circles around from wherever it is 360° from wherever its source is, in a soothing way . . .

Language Patterns

Bind, or "illusion of choice": the presupposition is that the subject is in a trance; only the depth is in question.

Wordplay: "In trance in/entrancing."

Repeats the process, and then presents the subject with a bind (illusion of choice) by asking which trance "feels more like a trance that you want?" This presupposes that one of the two will be the trance the subject wants.

Dissociation.
Presupposition.

Suggests feelings (eyes down and to the right) should be linked with recalled visual imagery (up and to the left), then overlaps to auditory channel, manipulating the integrated triple-sensory representation so that it enfolds the subject "in a soothing way." This is characteristic of RB's use of hemispheric integration (bringing both halves of the brain into play).

Trance-script	Language Patterns
. . . and as you do this notice, if you hear your internal dialogue are the sounds that soothe you from the inside from one point and it begins to move around to the point at which you feel yourself floating down and often realize that from wherever it is, the sound can begin from above you or below you so raise it and lower it, both in height from where it comes from, but also do it in pitch.	Temporal predicates. Shifts internal representation from auditory digital to kinesthetic, manipulating both to deepen trance. Illusion of choice ("from above you or below you . . ."). Presuppositions.
Now I want you to *notice something* before you *go even deeper into trance* because you can sit there and *feel yourself breathing* and with each breath you are able to *enjoy, even more, any changes that you're capable of producing* because the hypnosis you're learning here is not about controlling other people; it's about controlling yourself and about being a **biofeedback mechanism** to *give somebody else control.*	Simple and comparative deletions. Modal operators. Comparative deletion ("even more").
If you want to be somebody, you know, you can do things that help people to be able to, as we put it, drive their own bus . . . *imagine*: hypnosis can help you to *control your blood pressure*, your heart rate, can make you *feel more confident*, it can *give you more courage* hopefully in a time that is useful . . . whatever your brain can do and whatever you've heard of anybody doing with it, any **state** that you've been in and the ones that you just *fantasize it might be possible*, **hypnosis** is one of the things that has made it possible . . . now . . .	Implied causative. Modal operators of possibility. Embedded commands ("imagine!"). Lost performatives. Modal operators.

Trance-script	Language Patterns
. . . what I want you to consider at this moment, is that whatever **feedback** you can provide that helps someone to alter their **state** in such a way by using whatever means of language or tone or to assist you to have **choices** that you want and need for yourself that will last you for years.	Factive (awareness) predicate. Shifting referential index. Who is RB talking about here?
Now, being able to go *into your trance deeply* and be able to *make changes in yourself* is a **tool** that you are learning, not only to have, but to do as well, and having the **variety** and **choices**, is what will assist you.	Qualitative adverb.
NLP itself was born when we realized that if the mind could do these hypnotic phenomena in an altered state, the human brain was capable of doing it, and how do we know how to *get those unconscious responses* and your unconscious knows how to do these things. NLP is only to assist you in being able to *have conscious control of the skills* that you own.	Modal operator of possibility. Cause and effect. Unspecified noun. Phonological ambiguity ("Your unconscious/you're unconscious"). Complex equivalence.
Now what I want you to do, very slowly and in your own regular speed, is to return back here, but only when your unconscious has made all necessary adjustments so that you will *discover something of great interest and importance* to you . . .	Paradoxical bind. Phonological ambiguity. Nominalization layered with embedded command to prompt transderivational search.

THE STRUCTURE OF
Trance-formation 2

Note: Embedded commands are *italicized*. Nominalizations are in **bold text**.

Trance-script	Language Patterns
Here's a really rapid induction. Just before I give it to you, though, what I want you to do is to just close your eyes for a minute and pretend that *you're in a trance*, just for a second . . .	**Distraction** ("**Just before I give it to you**"). Lost performative.
It's more fun to pretend anyway	**Comparative deletion**
Just, like, for example, just reach over and touch yourself on the arm and go into a **trance** deeply and, as you do so, first, I want you to remember a time when you had a **really wonderful feeling**, and then, as *you remember*, I want that **feeling** itself to begin to spread and start to spin, so with each breath it's going to grow and become wider and bigger, and spin faster, and then stronger, especially if it has a giggle attached to it . . .	Ordinal and temporal presuppositions. Cause and effect. Comparative deletions.
Now, as I continue to speak, with each word I say I want that **feeling** to grow stronger and stronger and stronger and I want whatever it's about to become faster . . . there you go . . . put it in hyper-drive, now I want you to spread that **feeling** all and up and down each leg right down to your toes and then make it stronger in your toes and have it rush up the inside of your legs right across your stomach and up to your nose.	Implied causative. Presuppositions. Comparative deletions.

Trance-script	Language Patterns
Now, playing with your **feelings** is fun; playing with other people's feelings is also fun, so now I want you to come out of **trance** for a moment, and you don't have to come all the way out though, just as much as you want to, before you go in again . . .	Fractionation. Temporal presupposition (that subject has been in trance one time—and will go in again).
So just put your feet on the floor and your hands on your thighs and pretend that you're going into a trance again, and think of what it is that you would do in trance . . . You can pick anything you want . . . very good. But if you learn how to get other people to do things, and then think that you're an important person, you're going to end up that way. Act like you're an important person and you're going to end up an important person . . .	External, sensory-based, verifiable facts followed by nonverifiable injunction. Phonological ambiguity ("important/impotent").
Now, again, what I want you to do is to close your eyes and I want you to visualize for yourself a long, long, long tunnel . . . and the more you smile and enjoy yourself and breathe because sometimes you forget about that . . . breathe in through the mouth and out through the nose, then, as you breathe in, the more I want you to *feel your hands*, and lift one of those hands . . .	The more/the more pattern (cause and effect). Utilization of the natural sensation of physical lifting on inhalation.
And you already know how to do it your way, so now do it my way. Your eyes are closed and you're beginning to see a long tunnel, and I want you to lift one of your hands as slowly as is humanly possible, a neuron at a time, and that you, that's one neuron at a time . . . there you go . . .	Unspecified verb. Pacing and leading.

Trance-script

Continue to breathe and take a breath, like take—breathe in and . . . out . . . in . . . and out . . . slowly but deeply, and with each breath you're still lifting that hand as slowly as is humanly possible, and as that hand lifts, I want you to go back to **some pleasant memory** from your childhood. Something perhaps that's a bit and a piece from here and there is something you haven't thought about in years . . . and what I want you to do is to continue one neuron at a time to *lift that hand* . . . and as you lift that hand, I want you to go and find unconsciously the necessary **ingredients** in your unconscious to prepare to make **a change**. Now, lifting your hand up is something you've done involuntarily for years. When somebody reaches out to shake your hand, you don't need to struggle. Your hand knows where it's supposed to go now if you take another deep breath . . . and literally of your own accord as you lift that hand as slowly as you can, I want your **mind** to wander a little further . . . into the soothing idea that **unconscious learning** has always been your most thorough means . . .

See, for example, when you learned the task of reading and writing, it was very conscious and for some of us harder than others, and I don't know whether or not you realized at the time that it would be the basis of reading and surviving in many ways . . .

Language Patterns

Prompts transderivational search.

Phonological ambiguity ("piece/peace").
Punctuation ambiguity.

Dissociation ("that hand").

Equates universal experience (handshake) with desired action (hand levitation).

Punctuation ambiguity.

Phonological ambiguity ("wander/wonder").

Selectional restriction violation.

Modal operator.
Scope ambiguity.

Trance-script

See, when you drive down the road
and you see a stop sign . . . you don't
have to read it one letter at a time; it
jumps out at you and, when . . . it . . .
does . . . it . . . allows you to *pay attention*, to *do something different*. It also
tells you when to *continue to move
ahead* because as you lift that hand, I
want you to imagine that you hear
your own internal voices moving
down that tunnel, and as it moves
down that tunnel and you listen to
any sound in your mind, I want it to
become more distant . . . and let that
hand lift up . . .

Because I want you to, since you know
where your nose is, to feel a rubber
band between your finger and your
nose, that's only as strong as any
attraction you have to being able to
learn. But I want it to be the hardest
thing in the world at this moment for
that rubber band to *pull your hand up
toward your nose*, because I want your
hand to lift only as fast as unconsciously you find a way to surprise
yourself delightfully . . . because, soon,
your **unconscious mind** could signal
you that since . . .

Language Patterns

Utilization of subject's head movement ("move ahead/move a head").

Comparative deletion.

Unspecified verb.

Qualitative adverb.
Modal operator of possibility.

Presupposition.

Trance-script

Language Patterns

. . . it's always protected you through the years. It made you blink if something flew toward your eye; it digested your food and kept your heart beating. It wasn't the one that needed the wrong person. It wasn't the one that made the bad investment and bought the wrong car . . . but it is the one that allows you to *realize* that when that hand touches your nose, *the strength of your belief* that you can *change your mind* and *expand the quality and quantity of pleasure you can have* by sometime making something taste inordinately good, or feel inordinately good, or sound so overwhelmingly nice, and if you're married to them, look at the most beautiful thing in the world . . . your unconscious knows you can do this because as your hand continues up toward your nose, as close as you get to your nose, the closer you'll be to your unconscious making all the **appropriate changes** in you to allow you to start to find that **useful happiness**, and when your hand touches your nose, your hand will go back down toward your thigh.

If your hand doesn't touch your nose . . . it will when it's ready . . . and what I want you to do in either case is to realize . . . what you're doing now is no different than anything else . . .

Universal quantifier.

Conscious/unconscious dissociation.

Unspecified noun.

Universal quantifier.
Phonological ambiguity ("knows/nose").

Phonological ambiguity ("your unconscious/you're unconscious").
Punctuation ambiguity.

Presupposition.
Bind.
Phonological ambiguity ("no different/know different").

Trance-script	Language Patterns
. . . **some part** of you is *moving, thinking, and breathing comfortably* and your unconscious is in control as much as your conscious mind knows it or not . . . the thing about true control is to *control yourself in a way that makes you happier,* because when your hand floats back down to your thigh, you think of **something** you haven't thought of in years let your **unconscious mind** crystallize the thought that lets you know you can **stay here and learn** how to have pleasure and enjoy, in a way that's your birthright and you earned it.	**Bind.** **Comparative deletion.** **Presupposition.** **Cause and effect.** **Complex equivalence.** **Phonological ambiguity** ("stay here and learn/stay, hear, and learn").
And what I want you to do is to take that crystallization and return back here at the same rate and speed . . . as it takes you to count from one to ten . . . now . . . I want you to do this so that you can feel yourself floating up . . . one . . . and two . . . because part of learning about trance is learning about how to feel when you're going up and when you're going down . . . three . . . four . . . three . . . two . . . three . . . four . . . five, six, seven, eight, nine, ten . . . now as you learn to separate **those particular feelings** that constitute trance, what will happen is that you learn what it feels like to *float down* and *float up* and you learn how far you have to go to *get something* that may be familiar, both in and out of trance, depending upon the trance. Now. That was just for the sake of pretending . . .	**Temporal predicate** (hypnotized subjects need to be told when to carry out instructions). **Fractionation.**

Fear of Needles

Trance-script	PROCESS

RB: So, what's the problem?
Needles.

RB: Needles—what about needles?
Er, the last time I had to have some-thing . . . I had blood taken from my arm two weeks ago and I have never passed out in my life. I passed out. The needle's in but . . .

RB: Yeah, the needle was in, so it's not seeing a needle?
It's not, well, I don't know but I've never had that sort of reaction to any situation where, you know, completely er . . .

RB: But you had shots before and it didn't bother you?
It's gradually got worse over the last two or three years. I was okay, but, now I don't like it at all.

RB seeks exceptions to the response.

RB: Okay, well you don't like them but again . . .
Passing out's proof.

RB: Pardon?
Passing out.

Trance-script	PROCESS

RB: Passing out's pretty extreme, but it doesn't always have to do with the needle by the way. A lot of times people tense up a little bit, and if they're a little bit hypoglycemic they pass out. So . . .
Right.

RB begins to reframe the "purpose" or "intention" of the subject's response.

RB: Your brain may associate things, but if it's progressively got worse over time . . . how did you make it worse by the way?
Thinking about it.

Begins to elicit process rather than content ("story") or opinion.

RB: Yes, and just exactly how did you think about it to make it worse.

Subject notices visual channel.

Pictures of . . . pictures have.

RB: Every time you do it by the way, the needle gets bigger. I just noticed that. You started out like this [gestures], and then it was like this [begins to exaggerate gesture], and then you opened your hands like that [hugely expansive gesture; client laughs].

RB identifies how the subject changes her submodalities to become filled with "dread." By making the image of the needle bigger, the kinesthetic increases.

You see I get paid the big bucks for paying attention to things like that, and when I said, "How do you make it worse?" you stopped and you went like this [big gesture], and you went like this [bigger gesture], and then when you came back the needle was huge. If you had a needle that big it would scare the crap out of me, too.

Trance-script

I tried to watch it last time because she tried to get it in there, wouldn't go in, and then she tried to get it in there and I said, "Two injections, why two?" and she said, "Ah sorry, it didn't work the first time." So I watched her do it the second time, and that happened, and, you know, I'm dreading the next time I have to have one.

RB: Okay, so you're already dreading it. It's a recurring thing? So if you're going to dread something you make a series of images.
Yes.

RB: Okay, let's say what we wanted to do is, let's say, if somebody hired you and said they'd pay you a million dollars if you could teach someone else to dread needles, okay?
I could do that.

RB: You could do that? Now, what would you do to the guy you're teaching?
I'd tell him that story. I'd tell that story and give him lots of horrible images.

RB: Okay, but it's the images that do the work. The story isn't the important part. The story is designed to get the images inside his head. Now, there're two ways you can do it. One is, you can leave your body the same size and make the needle bigger, and the other is you just keep making the picture bigger.
Yes.

PROCESS

Elicits further information about how the subject creates "dread" (when she creates multiple images).

This is a variation of RB's "temp" question: "If I could be you for a day, while you take a holiday from your problems, how would I know to . . ."

Unconsciously confirms the need to create multiple images.

Seeks finer distinctions. "Making pictures" is not enough information. Does the subject make the whole picture, or just the needles, bigger?

Trance-script

RB: Which do you do?
Erm, the blood is, you know, it comes from my . . . The first time, where they took one [sample] out I thought: I'm not scared, I don't do fear, I'll conquer this and I watched them draw blood and went, oh shit, and that sort of, you know, even at the last time they were putting stuff in, they weren't taking it out, I still kind of had the . . .

RB: Picture?
The picture of the . . .

RB: Yes, that's what you told us that you did it with a picture, but I asked a much easier question. Is your arm the same size as your arm and then the needle gets bigger? In other words, you can make a picture and it's bad. How do you make a picture that's worse? Do you make the whole picture bigger, do you make the picture closer, or do you make the picture the same size and make the needle bigger?
Er, er, erm . . . I don't think I make the needle bigger. I think I remember the pain more intensively than it was.

PROCESS

RB declines to discuss content and directs the subject back to sensory-specific details.

Submodalities drive changes between the stages of a strategy. RB seeks more information about these transitional phases.

The feeling is the *result* of making pictures, not the cause. RB persists in focusing on submodality changes.

Trance-script

RB: Okay, all right. To remember the pain more intensely you have to do something to the picture. So I'm just trying to find out, okay, if we were to make it so that instead of making this better we made it worse, you'd have to do something to the picture, you'd either make the picture bigger . . . It's an easy thing to find out.

What you do is, you look at the picture that creates dread and the first thing you do is you make the whole picture bigger and find out if you dread it more and then you try making the picture closer—does it make you dread it more? Or do you make just the needle bigger or do you make the blood come out more dramatically. Any element that you can adjust that increases your dread . . .

I think for me it's like it's the vividness of the picture, the blood . . .

RB: So you actually just have the image become more vivid?

Yes.

RB: Does it become more three dimensional?

Yes, like it's real, it's real. I'm not . . . I struggle because I don't feel I'm very good at visualizing, but I get that picture of really . . .

PROCESS

Begins to explore what the subject means by "vivid."

Trance-script

RB: Okay, you have the images . . .
but, see, there's a couple of sides to
this. Now let me tell you, I'm not
asking this because I'm not even that
interested in whether you pass out
when you get a shot. What I'm interested in is the intensity with which
you create feelings. Now, if your feelings become more intense because
you have a more vivid image, okay, a
more focused image . . . what I want
is for you to start to get where the
magic is in this. The magic is that
you can create something that is a
big, bad problem, okay?

What it really means is that you have
this machine inside your head that's
capable of making things intense.
Now, if your ability to increase
dread, okay, gets in your way, okay,
because if you keep doing this, eventually you'll get to the point where
there'll be a diabetic in the room,
they'll pull out a needle and you'll
instinctively pass out. Or you'll
watch one of these doctor shows on
TV. There are people who have
phobias of sharks this bad. One of
the worse shark phobias I've had—
the woman couldn't read magazines
because there might be a picture of a
shark in it. When she told me that
she said she tried to only read certain
kinds of magazines, but every once
in a while she'd flip the page, there'd
be a picture of a shark on the page,

PROCESS

Establishes the existence of a strategy
(or "machine") whereby the subject
creates "dread" in preparation for uti-
lizing it more resourcefully later.

Begins to create an "away-from" pattern to discourage the subject from
focusing on the problem instead of
more resourceful responses.

Trance-script

PROCESS

and she would feel intense pain in her leg. That's because she kept imagining walking out into the ocean and being bitten by a shark. She saw this in a shark movie or something, and when she was a little kid, she'd been in a pool and guppies swam around her legs and scared her.

She collected together all these memories and made up this horrible experience to the point where she had really intense feelings. Now, she didn't even come to me to get rid of that. She came to me because she said, "I feel numb around my own children." She wanted to be a good mother but she felt impatient with them and intolerant of them, probably because they outnumbered her—she had five of them—and she said, "Well, I don't feel that I have enough time for them" and blah blah blah. But the truth is that she hadn't taken the same machine and applied it to her feelings, because the same machine that can create crap can create something really good in the appropriate context.

Explains process of generalization by analogy.

Reinforces the potential value of the behavior in a more appropriate context.

Trance-script	PROCESS

Now, psychoanalysts would want to go into your childhood and say things like, "Well, needles, they're like a penis so it must have something to do with penises." They'd say, "It's all in your head, it must be a penis. It's shaped like that." When I started out, you know, about 50 percent of all clinical written material was about this psychoanalytic horseshit, where, whatever people said, you distorted it into the least likely thing it could possibly be, and then spent five years trying to convince the client of that. And, in the process they would also say things like, "What other fears aren't you admitting to yourself?" I love that one. People go, "I can't think of any," and they go, "A-ha, denial!"

Uses humor to loosen up the subject's serious attitude (note the implication: "It's all in your head, it must be a penis. It's shaped like that.")

Now, as far as I'm concerned, denial is only a river in Egypt. So, now, let's try a little experiment, okay? Because, if you make a really vivid image of this, it creates a new dread—true? So let's try a little experiment . . .

Thought experiments work this way; the first thing you do is go back, look at that vivid image of having the blood drawn, and just blur it. First think it flat—can you make it flat? Flat?

RB begins experimenting to find the submodalities that will drive change.

RB: Yeah, like a picture in a magazine? Yes.

Trance-script	PROCESS
RB: All right. Now defocus it. Okay.	
RB: All right. Now in this state right there, do you feel dread? No.	Tests. Defocusing image proves effective.
RB: Okay. Now if we can get your unconscious to do that automatically at the sight of a needle, right, then we're headed in the right direction. This is a little tiny problem okay? It's a good test because I like good tests right, and in fact, being a diabetic, I have loads of needles.	Produces hypodermic needle and begins to school the subject in developing the ability to visualize both needles and the problem as smaller than before, and, also, potentially, something at which she can learn to laugh.
I don't know why heroin addicts hide. Diabetics don't have to; it's not against the law. In fact, if we don't shoot up we'll die.	Indirectly suggests that some injections can be lifesaving, and that the subject can learn to tolerate them.
I have childhood diabetes, the kind that's genetic. It's not like there's something you can do about it. So, at first when I was diagnosed, I used to hide in the bathroom and do it, and then, one day, I was in a restaurant and this waitress offered me something and I said, "I can't have it, I'm diabetic," and she said, "Did you take your shot?"	

Trance-script

PROCESS

I said, "Well, I'm going to go to the bathroom," and she said, "Why? My husband doesn't because he thinks that's crazy. Just open it up and spike yourself," and I thought, *Well that's a very liberal point of view,* and as soon as I did, some people nearby freaked out. She burst out laughing and she says, "Oh, I love doing that." It was like instant therapy. Suddenly, I thought, *I could really enjoy this!*

The next day I was on an airplane flying and they were serving us lunch and I opened up my little kit like this and the woman sitting next to me looked at me like this, and I pulled out the bottle and went *sloooooooop,* like this and sucked out the stuff and looked at my arm and I rolled up my sleeve like that and I said, "Would you like some?" and she goes, "What is it?" *Interesting answer,* I thought. I said, "Oh, I'm a diabetic. It's insulin," and I said, "If I don't shoot this, I'll die and they don't really like dead people on the airplane." But, you know, after a while, you know, you get used to such things, but, you see, if you have a bad experience, and it doesn't matter what that bad experience is, by the way, and it's more vivid that your other memories, a psychiatrist will tell you that's an "imprint," okay? But the truth is that at that moment you had blood drawn you were more alert than you are most of the time, that especially when she missed the first time and had trouble finding a vein and started hunting around in your hand, you came to your senses.

Continues making light of the process of using needles. Humor is an important tool RB uses to depotentiate fear and anxiety states.

RB begins to switch referential indexes ("I" and "me" become "you") coupled with embedded commands ("get used to such things") to install new responses in subject.

Trance-script

Now, that's an inborn thing. That's a self-defense mechanism. We have to be like that. If we were like walking through the jungle, like mellowing out, and a tiger jumped out in front of us, it's really time to come to your senses, you know. That's a time when you're really alert, fully alert, and so that memory is going to be crisper. Now in modern society, we do have things jump out and attack us. Like in New York City . . . we have stupid muggers and irate taxi cab drivers and, every once in a while, a stray dog, but, you know, your body is designed to do this. Now, what your body did is it took that mechanism and created a vivid memory—but it doesn't mean you have to keep it that way. The more important part of it is the other side of the coin. Now, think of what you would like to be a stronger feeling more of the time?
Erm, passion?

RB: Any kind of passion?
Erm . . .

RB: You're the only one that has to know the answer to this. Do you know the answer? If you're going to be passionate, you want to be passionate about something, right?
Love.

PROCESS

Continues to reframe response as essentially positive. The recurring phrase "come to your senses" prompts the subject to deal with data gleaned from her senses, rather than collapse back into a habituated response.

More reframes.

Trance-script

RB: Well, that's a little vague, you have to pick something specific. You start with one thing, okay? You don't have to do everything at once. See, remember, the brain is designed to do the following things. The brain is designed . . . when I wrote *The Structure of Magic*, every graduate student who ever studies NLP in college wants to write a dissertation and they write Dr. Bandler the following letter; they go, "You didn't document the resource for the three universals of human modeling." That's because I made them up. But I defined them. Their being there is evident in everything. To build a generalization, you have to delete some things and not others. For you to know what doors are, even though you encounter new doors all the time, first you have to say: "This is separate from the wall."

Your brain has to know so you delete some things and pay attention to others. And, yet, every door is different. They're different colors, they look different. Some are glass, some are wood—at the molecular level, they're totally different, but somehow, we have to make them the same. So we have to first separate out part of the world, and then we have to generalize, so we have to distort and make all doors fit into this category. This makes us functional. So

PROCESS

Rejects nominalization and pushes for specific, quality data.

Trance-script	PROCESS

what you can depend on is that, if you build a category in your brain, your brain will generalize the rest of things. So all you have to do is pick an example of where you want to be more passionate. It can be just about anything. Did you pick something that's important to you?
Yes.

RB: Okay. Got it?
Yes.

RB: Right, so you know what it is. Now, when you think about it, is it as vivid as that needle?
Erm . . .

RB: I would take that as . . . it is?
It's pretty vivid.

RB: Oh it is, huh?
Well, I'll tell you what I'm doing. I'm trying to think of being passionate about my friendships with people.

Notes subject's lack of conviction and gently teases her.

RB: All you have to pick is *one* situation.
Yes, and of course I picked one that's quite passionate because that's one that comes to my mind first but it's the other ones where . . .

RB: But you said you *wanted* to be more passionate, right?
Yeah, yeah.

Trance-script	PROCESS
RB: Okay, okay. So you picked one where you *were* more passionate? Yes.	An important distinction.
RB: Okay, right. Pick where you would *like* to be more passionate. Okay.	
RB: Okay, is that as vivid? No.	
RB: No, it's not. It's also not in the same place either. Look at the needle. Where's that image? It's over there, okay, and you know how far away it is and how big it is. Yes.	
RB: Now, pick this other image, right? Push it over to the wall, pull it around and pull it up to where this one is and literally adjust it so it's just as vivid. Now as it becomes more vivid, do your feelings become stronger? Yes.	Since RB has established that "vividness" increases the intensity of the subject's fear of needles, he begins to transfer the submodalities of intensity and position over to a more useful and appropriate context—that is, increasing passion in a friendship.
RB: Okay. Is it three-dimensional? No.	

Trance-script

RB: Okay. Right, first step—pop it out to three dimensions. It has to have that characteristic called "parallax," okay? When people make pictures, we look at flat screens a whole lot. We spend our days looking at computers, looking at TVs, looking at magazines. We look at two-dimensional things all the time. Our brain itself is actually very holographic. Now, parallax is this: it's where you take an image and tilt it slightly and let everything come out front and behind, in such a way that you can take the image and turn it like this. Look at it from the side, because our brain is capable of doing this. In my lab, I have a great hologram of three chess pieces and a magnifying glass. When you looked at the magnifying glass and you looked from an angle, it would magnify the first chess piece, and as you moved, it would magnify the second chess piece and then the third. Now, when I pick the hologram and flip it around like this and ask people, "Do you see anything?" they look at it and say, "No." Then I put my finger on the plate and pull it out to here, where the image is, because the image is no longer behind the plate, it's in front. As soon as they follow my finger to the right place, *bang*, they can see it—and from that day forward, they can never not see it, because it's simply a matter of teaching your brain to do this.

PROCESS

Adds third dimension to the subject's representation, using several examples and analogies to assist the change.

Directs subject's attention to where image is.

Switches referential index to install learning in subject.

Trance-script

So go back and look at the same image and make it flat and then turn the image slightly and pull the thing so that it's in front of the flat plane and behind the flat plane and continue to turn it so that you can look at part of the side, then turn it back straight again and turn it to the other angle and look a little bit at the other side. Now, this is what your brain is capable of, and, when you do that, your feelings become much more intense—true?
Uh-huh.

RB: Okay. Now, the other thing is about crispness. Anybody who's done photography knows that there's quality of lens. The human eye is capable of much more precision than any lens. The trouble is that people are thinking too much, and if you're not focusing your eyes, you don't actually even look in the right place. When I first started out I couldn't see nearly as much as I can now, and over the years I've learned to focus three dimensionally. Now, the more you look at internal images that have the quality of parallax—that is, beyond three dimensional, where you can actually make an image and rotate the image and look at it from every side—because the human brain is capable of this . . . in fact, one of the measures of intelligence in

PROCESS

Prepares for more submodality changes.

Trance-script

PROCESS

advanced IQ tests involves showing young children three things, then hiding the three things behind a big block, and asking them to draw what's hidden by the block. They ask the children to draw from a particular angle. They say, "If you're up over here drawing this, what would it look like?"

At a certain age, kids can't do that. Then, as they develop past the age of five or six or seven, they suddenly develop the concept of parallax in their minds, so that you begin to realize that when you're talking to somebody they have a back. In other words I'm not looking at your back; I can look at the front of you and I've seen enough people in my life that I can construct what must be behind you, having seen these chairs, and to the degree you pay attention walking in, you look at somebody, you look at what they're wearing and you can turn around and figure out where the back of the chair is and all of these things.

RB begins to regress the subject to childhood, installing or reinforcing abilities to create detailed internal representations by switching referential index from "they," "them," and "I" to "you."

Now, when you want to create more passion, there's two parts to it. One is, you have to make the image crisper and crisper, and the other is you have to do the things that intensify feelings. But which feelings is something you need to determine, because you can make something so vivid you have a panic attack . . .

Adjusts focus and crispness of image.

Trance-script

Now, you did something okay with a needle. Actually it wasn't you who did it. She did it for you. She wasn't obviously that great a nurse; she missed the vein. I know someone who almost never misses. He puts in the IVs, and he can do it in his sleep. When I was in the hospital, I had nurses who tried five and six times, searching for a vein. One of them, I actually did myself because I got tired of them poking me in the middle of the night, going, "This'll only take a minute," smacking me like this, and saying, "You'll be back to sleep before you know it." Then, they'd go, "Shit!" and start to blame it on my vein "running away." I'd say, "Yeah, it does that all the time. Sometimes I'll wake up in the morning and my veins are out partying." But one night I got so frustrated one night, I said, "Can I see that for a second? I just want to look at it," and I stuck it in, and the blood came out, and she said, "Are you a doctor?" I said, "No, I'm just a frustrated person." I said, "How long have you been doing this?" and she said, "Well, you're my second person." I said, "I believe you." But it's one of those things you get good at.

PROCESS

RB makes light of the process of drawing blood. Note how his story matches the experience of the subject's. This is teaching by metaphor, obliquely encouraging her to look at what is happening, to be able to see the blood coming out, and choose a response other than "dread."

Begins to amplify and anchor laughter to situations where the subject would like to have a better response. Suggests "it's one of those things you get good at."

Trance-script

Now . . . one of the things psychology figured out is that there are "root experiences." The truth is, they are actually more than root experiences. We have all kinds of experiences through life, and we learn to have certain emotions. Then you learn an emotion like dread because you've dreaded a whole bunch of different things, and you save it up and attach it to something new. I think it's infinitely more complex than psychology views it, but I also don't think it's the important part of it. The important part of it is: if you have a strong emotion, it takes a strong emotion to knock it out. So I'm going to ask you to try a little experiment, okay? The experiment goes like this. What I want you to do is to recall the funniest thing that ever happened to you.
The funniest thing that happened?

RB: Yes.
I played a very silly practical joke on someone.

RB: Okay. When you think about it, does it make you laugh?
Yes.

PROCESS

Since emotions may be learned, the implication is they can be unlearned. This can only be accomplished by extinguishing the strong emotion with an even stronger one—preferably humor.

Trance-script	PROCESS
RB: Okay. Can you make that as vivid as this picture over here. Close your eyes, go back to it, and remember that good feeling. See what you saw when you were there, hear what you heard, remember what you did. Does it feel funny? Oh yes (starts to giggle, and then laugh with gusto).	Has subject associate fully into the memory.
RB: So look at the other picture. The needle— Can't. Can't see it.	
RB: Well go ahead, take a look at it. Can't see it.	Tests repeatedly to ensure pattern has changed.
RB: Can't see it? Now what does this mean? It means the next time somebody says to you, "Well I have to draw some blood," you're not going to make that same old picture. In fact, you put it exactly where the other image was, the thing you were having trouble being passionate about . . . it's already over here. I didn't ask you to do that, your brain did it all by itself, see? Your brain's already got a way of deciding, "This, we water down, this we make vivid."	RB has effectively "collapsed" two anchors. By creating a strong, positive state then inviting the subject to reaccess the unwanted state, the original response becomes neutralized. A new "sorting" mechanism is installed.

Trance-script

It's just that the conscious mind is the one that should decide which pictures go where, because if you let your unconscious do it, it doesn't care if you're scared or not. It just isn't important. It doesn't make distinctions that way. This is one of the simple things I've found through the years. I've had people who've been through fifteen years of therapy and spent and spent fifteen minutes with me, and when I'd say, "What other problems do you have?" they'd start giggling, right? I get a lot of laughter when I'm working. That's why I got kicked out of my first office. All the psychotherapists there said I wasn't being sincere enough. But the one thing I'm sincere about is giving somebody freedom. Freedom isn't built upon dwelling on your problems; it's built upon dwelling on the future and taking a good resource and placing it there . . .

PROCESS

Outlines and reinforces a powerful formula to be applied in the future in the pursuit of freedom and change.

THE PROCESS OF
Trance-formation 2

Fear of Flying

Trance-script	PROCESS

I fly a lot, fifty or so hours a month on average.

RB: Yes.
And I, er, from time to time I have a really serious problem right before I start, I'm convinced the plane's just going to [claps hands sharply] wipe out shortly after take-off and landings. It can be like to the point that . . . it's over as far as I'm concerned. When I'm up, I never think like that unless there are like severe changes in air pressure, and it doesn't happen when I'm really, really . . . when I have a ton of things that I have to do.

RB: So you only torture yourself in your spare time?
Yes, or when I'm really tired. I was flying to New York about a month ago and I ended up luckily very far up in the plane, but I felt so close to the nose, whatever else, so I felt like closed in up there for whatever reason then. You know, sometimes before you take off, the airplane stinks of fuel because they're filling it up and, I get this feeling I need to get out the plane before

Humor, irony, and gentle chiding is characteristic of RB's work.

Trance-script *(continued)*

PROCESS

they close the door, you know, and I actually got up and walked up to where you're going to get off and the stewardess came up and said: "How can I help?" I can't step off the plane, so I'm standing there, you know, should I, should I not . . .

RB: Back up, back up, because you're already acting like an idiot at that point. But before you act like an idiot . . . what happens? Just back up for a minute, okay? So, you're sitting in the seat, how do you get yourself nervous enough to want to leave? Sounds like your mind is racing through a bunch of . . .
Yeah, well when that happens that . . .

RB seeks to identify starting point of the subject's strategy for becoming fearful. His intention is to install more resourceful response *before* the strategy has a chance to run.

RB: No, no, no . . . back to the beginning, okay? So you're sitting in there, you're either thinking about all the things you need to get done or you're thinking what? The plane's going to crash? What?
Yes, I mean, you know, I mean it's not an either/or. It's normally when I'm very tired and I don't have tons of stuff to think about, or I'm too tired to think, so when my mind is just too exhausted then I . . .

Discourages subject from content and story and steers him back to sensory-based information.

Trance-script	PROCESS
RB: Well, yeah, great—but what do you do once you're exhausted or tired, or have too much spare time? You don't go inside and say anything calmly to yourself, do you?	Seeks greater specificity.
I'm not much fun to fly with because when I get on an airplane, I fall asleep. I'd never been able to sleep on airplanes before, until once there was a guy sitting next to me and he stuck his thumbs in his seatbelt, leaned back, and was snoring before they'd even started the engines. So I woke him up and said, "Excuse me, sir," and he looked up and said, "What's wrong?" I said, "Absolutely everything. You want to be sound asleep and unless you want me to be talking to you for ten hours, tell me how you do it."	Begins to induce altered state by story, analogy, and changing the tonality and rate of his speech.
He thought a moment, then he said, "I never used to be able to sleep on planes, but I discovered if I take my thumbs and turn them inside, put them in the seatbelt, and then tell myself I should go to sleep now, close my eyes, and then just watch the little lights go by, no images. Just dots. The white dots would come by, every once in a while a green one, and when you see a blue one, focus into it, and step inside."	Quotes pattern permits RB to instruct subject in relaxing without arousing resistance. To effect change, the subject needs the experience of being able to choose to be relaxed and comfortable on a flight.

Trance-script

Now, it turns out that's very much like a Vedic meditation that they use to teach insomniacs how to sleep. In this Vedic meditation, you go inside . . . see a red circle, . . . then a green circle . . . and then a blue circle . . . then you see a green circle again . . . a red circle. Then you make the red circle bigger, then you shrink it down. You make the green sort of bigger and you shrink it down. Then you make the blue circle big enough that it wraps around you to the point that in your mind you can turn 360° inside the blue circle . . . then you shrink it down inside your head and you . . . go to sleep.

Now, when I was in India, I met this lovely guru and I asked him, "What exactly does a guru do? I've heard about you guys, but I'm not really sure what it is you do." He said, "People come tell me what's wrong with their lives and I give them meditations to change their lives. We have several Vedas that give us a set of mental things to do." For example, he told me about one technique where, as you . . . breathe in, you follow the center of your body down, down the center of your legs, then, as you . . . exhale, you come up the back of your legs, and then you visualize blue rings around each vertebra going up your spine. Then, as you blow air out and make an image of it, and inside the image, you . . . concentrate on the things in your life you need to change.

PROCESS

Variations on the theme of entering a sleeplike state. Voice continues to slow and deepen.

Embedded command: "Go to sleep!"

Switches referential index to "you" as he continues to deepen the subject's state while apparently just recounting an anecdote.

Instructions on how to relax become increasingly specific. RB also installs the need to know what changes are desired, as opposed to simply "not having" the problem.

Trance-script

PROCESS

Now . . . you have a meditation when you get on airplanes. Your meditation is either: think about work, or think about your imminent death. As you continue to think about your imminent death, you do it in a way that it actually affects you viscerally, does it not? Otherwise you wouldn't get up and try to get out of the plane, right? These particular images are strong enough that they affect you physically. Are they very vivid?

Compares and contrasts the peaceful meditation with the subject's viscerally disturbing "meditation."

Begins eliciting submodalities.

You know, it's not really [subject makes a dismissive gesture near his head and turns his head away from his hand] . . . I mean, it could be like there's a delay on the plane, for instance, the mechanics are running back and forth, and while I don't see crashing or burning planes or anything like that [repeats gesture]. I just know it's going to [claps hands], you know, be over. Once I come to that conclusion that's when, you know . . .

RB: Right good. You don't think that conclusion is in an image?

Internal images are always present. Not recognizing this can be the source of considerable confusion and pain.

Yes . . . I think. It's not very . . . It's very quick . . .

Trance-script

PROCESS

RB: Okay, but nobody said you dwelt upon the image. As you say, it's a very quick image. You make the quick image, and then, it just becomes a matter of fact. You think, *Oh God, I didn't transfer funds into the right bank account . . . I forgot to fill out the insurance policy . . . Good God, I have the car keys with me. How will they drive the Volvo?* But, you know, that's the voice of somebody who's already dead in the picture, you know. These are regrets that you can have in your afterlife. Yeah, you're right.

Humor, irony.

RB: Yeah. But you're not the only person who does this. I once knew a guy who interrupted his own suicide attempt for the same reason. He thought he had cancer, took a bottle full of pills, then suddenly stopped and thought, *I didn't leave my life insurance policy where anybody could find it. And, no one will know where I hide my car keys . . .* So he called the paramedics and asked them to sort out those things for him. But paramedics are not terribly cooperative that way. He told me later in the hospital, "I told them I'd taken these pills and asked them to get my keys out of the top drawer upstairs and bring down the papers in the third drawer so I could sign them really quick, and the paramedics said, 'Shut up, tell us what you took.'"

Normalizes the subject's experience and recounts story of someone who felt hopeless, but was helped to learn how to change his state. This is an example of Milton Erickson's "My Friend John" pattern, which allows the practitioner to explain and advise the subject directly in a way that doesn't arouse resistance, because, consciously, it is perceived as being all about "John."

Trance-script

PROCESS

The next thing he was in a hospital, and, unfortunately for him, was assigned a conservator, which in California means some stranger gets put in charge of your affairs. I was sent in by the courts because there had been some problems with the conservator stealing money from people, and the courts wanted me to find out if this guy really needed a conservator. I tried to talk him out of suicide. I said, "There are better choices than suicide," and he said, "Well, I can't stand the pain," so I said, "Then, one of the choices would be to get rid of the pain." He said, "There's no way in the world anybody could control the pain," and I suddenly screamed at the top of my lungs and whacked him, right above his throat. Then I looked at him and said, "How much pain did you feel when I did that?" and he looked at me and he said, "None," and I said, "Now all we have to do is get you to hold that state," because the problem can be the kind of judgments that people make.

So, as soon as you run that picture in your head, right, my guess is that, as you've done it a number of times, you've gotten better at it.
Oh, I'm really good at it.

RB has already observed that the subject responds on a flight as if he is already dead—i.e., he is repeatedly and metaphorically committing suicide. Here, the subliminal message is: *There are better choices than suicide.*

All that's needed is to create an alternative state and then learn to hold it.

Trance-script

Now, if you go back and think . . . you kept saying the images are important, but when you did that, you made this lovely gesture [imitates subject's dismissive gesture]. You went, "No, no" it's not that the image is important. It's like . . . what's important about it is that you're not looking at it because if you looked at it and started to think how silly it is, maybe you wouldn't go through all the unpleasantness.

Because the other thing you can do is think that the reason mechanics are outside is that they're fixing the plane. That's actually a good thing, you know. Instead of reassuring yourself, you're scaring yourself to the point where you feel you're already dead. And it's nice that you don't make it a long, suffering process.

Some plane phobics actually die slowly in the fire and imagine crashing to the ground at a very slow speed so that their death is maximally unpleasant. They drag it out for thirty-five minutes in slow motion and feel every cell of their body burning up, and of course, that's crazy isn't it?
Erm . . .

RB: You look shocked. Why would anybody do that? Well, my question is: why *would* anybody do this? *Just because it's a bad habit.*

PROCESS

Reframes the events that trigger subject's anxiety as actually protective.

The subject has overgeneralized his response, and RB is implying that this "bad habit" can and should be changed.

Trance-script

So . . . as long as you're making the picture . . . of course it's true, every time you get in a plane it can crash. But, then again, other than elevators, planes are one of the safest ways to travel. Actually, you're more likely to die crossing Kensington High Street than you are flying in an airplane. In some cities in the United States, they pay cars to run you down. In California, we train drivers to stay away from pedestrians, but there are some cities, like Seattle, where pedestrians don't have right of way, so they might as well paint targets on themselves and walk into the streets. New Orleans is a lot like that. In Los Angeles, drivers have right of way unless there's a certain light, a certain color, or something—but I'm very suspicious of that. I try to wait until there are no cars that could possibly hit me and then cross the street. I think the best defense is armor plating. People have always criticized me because I drive big cars, but I find if I'm in an accident I want to win. Back in the seventies I drove this humongous Lincoln Continental that I bought for nine hundred dollars and put steel bars around the side. People said, "Why do you drive that big tank?" and I said, "Because I have children, that's why." I said, "If somebody hits me I want them to die, not my kids . . ."

PROCESS

First, however, he anchors in a state of safety along with that of comfort.

A succession of scenarios shift the subject's state from that of a victim, at the mercy of uncontrollable feelings, to one in which he can take steps to protect himself from worrying excessively about events out of his control.

Trance-script	**PROCESS**
The trick is . . . how do you ever see that image you weren't looking at? Where is it, by the way? [Subject points.]	Begins to introduce the means of changing the "bad habit."
RB: It's right there? Okay. Now, there are, there are things that you just know are not true, aren't there? For example, there are some people that work at your company who tell you things you don't believe? Oh, yes.	
RB: Richard's really good at finding those. I have some inside information about that . . . So, now, when you think about the example that came up in your mind, the thing that somebody told you that you absolutely didn't believe. Okay? Where is that picture? In exactly the same place? Yes.	
RB: Okay. What's the difference between that picture and the other one? Are they both movies? Is there any difference in the size? Is one more focused than the other? No, it's that . . . I can see that [the picture of disbelief] very clearly exactly for what it is, but the other one is very . . . I can't really get a grip on what's in that image.	
RB: Is it seeping in yet? Yeah, yeah.	Ambiguous statement. Is understanding "seeping in," or detail that has been missing from the image?

Trance-script

PROCESS

RB: Okay. Now look at the one where you can see it for what it is, the one that tells you this is complete bullshit, right? Now pick the vague image and make it like the one that you know is bullshit.
Right, that's very . . . You see, the image of the not so good thing, crashing the plane, it's not even a defined thing.

RB: No, it's not. It's absolutely not a defined thing. That makes it easy to fill in the blanks. As soon as you define it, doesn't it seem like bullshit? That's why you said this isn't going to work.
Yeah, of course.

RB has already noted that the subject's fear arises out of unclear images. Now he begins the process of helping the subject apply the resources he already has (knowing when something should not be believed) to the vague impressions that have been causing him distress while flying.

RB: Right, so just try it my way. Okay, since you don't know how it's going to crash, you don't know what's going to happen, as soon as you define it, it becomes a problem that can be dealt with. Okay, because one of the choices is you could be shot out of the sky by an alien spaceship.
[Laughs.] Yeah, okay, it's not that . . .

Since the image is unclear, RB sets about filling in details that the subject will clearly find funny and dismiss as unbelievable.

RB: Okay, so are you going to die going down the runway?
[Subject shrugs.]

RB: Okay, all right, but how specifically?
I don't know.

Trance-script	PROCESS
RB: Well you don't know, so why not be shot down by a spaceship? You're right [laughs].	
RB: Well, if you made it clear then probably your brain would go: "This is bullshit," don't you think? Isn't that how you decided that the other thing was bullshit? You could see it for what it clearly was. That's exactly what you said to me. All I'm doing is what you told me to. Now, if you take this image and you make it clear, you will be able to decide if it's rubbish or not. Yes.	Subject accepts the reasoning.
RB: So the choice is, you either leave it vague and scare yourself. In fact, you could scare yourself about everything this way, think about it. You're right, yes.	RB reinforces the fact that the subject has choices and that making the less resourceful choice could ruin other areas of his life.
RB: Yeah, you could. You could be . . . are you married? Yes.	Begins to attach increased emotion to the response.
RB: Yeah. Well, you could make vague images of your wife running off with another man, draining your bank accounts and some worthless unknown figure . . . Every day, you could scare yourself . . . or you could see this BS for the nonsense it is and not do it. Yes.	

Trance-script	PROCESS

RB: You understand?

Yes.

RB: Okay. You see, I realize that a lot of times when I do stuff with people they'll turn around and look at me afterward and they'll go, "And you get paid for this?" . . . You see, the anxiety you create is created out of not having a clear image that tells you whether it's bullshit or not. My guess is that if you clear up the image, sometimes it's going to come out bullshit and sometimes you're going to go, "This is right." But as long as the image isn't clear . . . for example, to tolerate relatives who borrow money from you over and over again and don't pay you back, you would have to keep the image blurry, right?

Okay. When I was married the first time, every relative my wife had would borrow money from me, and after the second or third time I knew they weren't going to pay me back, even when they said, "I'll pay you back the money I owe you as well as this money." It would pop up in the bullshit image, and then I'd make the image of having to argue with my wife about it and I'd just blur the image and give them the cash.

By analogy, RB sets up a sorting mechanism between what is "real" and what is "bullshit," using the sub-modalities of clarity and "blurriness."

Trance-script

But I was smart enough to go upstairs and *not* put it in the "I'm going to get paid back" column. I have a page of people that are never going to pay me back. There's only one advantage. When it hits a certain level they won't come around and ask for more because they know you're going to bring it up. And I try to compute how much that it's going to be ahead of time. I make lists of the people in my life who come to borrow money and try to figure out how much it's going to cost me before they avoid me for the rest of my life and I consider whether that's a worthwhile investment, or whether it's cheaper to tell them to shove off. With some people it's really not that expensive. For some people it's less than a hundred bucks. As soon as they owe you fifty bucks—they'll keep asking for twenty, but you look at them and you say, "Say, why don't I loan you fifty and you pay me back seventy the next time you see me?" *Pffffft*. They're history and never come back again. Now, I used to just pull my hair out by the roots over and over again about it until I made the decision to make it so that I knew what was bullshit and what wasn't. So, what you're asking about is how to simplify your mind. Learning how to have more good feelings at the right time. Keep it in mind . . .

PROCESS

The subject is already in a profoundly altered state, and Bandler continues with the following trance. . . .

A TRANCE TO FLY BY

Exercise

The reader will greatly improve the ability to construct elegant and productive trances by deconstructing the example below. Note language patterns and process instructions in the right-hand column.

Trance-script	Language Patterns/ Process Instructions
. . . My goodness, I went to a particular country once, and after I gave a lecture, somebody came up and *actually* criticized me for dwelling upon feeling good so much. They told me that good feelings weren't real and bad feelings were. No, I thought. As a national model for a country, this would lead to massive depression. Fortunately, not everybody in that country agreed with him, but he told me that you can't trust good feelings; you'll always end up having a bad one anyway. So he'd rather feel bad all the time and be disappointed.	
Me, I'd rather live in a state of self-deception and . . . feel good most of the time, and if I'm going to feel bad, keep it as short as possible. It's not that people won't disappoint you and that crap won't happen . . . Who knows? Maybe some day the plane will come out of the sky . . . but all the worrying and fretting isn't going to make it happen less.	

**Language Patterns/
Process Instructions**

So, therefore, you might as well make your time on planet Earth as comfortable as possible. So wiggle your toes a little bit and let a feeling come up your legs that ends up in a smile . . . That's right.

Throughout your life, you've smiled hundreds and thousands of times. Without thinking about it, your heart will beat over two billion times in your lifetime. Sometimes it beats a little faster than others, sometimes it beats a little slower . . . Your blood pressure will go up . . . and down . . . sometimes it goes up a little too high and sometimes . . . it drops a little low. The natural process for human beings is for things to fluctuate and to . . . achieve a balance.

Now this means, in mental activities . . . when you're out of balance it should be a natural inclination to . . . find some homeostatic response. If you're going to create massive dread, you should also be able to . . . create a sense of humor about it. I find that a giggle goes a long way in this regard . . .

And if you're going to create plane disasters in your mind, you might as well have them be by flying saucers. You might as well decide that aliens have traveled across the universe to shoot just your plane out of the sky

because if you do that you can . . .
get it to the point where it seems as
silly as it is.

If you leave your anxiety amorphous, vague, hidden in blurry pictures, and it creates in you distress.
You're better off . . . creating intense
focus, clarity, three-dimensional
images, and then . . . select what you
put in them. Practice, practice, practice. If you begin to see yourself
being more successful in the ways
that you want . . . as you drift down
deeper and deeper still into what it is
you do not know yet, but in the
process of dropping into a deep
trance . . . it's very easy to learn. . . .
If you talk to yourself too much . . .
go inside and just slow down your
internal dialogue. If you must sleep
. . . talk to yourself in a *sl-e-e-e-py*
voice. If you're having trouble listening, it doesn't matter . . . I'm not
speaking to that mind but to your
other mind . . . the other mind . . .
the part of your mind that understands language, the part of your
mind that understands how to . . .
have a function, like getting him
into the future.

Now, one more time, just force yourself to smile and think something
happy. Think a little bit of that feeling and let it spread, feel the back of
your hands, the back of your arms,

**Language Patterns/
Process Instructions**

the back of your elbows, the back of your shoulders, and literally smile . . . and you'll discover that when that serotonin hits your bloodstream it makes the hair on your arms tingle a little bit. It's a natural hardwired response. Even people in Borneo do it. Smiling and laughing is hard-wired and it's hard-wired to learning. The reason children play and laugh and giggle as they prepare for life is that if you practice things as a game and you make the game enjoyable, it means that you use the learnings more often. Too many times people try to struggle to understand and to learn. If something is a struggle and you attach new knowledge to struggling, it's just harder to use the knowledge.

Now, I asked you to just try doing something in your mind. Remember what it is that I told you, and start to try it. But before you try it, start to feel good. Go back and find a really happy memory. Everybody's got at least one, go back and see what you saw at the time, hear what you heard. Make the image life-size, so that you can recapture some of whatever good feeling you had, whether it was the birth of your first child, whether it was winning an award, whether it was getting a date . . . it doesn't matter what it is, because that's only content . . .

**Language Patterns/
Process Instructions**

As you go back and you see what you saw and hear what you heard at the time, it gives you a chance to get back some of the chemicals inside of you that make good feelings.

Now if you increase the size of this image, your feelings will get stronger. If you pull it a little bit closer, your feelings will get stronger. If you turn up the brightness, your feelings will get stronger. If you turn up the volume—in fact, if you put bigger speakers in your head so that you have that surround sound—you get more of the memory . . . and the more of the memory you get, the more of the . . . good feelings will begin to flow through outside your body. From the tip of your toes to the bottom of your head, from the back to the front, from the outside in, as you let these feelings spin through your body and move around and circle inside you, it gives your unconscious a chance to pre-pare. And keep that good feeling spinning and smile. If you're not smiling when you have a good feel-ing you're only getting part of the goods. It's like having sex with a magazine instead of a person—just not the same thing.

In fact, go back and put more paral-lax in your image; make it more three-dimensional. Tilt the image to

**Language Patterns/
Process Instructions**

the right and to the left; take control of your brain. If it's not vivid enough, make it a little more vivid. Focus through your image and make it a little clearer. Every inch, every pixel, you add, every little bit that gives you more of the good feeling prepares you better . . .

Because if you can smile in your body, if you can smile in your heart, then you're prepared to start to confront your demons—the demons we live with. Because the chains of the free are not jails and starvation and poverty. The chains of the free are built out of the way in which we think inside our minds. What we feel is possible and what we feel is impossible, what we believe about the kind of person we are and the feelings that we allow ourselves to have. Because when you go back and you look at the beliefs you have that limit you . . . and, this time, literally turn it around and see what's on the other side and it might not be clear at first but your unconscious now wants and needs to go further . . .

So, take that thing that was most immediate and imagine thinking about it differently. Imagine doing it in a relaxed, quiet way for just a moment when your unconscious comes up with another way to feel, I want you to start doing it. Because this is just a step in the process. This is designed from the beginning to the end to accomplish one thing, which is to reclaim your life, so that you . . . start accomplishing the things that you want more.

You are already very successful, very good at what you do. Now if you can optimize, it just means that you'll do it that much better. And you have been struggling with (this problem) for a long time. I recommend you give up struggling and just get on with it. The more you struggle, the more you get good at struggling; the more you relax and start enjoying the process, the more you find an easier, happier way to get things done quicker.

Now in a moment, I'm going to ask you to come out of this trance, but for a moment let your imagination run away with you. Begin to think maybe there are a few other things in your life that you could make more exciting, some things that you could just make unimportant, because some things we make so they just don't matter.

Now, some things don't matter and some do . . . Maybe you need to move some of the things that don't matter into things that do matter, and some of the things that do

**Language Patterns/
Process Instructions**

matter into things that don't. If we recategorize our lives and just imagine sorting through your thoughts and your feelings and being able to place them more methodically . . . well, unconsciously . . . that's what you do each night while you sleep and while you dream.

So, tonight, while you sleep, while you're dreaming, your unconscious will remember this trance . . . and in a moment I'm going to count from one to ten, and with each count, I want you to wake up as much as you need to, and I want your unconscious to keep doing exactly what it's been doing in a new way.

Now . . . one . . . starting to wake up . . . two, waking up a little bit more . . . three, smiling, smile, smile, smile . . . come on . . . smile, four, five, six, seven, eight, nine, ten . . . *Aaahh* . . .

Twenty

IN CONCLUSION

W<small>HEN</small> I <small>BEGAN WRITING</small> this book, I described myself as an optimist. In spite of everything that's happened in the world and some of the things I've seen, I'll always remain an optimist, because I believe in our human capacity for learning and change.

There will probably always be people who say "it can't be done," and those, I believe, are the true pessimists. When I was a kid, they used to tell us it was impossible to go to the moon. We've been to the moon. We've been several times, even though we're absolutely convinced there's nothing of value there.

Ultimately, we will go to the stars. We'll figure out how to get across space rather than through it—and this is going to come from our believing in what's possible . . . and then doing it.

Psychiatrists told me many times that the schizophrenics in their care were "chronic" and without hope. I didn't believe that, and so I went in with the idea that they were wrong, and that even the chronic and the hopeless could be set free.

And many of them were set free, because we have the ability to learn and grow. There are many things that were important in our childhoods and no longer apply. We can switch things around in our minds so they completely change their meaning. We have the ability to distort our generalizations, and that's what makes us so smart and able to do such clever things.

My interest in hypnosis and altered states led me into many different and rewarding areas. Because I wanted to find out how far we could push things and whether there were limits to our ability to grow and develop, I created three important behavioral technologies.

Neuro-Linguistic Programming, sometimes described as the study of subjective experience and what can be predicted from it, demystified hypnosis and brought its underlying structure into conscious awareness. Design Human Engineering (DHE) demonstrated that we could create entirely new states and experiences for ourselves, limited only by our imagination. Neuro-Hypnotic Repatterning (NHR) was designed to use the hypnotic process to restructure people at the level of their cortical pathways.

It exasperates me that some people still cling to their limiting beliefs about all this stuff. I meet people, fundamentalist Christians mainly, who tell me that hypnosis is the devil's work. I disagree. Stupidity is the devil's work.

Sometimes just the sound of a word makes certain people feel bad—so, I say, call it something else. Call it hypnosis or call it altered states. But in practice, I really don't care which word we use; I care about what we can accomplish.

Early on in my work, I realized that people get themselves into trouble because they engage in habitual behavior that keeps looping. I remember reading in a book, at least thirty years ago, that schizophrenics lived in a small but repetitious reality. When I got inside mental hospitals, I found the author was absolutely right. These people had a very limited behavior pattern that just looped and looped and looped. There was no variation . . . except sometimes at dinnertime.

It fascinated me to see how they could set aside their schizophrenia for just one little event. But it also meant that if they could do it then, they could do it at other times.

Many years ago, at Thanksgiving, I used to take my kids to feed homeless people at a church every year. The way we did it was different, because these were elderly people without homes or families. Many of them were seriously mentally disabled, because at that stage Reagan had closed many of the mental homes and put the majority of the residents out on the streets.

So, instead of having them standing in line and getting food slopped on to a tray, we set things up like a restaurant. We had tables and chairs and tablecloths and napkins. And the people were met at the door and taken to wash up before their meal, and when they got back, they found people waiting on them. We put people in parties of two or four, mixing them in with people living in the community.

What amazed me was that, even though some of these people were absolutely crazy, the way they were treated fired off some old anchor, and they all regressed to the point where they left their illness at the door.

Nobody acted crazy. Table manners and courtesy kicked in. It was so weird that I thought it was just going to be one group. But they kept coming, and no matter how terrible their state when they arrived, they switched immediately. They sat at the tables, chatting to each other politely, being courteous to each other and the people who were serving them. These were people who were stealing food from each other on the street and beating people up, but we didn't have a single fight. We didn't have a single loud word. They would get up and start to clear their dishes, and we'd say, "No, no. Leave that to the busboy."

The truth is, if you put people in the right environment, their behavior will change. The worst environment of all is mental hospitals. There's so much competition for who's the craziest there that people have to accentuate their craziness to get noticed.

I remember a paranoid schizophrenic in a hospital once, hiding behind a couch. He spent all day popping up and peeking out. So I went and sat on the couch, and when his head came up, I yelled, *"Boo!"* and scared the hell out of him. I kept it up for an hour, moving to a slightly different position each time, and yelling "Boo!" each time.

After a while, he started laughing. Then I pulled him over the back of the couch and made him sit next to me. I said, "If you don't sit next to me, they're going to get you."

I kept looking over the couch suspiciously, as though something bad was behind there. A little later, he was standing over at the coffee machine, drinking coffee and chitchatting with people.

The thing was, his psychiatrist had spent a whole year telling him that there was nothing to worry about . . . but, excuse me, if I keep looking at you and saying, "Now, there's nothing to worry about," you'd also probably freak.

The psychiatrist wasn't listening to his own language and didn't realize that he was actually inducing even more paranoia in this guy. My feeling was: give him something to be paranoid about, and then he'll stop being paranoid about nothing.

Over and over again I've been in the position where I've been hired by a family to help someone recover from hospitalization. Now, I know it's not the hospitals' fault they got there in the first place, but it certainly is their fault that they stayed there. Tolerating people's lunacy and having them interacting with other lunatics is bound to have an effect. They really need to be in a situation that demands and triggers their best behavior.

I realize that it's not a popular view, but I think Reagan did a good thing in getting most of the people out of mental hospitals and forcing them to cope. True, some of them became homeless, but a lot of them got jobs and places to stay. Some of them functioned better than others, and the more we force people to be able to function, the better off they're going to be. Maybe they're still crazy—but then, I meet crazy people everywhere, every day.

So, with this book, I hope to pass on some of my optimism—and a whole lot of other things that I don't want left behind.

I've developed many patterns that haven't been written about. Some have been written about, but the books are no longer readily available.

I want people to have those older things, and some of the new things, because the kinds of things that I do with people have worked. My clients get better, and the clients of so many of the people I've trained are getting better.

The problem is, it's like being a cookie cutter. If you make your cookie cutter out of my cookies, and then somebody else makes a cookie cutter out of those cookies, as it goes down the road you have copies of copies of copies, and it's just no longer as clear as it should be.

I've always done things the simple way. I look at how other people do training, and see people come out of their seminars with Practitioner and Master Practitioner certificates, and they can't even fix a phobia. *Frogs into Princes* told you exactly how to do it. People read the steps in the book, followed them, and sent me postcards that said things like, "I got rid of my phobia for $8.95, after spending $160,000 on therapy. Thank you very much." And I'd write them back and say, "Doesn't the word 'refund'" pop into mind?" It certainly would with me.

My concern is for the people who want to fix themselves and the people who really want to fix others. I want them to have the basic tools clearly defined and not mitigated through all the nonsense that's out there.

Some people say that the things I've developed are common knowledge, so therefore everybody's entitled to them. My feeling is that everybody's entitled who does them right and can make them work. The rest of them are not entitled to write books about my work and aren't entitled to talk about it. This is all about intellectual property rights.

Now, I could be suing everybody under the sun if I wanted to, but I think the best solution is to put clear representations out there so people who are serious about wanting to do this—learning to change their life, learning to change other people's lives—have the resources they need.

Over the years, I've written a number of books. They all have different material in them, but as they become less available, I don't want the knowledge in them to be lost. I also want some of the things that aren't yet in books to be there so they're not lost.

I'm not going to be around forever. I'll be doing training for quite some years, but not everybody can get to a training seminar. Some of the people who have no training are going to want to learn from books. I have people who study my work in countries I didn't even know existed. There are also some people who took bad training who want to clean up their misunderstandings.

Once this book comes out, it will get translated into other languages, and once again it will be the cookie-cutter effect. It will get a little distorted. But the people who want to read what I actually said in my own native tongue should have everything available to them. Those who don't will at least have translations of what I was saying—not what somebody else said I was saying.

I am hopeful that my message about learning and change will endure. I think we need anything that helps us overcome our present limitations and move into the future.

The signs are good. I work all the time with Muslims and Hindus and Christians and Jews and atheists and pagans. All of them are in the same room, getting along perfectly well with each other.

This is one of the things I enjoy about my seminars, especially in cities like London, where they are cosmopolitan and polytheistic; there are people of every race, color, and creed, and often from twenty to thirty different countries. I did a seminar in Florida where we had people from Kuwait and people from Jerusalem. We had Jews and Arabs doing exercises together.

This is possible because one of the things we all have in common is thinking. We all think and we all believe—and once you realize that you can alter your thinking and beliefs, it changes the way you behave.

Beliefs aren't about truth. Beliefs are about believing. They're guides for our behavior.

There are many people who have the same religious beliefs but behave totally differently. There are Muslims who are very peaceful people, and there are Muslims who are murderers. There are Christians who are murderers and Christians who are pacifists.

It has nothing to do with which God you believe in. It's about how you build your beliefs to guide your behavior. The more we get people to understand this, the less they're going to build beliefs that require them to kill other people—and I think that's ultimately a very important thing.

Glossary

accessing cues. Subtle behaviors that indicate which representational system a subject is using to think with. Accessing cues include eye movements, voice tone, tempo, body posture, gestures, and breathing patterns.

anchoring. The process of associating an internal response with some external trigger so that the response may be quickly reaccessed. Cues may be visual, auditory, kinesthetic, olfactory, and/or gustatory.

auditory. Relating to hearing, or the sense of hearing.

behavior. Physical actions and responses by which we interact with the people and environment around us.

behavioral flexibility. The ability to vary one's own behavior to elicit a response from another person.

calibration. The process of learning to "read" the unconscious, non-verbal responses of others.

congruence. Full alignment of a person's internal beliefs, strategies, and behaviors, oriented toward securing a specific outcome.

context. The framework surrounding a particular event. This framework will often determine how a particular experience or event is interpreted.

criteria. The values or standards a person uses to make decisions and judgments.

deep structure. The internal, sensory maps (both conscious and unconscious) that people use to organize and guide behavior.

eye accessing cues. Eye movements that reveal which representational systems the subject is using to process information.

future pacing. The process of mentally rehearsing a future situation to help ensure that the desired behavior will occur naturally and automatically.

gustatory. Relating to the sense of taste.

installation. The process of facilitating the acquisition of a new strategy or behavior. A new strategy may be systematically installed through NLP techniques.

kinesthetic. Relating to body sensations. In NLP the term "kinesthetic" is used to encompass all kinds of feelings, including tactile, visceral, and emotional.

Meta Model. A model developed by Richard Bandler and John Grinder that identifies categories of language patterns that can be problematic or ambiguous.

metaphor. Stories, parables, and analogies. Used in NLP and hypnosis to facilitate change.

Milton Model. A model developed by Richard Bandler and John Grinder through the study of the hypnotic language patterns of Dr. Milton H. Erickson.

modeling. The act of creating a calculus that describes a given system.

Neuro-Linguistic Programming (NLP). The study of the structure of subjective experience and what can be calculated from that.

olfactory. Relating to smell or the sense of smell.

outcomes. Directions, goals, or desired states that a person or organization aspires to achieve.

overlapping. Extending processing ability and expanding experience by moving from one representational system to another.

pacing. A method used by communicators to quickly establish rapport by matching certain aspects of their behavior to those of the person with whom they are communicating; matching or mirroring of behavior.

parts. Anthropomorphic or metaphoric description of programs and strategies of behavior that may appear to function independently from the subject.

predicates. Process words (like verbs, adverbs, and adjectives) describing a subject. Predicates are used in NLP to identify which representational system a person is using to process information.

rapport. The presence of trust, harmony, and cooperation in a relationship.

representational system preference. The systematic use of one sense over the others to process and organize experience in a given context.

representational systems. The five senses: seeing, hearing, touching (feeling), smelling, and tasting. Also known as: Visual, Auditory, Kinesthetic, Olfactory, and Gustatory (VAKOG).

revivification. Reliving a past experience in trance as if it is an event in the present, rather than a memory from the past.

sensory acuity. Using all senses as fully as possible to gain maximum data from an encounter with another person.

state. The total ongoing mental and physical conditions from which a person is acting.

strategy. A set of explicit mental and behavioral steps used to achieve a specific outcome.

submodalities. The special sensory qualities perceived by each of the five senses. For example, visual submodalities include color, shape, movement, brightness, depth, and so on; auditory submodalities include volume, pitch, tempo, and so on; and kinesthetic submodalities include pressure, temperature, texture, location, and so on.

surface structure. An utterance.

synesthesia. The process of overlapping between representational systems, characterized by phenomena like see-feel circuits, in which a person derives feelings from what they see; and hear-feel circuits, in which a person gets feelings from what they hear. Any two sensory modalities may be linked together.

transderivational search. The act of exploring subjective experience to understand the statement of another person.

visual. Relating to sight or the sense of sight.

well-formedness conditions. In NLP a particular outcome is well-formed when it is (1) stated in positives, (2) initiated and maintained by the individual, (3) ecological, and (4) testable in experience—that is, sensory based.

Resource Files

RESOURCE FILE 1
Anchors and Anchoring

AN ANCHOR IS A "trigger" or stimulus that evokes a specific response, and may be set in any of the five senses. Anchors occur in the form of language, physical touches or actions, specific sights, or distinctive sounds, or they may occur internally, as trigger words, self-talk, imagery, or sensations.

Words are probably the most commonly encountered form of anchor. Since the description (the word) is not the "thing" it describes, it must trigger associations, to a greater or lesser degree, out of which the listener "makes sense."

Anchoring may occur outside of conscious awareness or can be deliberately set. Anchors can also be accidentally installed, as with the "one-pass learning" experienced by phobics. Some may be genetic—for example, the response to a baby's smile. The firing of an anchor may have a positive or a negative effect on the subject.

Anchoring is used in NLP to facilitate state management, either by a practitioner or by the subject. To this end, a strong, known, desired state is set up and deliberately attached to a trigger. This facilitates reflexive access to the desired state at will.

Effective anchors need to meet several criteria. They must be:

• Unique and specific (in the same place, using the same volume and tonality, etc.); otherwise conditioning will not occur.

- Set as the response peaks, to avoid anchoring the state as it subsides.
- Frequently refreshed; otherwise the effect will naturally fade away.

Anchors may be:

- Stacked (similar states anchored to the same trigger to create a more powerful "composite" state).
- Chained (a series of anchors, each of which fires the next).
- Collapsed (two dissimilar anchors fired simultaneously with the intention of either neutralizing each other or creating an "integrated" state).

Exercise: Setting an Anchor

1. Remember a time when you experienced a particularly heightened, positive emotion—for example, joy, bliss, excitement.
2. Re-create that experience as fully as possible, seeing what you saw, hearing what you heard, and feeling what you felt.
3. Intensify the feeling by noticing the direction in which it is moving and spinning it faster and faster. Increase the intensity of the other submodalities, brightening the colors, bringing the image closer, and so on.
4. As the feeling begins to peak, firmly press the back of your hand, then let go just before you sense the feeling will start to subside.
5. Change your position ("break state"), then test the anchor by firmly pressing the back of your hand in exactly the same way as before. Notice how much of the original feelings return.

6. Repeat if necessary until the anchor is reliably in place.
7. "Top up" regularly if you wish the anchor to last, since the effectiveness of anchors tends to decay with time.

Note: You can stack anchors by linking several responses to the same trigger. The response will be a synthesis of all the separate anchors but should be more intensely experienced than any of them individually. They can also be chained—that is, set to run in sequence, as demonstrated in Chapter 17.

Where a simple response is causing problems (e.g., irritation at the sound of other people's cell phones ringing), the anchor may be effectively collapsed.

Exercise: Collapsing Anchors

1. Create a strong resource state by first remembering a time when you responded appropriately, stepping into and intensifying it, then anchoring it on one part of your body. If necessary, stack the anchor to ensure that the state is powerful and the anchor properly set. Change state.
2. Now, think of the state you wish to change, and as you reexperience that, anchor your response on another part of your body. Change state.
3. Now, fire both anchors simultaneously. The effect of the two contrasting anchors integrating is usually mildly confusing. Hold the anchors until any confusion subsides.
4. Slowly lift the anchor of the unwanted state, followed a few seconds later by the anchor for the resource state.
5. Test by trying to trigger the unwanted response. Instead, your response should be more neutral, or even to enter the resource state.

RESOURCE FILE 2
Sensory Predicates

IDENTIFYING THE SPEAKER'S SENSORY predicates may indicate
(1) the subject's preference for one channel over the other, or (2)
the sequence the subject uses to motivate himself to act (his strategy). Matching the speaker's sensory preference is a means of gaining rapport, while leading him into other systems increases the
flexibility of his behavior.

When a speaker uses sensory predicates that mismatch her eye-
accessing cues, there is a strong possibility that she is acting or
speaking under the influence of material outside her conscious
awareness (e.g., if she looks up and to the left, then down to her
right while saying, "I just feel bad for no reason," she is likely to
be responding to an unconsciously accessed eidetic image).

The following list is far from complete.

Sensory Predicates

Visual	Auditory	Kinesthetic
Appears	Audible	Active
Angle	Call	Bear/bearable
Aspect	Click	Cold
Bright	Communicate	Cool
Clear (also Auditory)	Discuss	Feel
In the dark	Earful	Grip/s (get am ___come ___)
Dim	Earshot	Flow
Focus	Express	Grasp
Hazy	Hear	Gut feeling
Light (in __ of)	Hush	Handle
Look, Looks like	Listen	Heavy
Observe	Loud (___ and clear)	Hot/hotheaded

Perspective	Manner (of speaking)	Lightheaded
Picture	Mention	Lukewarm
Scope	Noise/noisy	Pain/painful/in neck, etc.
Shortsighted	Outspoken	Pressure
Show	Pronounce	Rough
Tunnel vision	Quiet	Sensitive
Vision	Ring (__true__ a bell)	Stress
Watch	Sound	Tension
Witness	Tell	Unbearable

Exercise: Recognizing Sensory Predicates

Choose one sensory system and spend one or two days listening for words and phrases not included in the list on the previous page. When you have filled in one column, move to the next system and repeat. Do the same for the third sensory system.

Sensory Predicates

Visual	Auditory	Kinesthetic
_____	_____	_____
_____	_____	_____
_____	_____	_____
_____	_____	_____
_____	_____	_____
_____	_____	_____
_____	_____	_____
_____	_____	_____
_____	_____	_____
_____	_____	_____
_____	_____	_____

RESOURCE FILE 3
Some Submodality Distinctions

SUBMODALITIES ARE THE QUALITIES that each modality can possess. This list is far from complete. Keeping notes of further distinctions will greatly improve your ability to understand and respond to your clients' or your own subjective experience.

VISUAL

Associated/dissociated

Color/black-and-white

Moving/still

Location

Size

Near/mid/far

Vivid/pastel

Framed/panoramic

Clear/vague

2-D/3-D

Single/multiple images

Steady/jerky

Flat on/tilted

Smooth/jumpy transitions

AUDITORY

Harsh/soothing

Loud/soft

Inside/outside head

Location (side of head)

Pitch

Tempo

Continuous/interrupted

Distance

Clear/diffuse

KINESTHETIC

Location

Movement

Direction

Pressure/Weight

Extent (where it starts and where it finishes)

Temperature

Duration

Intensity

Shape

RESOURCE FILE 4
The Meta Model in Brief

REMEMBER, THE META MODEL is designed to separate out what part of a person's model works from what doesn't. Even though the patterns are laid out here under the headings of Deletion, Distortion, and Generalization, always go for the biggest chunk question available to you. "Biggest chunk" refers to the question that will give you the maximum amount of information in the shortest possible time. The most useful question is usually, "How do you know?" To answer this, the subject has to use the language of process, rather than of content (story).

Note, too, that even though we sometimes refer to the questions we use to recover lost information, we need to avoid sounding like interrogators.

DELETIONS

Simple Deletion. Information is left out of the statement.

Example: "I'm anxious."

Question(s): "How do you know you're anxious?" "How do you know you're not really excited?" "What actually happens that lets you know you're depressed?"

Unspecified Referential Index. The subject of the statement is unspecified.

Example: "They just don't like me."

Question(s): "Who specifically doesn't like you?" "How do you know they don't like you?"

Comparative Deletion. A comparison is made, but it is not clear as to who or what is being compared. Be alert for words such as least, most, more, less, better, worse.

Example: "The way we're doing it is better."

Question(s): "What will let us know it's better?" "Better than what?" "Better than whom?"

Unspecified Verb. The author or agent of an action is unclear.

Example: "It's causing problems in my marriage."

Question(s): "Who/how/what specifically?" "How do you know?"

Nominalization. A process (verb) has been turned into a "thing." Nominalizations are abstract nouns. They have no physical existence in the world. European languages favor nouns over verbs with the result that many processes are perceived as being "set in stone," rather than as fluid events in motion. The test for a nominalization is: "Can I put it in a box—albeit a large box?" Examples of nominalizations include love, relationship, respect, truth, communication, freedom, anxiety, depression, etc. Questions are intended to restore process to the "stuck" state.

Example: "My relationship is in trouble."

Question(s): "What about the way in which you are relating is troubling you?" "How do you know the way you are relating is causing you to feel troubled?"

DISTORTIONS

Mind reading. The speaker claims to know, or acts as if he knows, what another person or people think, feel, or believe.

Example: "When I get up to speak, people will be critical of me."

Question(s): "How do you know?" "What makes you think they're not just considering what you say?"

Lost Performative. A value judgment is made, without stating who has made the judgment.

Example: "Right-thinking people agree that pornography is bad."

Question(s): "Right-thinking according to whom?" "How do you know they are right-thinking?" "How do you know they know it's bad?"

Cause-Effect. A particular action is taken to cause a specific response or reaction. Listen for words such as: because, if/then, makes, drives, compels, causes.

Example: "The way she looks at me drives me crazy."

Question(s): "How specifically does the way she look at you drive you crazy?" "How do you know to feel crazy when she looks at you?" "What happens exactly when she looks at you that makes you feel crazy?"

Complex Equivalence. In this situation one action, experience, or behavior is taken to mean another without explanation or proof. Listen for words such as: means, therefore, implies.

Example: "His e-mail was so brief, he must be angry with me."

Question(s): "How do you know a short e-mail means he's angry with you?" "Might he not have been very busy rather than angry?" "Have you ever dashed off a particularly short e-mail? Did that automatically mean you were angry with the person you were sending it to?"

Presupposition. An assumption or assumptions (unstated in the sentence), taken to be present or true for the sentence to be understood.

Example: "When are you going to start to show your affection?" The presuppositions include: that you are not showing your affection, that you could show affection (if you so desired), that there is some kind of relationship in which showing affection is appropriate. Answering the wrong part of the statement will often worsen the communication problems.

Question(s): "How do you know I'm not showing affection?" "What needs to happen that will let you know I am showing affection?"

GENERALIZATIONS

Universal Quantifiers. Universal quantifiers are very commonly encountered when people feel stuck or disoriented. They imply there is no exception to their experience. Listen for words such as: always, never, every, all, everyone, no one, everything, nothing.

Example: "I'm always depressed."

Question(s): Either exaggerate the generalization to lighten the effect, or use counterexamples. "What? Always? Even in the shower? Even when you're asleep?" "You laughed a little earlier today. You didn't seem depressed then."

Modal Operators of Necessity or Probability. Modal operators of necessity suggest something is required or not required to happen. Listen for words such as: must, mustn't, should, shouldn't, need to, have to, etc. Modal operators of possibility include words such as: can, can't, possible, impossible, will, won't, may, may not. Modal operators become problematic when they limit volition.

Example: "I can't get started in the mornings."

Question(s): Restore volition and challenge the limitation. "So, you're telling me you have never been able to get started in the mornings?" "What would happen if you did get started?" "What would happen if you didn't?" "What prevents you from getting started?" "How do you know when you can't get started?"

RESOURCE FILE 5
Milton Model Patterns

THE MILTON MODEL HYPNOTIC language patterns pace the listener's experience by the simple process of allowing him to supply meaning to the statements from his own, rather than another's, experience. This requires that the language be "artfully vague"—but systematically so. The Milton Model is sometimes described as the "mirror image" of the Meta Model, but it includes several environments not relevant to the latter. Since the patterns move the listener into higher levels of thought and more introspective states of mind, they are naturally trance-inducing.

1. MIND READING

Claiming to know someone else's thoughts or feelings without specifying how you acquired that information.

Examples:

"I know you're the kind of person who wants to learn how to go into trance."
"Many people feel as you do that things can only get better."
"I know you believe this is going to be difficult, but it's worth it."
"You realize how much of the way you feel is within your control."

2. LOST PERFORMATIVE

Value judgments that omit identifying the person doing the judging.

Examples:

"Relaxing is good once you know how."
"It is good to know that things are getting easier."
"One thing we know is that communication is a learnable skill."
"It is a known fact that people like people who are like themselves."

3. CAUSE AND EFFECT

Statements implying that a particular action causes a specific reaction.

Examples:

"Realizing you have a problem is part of the way you fix it."
"Seeing her expression makes me angry."
"Learning about NLP will make you a great communicator."
"By coming here, you will be able to learn many skills."

4. COMPLEX EQUIVALENCE

Suggests that one thing is related to and means something else. This may or may not be true.

Examples:

"Being here means that you will change easily."
"Your hand is coming down. That means you are going deeper into trance."
"Your face is softening. You must be starting to relax."
"You have chosen the most comfortable chair; therefore, you will go even more deeply into trance."

5. PRESUPPOSITION

Something that is unstated but is assumed to be present and true for the statement to be understood.

Temporal presuppositions are words suggesting the passage or importance of time (e.g., when, after, during, before, while).

Examples:

"When you close your eyes, you will begin to relax."
"After you've taken some time out to relax, I want you to consider what you will be doing next."
"As you go into trance, pay attention to the difference in feeling between your left hand and your right hand."

Ordinal presuppositions sequence the listener's experience by using numbers and position.

Examples:

"Just notice which part of your body feels more comfortable first."
"Think about what will happen after that . . . and just after that. . . ."
"The next thing that will probably happen is that your hands begin to feel warm."

6. UNIVERSAL QUANTIFIER

Universal quantifiers imply there are no exceptions to the current experience.

Examples:

"Everyone has had the experience of going into trance, even though
    they might not have recognized it as trance."
"No one need know your secret of staying calm in demanding
    circumstances."
"Each time you breathe out, you become a little more relaxed."

7. MODAL OPERATORS OF NECESSITY
    OF POSSIBILITY

Modal operators of necessity suggest something is required or
not required to happen.

Examples:

"You needn't even bother trying to relax."
"You can easily notice how much your whole system has already
    begun to settle down."
"We don't have to try to go into trance; we simply let it happen
    in its own way."

8. NOMINALIZATION

Processes presented as "things." Verbs turned into nouns.

Examples (italicized):

"As you drift deeper, you can come to a new *understanding*."
"*Trance* is a naturally occurring phenomenon."
"Your *unconscious* will help you make new *learnings*."

9. UNSPECIFIED VERB

Implies action without describing how the action has occurred or will occur.

Examples:

"You can imagine how things will be better."
"You can begin to make those changes now."
"We can get through this to a better relationship."

10. TAG QUESTION

A question added at the end of a statement/question, designed to increase compliance. Even though it is formulated as a question, it is downwardly inflected, like a statement or command. The effect is either strengthened or weakened according to where the tag question is placed in the sentence.

Examples:

"As you stare at that spot on the ceiling, your vision begins to change, does it not?" (strong)
"People can, can they not, decide to make important changes?" (weaker)
"Wouldn't you prefer to close your eyes and rest now?" (weakest)

11. LACK OF REFERENTIAL INDEX

The sentence fails to specify who is the agent or object of an action.

Examples:

"People can change more easily than they think."

"One can very soon feel the effects of exercising regularly."

"Meditation is good for those who don't need a very directive
   experience of trance."

12. COMPARATIVE DELETION
(UNSPECIFIED COMPARISON)

A comparison that is made without specifying who or what is
being compared.

Examples:

"You will start to notice feeling better."

"Even if you try harder you are unlikely to succeed."

"More people are starting to accept hypnosis as the useful tool
   that it is."

13. PACE CURRENT EXPERIENCE

Using sensory-grounded, behaviorally specific information to
describe current experience.

Examples:

"You are sitting in the chair . . .

". . . with your feet on the floor . . .

". . . and your hands in your lap, as . . .

". . .you start to relax . . ."

14. DOUBLE BIND

Also known as the "illusion of choice." Two statements that appear to give the subject a choice, although either will meet the speaker's intention.

Examples:

"Would you like to start now, or a little later?"
"Do you want to sit in this chair or the other one to go into trance?"
"You may notice changes immediately, or in a day or two. The important thing is to be alert to what's different and better."

15. EMBEDDED COMMANDS

A command that forms part of a larger sentence. The command is subtly "analog marked" to alert the listener's unconscious to its importance. This may be done with a change in volume, tonality, or body language.

Examples:

"So looking at needles doesn't make you *feel comfortable now*?"
"We are not saying that *change is easy*."
"It's good that you've decided to *become a nonsmoker*."

16. CONVERSATIONAL POSTULATE

A "rhetorical question" that, if taken literally, would require a response or action. Conversational Postulates may also include Embedded Commands.

Examples:

"Can you set aside the worries of the day and just put your feet up
   and relax?"
"Could you close the door and take a seat?"
"Is it possible to choose to change the way you've been communicating with your children?"

17. EXTENDED QUOTE

A succession of quotes designed to create mild confusion in the
listener, increase suggestibility and compliance, and embed
process instructions or commands.

Examples:

"Some time ago, when I was teaching a seminar in Oakland,
one of the delegates said to me, 'You know, my grandfather had
very similar ideas. He said, "You don't have to struggle to achieve
things. I always tell people, 'Know what you want and find the
easiest way of getting it,'" and he said he always found that planning is the best way. I always remember the day he said, "'If it
isn't easy, it isn't right.'"

18. SELECTIONAL RESTRICTION VIOLATION

Attributing intelligence or feelings to inanimate objects.

Examples:

"Your chair supports you in becoming more relaxed."
"The symptom is saying, 'It's time to change.'"
"Your outcomes want other people to change, not you."

19. AMBIGUITY

Words or statements that have more than one meaning. Several deep structures for a single surface structure, prompting trans-derivational search on the part of the listener.

Phonological Ambiguity (written differently, but sounds the same).

Examples:

"your unconscious"/"you're unconscious"

"delight at the end of the tunnel"/"the light at the end of the tunnel"

"by now"/"buy now"

a part/apart, I/eye, heel/heal, know/no, see/sea, write/right, not/knot, hole/whole.

Syntactic Ambiguity (syntactic function of word or phrase cannot easily be determined from the utterance).

Examples:

"Hypnotizing hypnotists can be tricky."

"Speaking to you as a person determined to change."

"The problems are caused by visiting relatives."

Scope Ambiguity (context is not clear as to which part of a sentence verbs or modifier apply).

Examples:

"The disturbing thoughts and feelings" (are the feelings also disturbing?)

"The long nights and days" (are the days also long?)

Punctuation Ambiguity (well-formed sentences joined by a word or phrase to create an ill-formed sentence. This prompts confusion and transderivational search in the listener).

Examples (link word italicized):
"I like your *watch* how your breathing begins to slow down."
"You can learn how to *relax* each muscle in your body."
"I like your *giggle* when the good feeling starts to spin."

20. UTILIZATION

Pacing the subject by incorporating the entirety of his or her experience, internal and external. Whatever happens can be utilized as part of the process.

Examples:
Client 1: "I haven't noticed any changes."
Response: "That's okay. You've been dealing with other things, so you haven't been ready to look for changes . . . yet."
Client 2: "I didn't hear a thing you said."
Response: "Not consciously. But you can be sure your unconscious did."

Utilization is also used to minimize the effect of external disturbances ("and all the noise and activity out there can remind you how good it is to relax inside"), or to mind-read the client's internal experience ("That's right . . .").

21. FACTIVE (AWARENESS) PREDICATES

Presupposing truth by the use of words such as: realize, know, become aware of, understand.

Examples:

"Have you noticed that your body has begun to relax naturally?"

"As you become aware of your breathing slowing down, you start to feel more comfortable."

"When you realize that you can make changes, there'll be no stopping you."

22. COMMENTARY ADJECTIVES AND ADVERBS

Words that predispose the listener to accept the quality of everything that follows, such as: kindly, usefully, surprisingly.

Examples:

"Happily, you don't have to do anything to relax. Just allow it to happen?"

"Interestingly, your unconscious is very protective of you."

"Clearly, your breathing has begun to settle down."

This section is not a complete representation of all the structures I wrote about in *Patterns of the Hypnotic Techniques of Milton H. Erickson, M.D.* However, after becoming familiar with the ones outlined here, the reader will have many tools to create pervasive change. By "becoming familiar," I mean to suggest that the reader should write out as many examples of each pattern as he or she can, then create various inductions out of these examples. Spend a day or two on each pattern. Also, practice delivering them aloud—to a friend, a voice recorder, or even your dog. Practicing hypnotic inductions in front of a mirror can be extremely state-altering.

RESOURCE FILE 6
Eliciting and Annotating Strategies

FORMAL ELICITATION OF A strategy requires systematic questioning and observation. Pay special attention to eye-accessing cues in relation to spoken replies to your questions. Strategies usually operate out of conscious awareness, and eye-accessing cues may reveal hidden aspects that need further investigation.

1. Begin by asking someone who is able to do something you would like to learn how they do it. Listen for sensory-specific information—that is, what they see, hear, and feel. Make sure they don't start too far into the strategy. Keep asking, "What happens just before that?" until the starting point has been identified.

2. When the starting point has been identified, keep asking, "And what happens next?" until the strategy is complete. Use the following symbols to record the answers.

> Visual = V
> Auditory = A
> Kinesthetic = K
> Recalled = ʳ
> Constructed = ᶜ
> Digital = ᵈ
> Internal to the subject = ⁱ
> External to the subject = ᵉ
> Transitioning = >

Examples:

The person who felt he couldn't draw was using the following strategy:

$V^r > A^r > K > A^r > V^r > K$ (recalling the sight and sound of see-ing and hearing his critical teacher, feeling bad, recalling his father's criticisms, feeling bad), which then looped back to the beginning, creating the feeling that there was no alternative to his problem situation.

The person who felt he could draw was using the following strategy:

$V^e > K > V^c > K > V^e > K$ (studying the scene, feeling and see-ing the "wire," tracing details of the scene, seeing and feeling the marks were "right").

Recommended Reading and Audiovisual Resources

BOOKS

Bandler, Richard. *The Adventures of Anybody.* Cupertino, CA: Meta Publications, 1993.

———. *Magic in Action.* Cupertino, CA: Meta Publications, 1985.

———. *Time for a Change.* Cupertino, CA: Meta Publications, 1993.

———. *Using Your Brain for a Change.* Moab, UT: Real People Press, 1985.

Bandler, Richard, J. Delozier, and J. Grinder. *Patterns of the Hypnotic Techniques of Milton H. Erickson.* Vol. 2. Cupertino, CA: Meta Publications, 1975.

Bandler, Richard, and Owen Fitzpatrick. *Conversations: Freedom Is Everything and Love Is All the Rest.* Dublin: Mysterious Publishing, 2005.

Bandler, Richard, and J. Grinder. *Frogs into Princes*, Moab, UT: Real People Press, 1979.

———. *Patterns of the Hypnotic Techniques of Milton H. Erickson.* Vol. 1. Cupertino, CA: Meta Publications, 1975.

———. *The Structure of Magic.* Vol. 1. Cupertino, CA: Meta Publications, 1975.

———. *The Structure of Magic.* Vol. 2. Palo Alto, CA: Science and Behavior Books, 1976.

———. *Trance-formations.* Moab, UT: Real People Press, 1980.

Bandler, Richard, and W. McDonald. *An Insider's Guide to Submodalities.* Cupertino, CA: Meta Publications, 1989.

Bandler, Richard, and John LaValle. *Persuasion Engineering.* Cupertino, CA: Meta Publications, 1996.

McKenna, Paul. *Change Your Life in Seven Days.* London: Bantam, 2005.

———. *I Can Make You Thin.* London: Bantam Press, 2007. Book and CD.

———. *Instant Confidence.* London: Bantam Press, 2006. Book and CD.

Thomson, Garner, with Khalid, Khan. *Magic in Practice: Introducing Medical NLP—The Art and Science of Language in Healing and Health*. London: Hammersmith Press, 2008.

Wilson, Robert Anton. *Prometheus Rising*. Temple, AZ: New Falcon Press, 1983.

———. *Quantum Psychology*. Temple, AZ: New Falcon Press, 1990.

DVD AND CD PRODUCTS

Bandler, Richard. *The Art and Science of Nested Loops*. DVD.

———. *DHE 2000*. CD.

———. *Personal Enhancement Series*. CD.

———. *Persuasion Engineering*. DVD.

LaValle, John. *NLP Practitioner Set*. CD.

These and many more DVDs and CDs available from: www.nlpstore.com.

Adventures in Neuro-Hypnotic Repatterning (DVD set and PAL-version videos), *Thirty Years of NLP: How to Live a Happy Life* (DVD set), and other products by Richard Bandler available from Matrix Essential Training Alliance—www.meta-nlp.co.uk; email: enquiries@meta-nlp.co.uk.

Tel +44 (0)1749 871126; fax +44 (0)1749 870714

WEBSITES

http://www.richardbandler.com

http://www.NLPInstitutes.com

http://www.NLPTrainers.com

http://www.NLPLinks.com

http://www.purenlp.com

http://www.paulmckenna.com

http://www.magicinpractice.com

http://www.medicalnlp.com

http://www.neuroing.com

http://www.meta-nlp.co.uk http://www.rawilson.com

The Society of NLP
Richard Bandler Licensing Agreement

The Society of Neuro-Linguistic Programming™ is set up for the purpose of exerting quality control over those training programs, services, and materials claiming to represent the model of Neuro-Linguistic Programming™ (NLP™). The seal above indicates Society Certification and is usually advertised by Society-approved trainers. When you purchase NLP™ products and seminars, ask to see this seal. This is your guarantee of quality.

It is common experience for many people, when they are introduced to NLP™ and first begin to learn the technology, to be cautious and concerned with the possible uses and misuses.

As a protection for you and for those around you, the Society of NLP™ now requires participants to sign a licensing agreement that guarantees that those certified in this technology will use it with the highest integrity. It is also a way to ensure that all the trainings you attend are of the highest quality and that your trainers are updated and current with the constant evolution of the field of Neuro-Linguistic Programming™ and Design Human Engineering™, etc.

The Society of NLP

NLP™ Seminars Group International, PO Box 424, Hopatcong, NJ 07843, USA

Tel: +1 (973) 770 3600

Website: www.purenlp.com